P9-CDD-203

Consciousness and Behavior

Benjamin Wallace
Leslie E. Fisher

Cleveland State University

Allyn and Bacon, Inc.

Boston London Sydney Toronto

To our children,

Jacob and Sara Wallace

and

Gregory, Patricia, Kathryn, and David Fisher

Copyright © 1983 by Allyn and Bacon, Inc., 7 Wells Avenue,
Newton, Massachusetts 02159. All rights reserved. No part of the
material protected by this copyright notice may be reproduced or
utilized in any form or by any means, electronic or mechanical,
including photocopying, recording or by any information storage
and retrieval system, without written permission from the copyright
owner.

Library of Congress Cataloging in Publication Data

Wallace, Benjamin.
   Consciousness and behavior.

   Includes bibliographies and index.
   1. Consciousness.   I. Fisher, Leslie E.   II. Title
BF311.W26669   1983   154   82-20768
ISBN 0-205-07892-3

Printed in the United States of America

10 9 8 7 6 5 4 3 2   87 86 85 84 83

Contents

Preface

In general, the major reason a professor chooses to write a book is because he does not find texts available in the area to be best suited for his course. This, of course, was one of our reasons; however, it was not the major reason for writing this book. Over the past ten years, one of us (B.W.) has been teaching a course entitled "The Psychology of Consciousness." The content for this course arose out of the interests of students who wished to learn about the peripheral areas of psychology. Although many wanted to study about and be given information on such topics as hypnosis, meditation, and psychedelic drugs, psychology as a discipline was not prepared to teach these topics in the traditionally established curriculum. As a result, interested students read about these areas on their own, often reading books by nonscientists. In and of itself, this was not necessarily bad, except that it tended to perpetuate and often accentuate the misinformation and misconceptions that students already held about these areas of interest.

As a professor who believed that the peripheral areas of psychology should not be neglected, I and other professors began to develop a scientifically based course in which students could discuss topics such as those previously mentioned. As the course began to take shape and become a part of a psychology curriculum, teachers and students began to discuss many of the peripheral areas of psychology in the introductory psychology course. Today, one cannot find an introductory psychology textbook that does not devote many pages and, in many instances, an entire chapter to topics that now fall under the rubric of "consciousness."

This book, then, is our contribution to the continuing development of the psychology of consciousness. As you shall see, this area of study began many years ago and many prominent psycnologists such as William James, Sigmund Freud, and Ernest Hilgard played a key role in its infancy. However, the study of consciousness disappeared from vogue (but not from sight or mind) with the rise of behaviorism (we discuss this in Chapter 1). We hope this book will serve to rekindle the flames of consciousness as an area of study within the behavioral sciences.

As you read through each chapter of the book, we hope you will begin to appreciate our discussion of each topic as an attempt to legitimitize a poorly regarded area of psychology. Many areas have already been legitimitized; others have not. Regardless of the present status of each topic, we believe that the psychology of consciousness is in the midst of a *zeitgeist*, which we predict will continue through the 1980s and into the 1990s. We shall see more research and more writings on these topics in the next few decades than we have in the entire previous history of the study of consciousness. This book serves to give an overview of these topics and acquaint you with the theories and experiments in these interesting, albeit controversial, areas of study.

We hope you are reading this book because you really want to learn about these topics. This book was intentionally written in such a style and manner that prerequisite courses or knowledge are not really necessary to appreciate and understand the topics of the psychology of consciousness. Thus, the book can be read easily by anyone who is interested, be they student or nonstudent. This book can also be used for a first course in consciousness, or as an adjunct or supplement for an introductory psychology course or for more advanced courses such as perception, cognition, and abnormal psychology. The reader can be assured that this book was many years in the works. We have attempted to bring you as up-to-date and as scientifically documentated a book on the topic of consciousness as was possible at this point in time. Enjoy reading it!

In developing this book, I (B.W.) would first like to express my gratitude to James Garrett for having introduced me to the psychology of consciousness, and without whose wisdom and discussion this book would never have been possible. Similarly, L.E.F. would like to thank Harry Kotses for introducing him to psychophysiology, the foundation underlying many areas in the study of consciousness.

As for the actual preparation of this book, we would like to acknowledge all the individuals who contributed their time and effort to the final product. Any errors that remain, of which we hope there are few, are our responsibility, of course, and not that of our reviewers. For reading drafts of chapters or the entire book, we thank Steven Coleman, David Grilly, Lester Lefton, Richard Rakos, and several anonymous reviewers assigned to our book by Allyn and Bacon. All of the reviewers provided many helpful suggestions that were subsequently incorporated into the final draft. Their comments were always constructive and they helped to make the book more readable. It is undoubtedly a more scholarly product as a result.

For typing the various manuscript drafts, we thank Sondra Lou Patterson and Bonnie Sharp. We also thank Sandra Zeppetella and Greg Fisher for providing us with many of our preliminary illustrations. We would also like to express our thanks to the staff of Allyn and Bacon, including Jack May, who persuaded us to do the book for his firm, and Merle Schlesinger for her fine editorial work in making the text more readable. In addition, we thank Anco/ Boston for helping with our final illustration needs. Finally, we wish to thank our families for having the patience to put up with us while this book was being written.

B. W.
L. E. F.

chapter one ══════════════════════

Introduction

In studying behavior, contemporary psychologists have been, for the most part, greatly influenced by the principles, laws, and theories of behaviorism (Skinner, 1964, 1974; Watson, 1913). Whenever a psychologist was interested in studying an aspect of behavior, he or she generally obeyed certain modes of collecting data, making certain that behavior was observable and, therefore, measurable. This is not a difficult rule to follow; nor is it necessarily one that we will try to change. However, in being so behavioristic, contemporary psychology may be incomplete. If we are concerned only with studying and reporting observable behavior or behavior that can be mutually shared, we may be side-stepping a great deal of human behavior that obviously is not observable. For example, should we ignore totally an individual's thought or feeling because it is not directly observable or capable of being mutually shared? Should we fail to study dreams because we (the scientists) cannot see them (share them) with the dreamer? Should we fail to study hypnosis or meditation because these phenomena are not directly measurable in the true behavioristic sense? The answer to these questions, obviously, is no. Yet contemporary psychology has downplayed the study of many interesting areas of behavior because of a seventy-year-old bias (Watson, 1913). We feel it is time to do away with this bias and yet not entirely abandon the school of thought, science, and methodology given to us by the behaviorists.

Our philosophical goal is to recover the tools of psychology that existed before the advent of behaviorism. Although we are well aware that behaviorism emerged as a reaction to the sloppiness and poor experimental control of such processes as introspection (Hamilton, 1880; Malcolm, 1964), it also did away with other ramifications of structuralism (Titchener, 1909). For example, during introspection, a process of self-observation, subjects were taught to verbalize everything and anything that they experienced during their participation in an experiment. In other words, they were to give a complete phenomenological report of their experiences with a stimulus event and with the environment. This reporting served as a means by which the scientist gained access to a subject's mental episodes.

In agreement with the behaviorists, we feel that much imprecision did exist during introspective assessments of experience. However, in reacting against this method of data assessment, behaviorism also reacted against most behavior that was not directly observable or that, at minimum, could not be mutually shared. This gave the use of individual verbal reports in psychological research (or, for that matter, in all behavioral research) a bad name. Psychology, as a science, witnessed a considerable decline in the use of such reports in research because they were not considered "scientific.' In fact, many psychology and behavioral science instructors still hold to this belief and try to proselytize their students to the "party line."

This strict adherence to behavioristic philosophy has been at the expense of much important data collection and of hypothesis, law, and theory construction. Not to deviate from strict behaviorism is to accept the dictum that thoughts or mental processes are not scientifically testable. We believe that such a view is untenable in psychology and other behavioral sciences in the 1980s. All behavior is fair game for study, whether it is directly observable or is speculated to exist via an individual's verbal report.

One area of research that has made great strides in attempting to assess unobservable behavior through verbal reports and other means, and therefore falls outside the legitimate realm of study by strict behaviorists, is what is now referred to as the *psychology of consciousness* (Ornstein, 1972, 1977). Although psychologists and philosophers have studied consciousness for many years (see Boring, 1929), it was not until very recently that this area of psychology reemerged as an important area of concern.

What exactly is the psychology of consciousness and when did the study of this area commence? Why is it reemerging as an area for psychologists to study after being in limbo for more than a half century? Most important, will science gain knowledge as a result of its reemergence? Let us examine these issues.

WHAT IS CONSCIOUSNESS?

Although philosophers have studied consciousness for nearly 400 years (see Natsoulas, 1978b), the psychology of consciousness can trace its beginnings only to the writings of William James (1842-1910). James, who founded the school of functionalism, saw consciousness as a tool that enabled individuals to select their own courses of action. He defined consciousness as the function of knowing (James, 1890, 1904). Knowing or the ability to know was to James a personal thought; therefore, what one individual knew or thought differed from what everyone else knew or thought.

Consciousness also, according to James, was forever changing. He meant by this that every conscious state is a function of the entire psychophysical totality, and that the mind is cumulative and not recurrent. Implicit in this is the belief that objects can recur, but sensations or thoughts cannot. James also urged that consciousness is a continuous process. There are time gaps, such as sleep; but when an individual awakens from sleep, he or she has not become someone else or another object.

Finally, James believed that consciousness had the important characteristic of being selective. Only a small part of the potentially effective world of stimuli could come to consciousness. The principle of selecting the effective stimuli was highly dependent upon relevance. That is, we attend to stimuli that are most relevant to us at a given time and place. Thus, consciousness is a highly selective process that is both logical and rational.

From the early thoughts of James, we come to more recent considerations of the concept of consciousness. Natsoulas (1978a) delineated seven separate definitions of consciousness from the *Oxford English Dictionary* (1933). The first definition deals with the topic as "joint or mutual knowledge." This definition characterizes a kind of relationship between individuals in which they are confidants. To speak of people who are conscious in this sense is to come close to the psychoanalytic definition of consciousness (Freud, 1913). This school of thought holds consciousness to be an expression, particularly as it is applied to efforts of comprehending what transpires in a patient during psychoanalytic therapy.

The "joint knowledge" definition of consciousness may also approach the concept as it is conceived by radical behaviorists (e.g., Skinner, 1974). To this group of scientists, individuals must be initiated into the practice of consciousness. Without such practice, people would be unaware of their private events. Since such events are not scientifically measurable unless they can be shared with others, they must be made nonprivate or public. At that point, the event becomes mutual knowledge.

Consciousness has also been defined as "internal knowledge or conviction." This refers to a certain cognitive relation to oneself or to being a witness to one's own behaviors. As such, one gains internal knowledge first hand rather than by hearing about it from someone else.

When James defined consciousness as a function of knowing (1904), he came close to the third definition of the concept as delineated by Natsoulas: consciousness is equivalent to a state of awareness. Such a state includes a knowledge of unobservable, private events or mental occurrences as well as a knowledge of external, observable objects or events. Therefore, the concept of consciousness involves the knowledge of being aware of something, generally through sensory confirmation.

Natsoulas describes the fourth definition of consciousness as "direct awareness." This is a "state or faculty of being conscious as a condition or concomitant of all thought, feeling, and volition," or what John Locke (1690) refers to as "what passes in a man's mind." Recently, Natsoulas (1978b) added to this definition by proposing that a person exemplifies consciousness by being aware of, or being in a position to be aware of, his or her perception, thought, or other occurrent mental episode. This definition differs from the previous one in that direct awareness has no involvement with sensory organs or receptors. To undergo a direct awareness is to have a thought that something is happening when there is no sensory confirmation of its occurrence.

Both Natsoulas (1978a, 1979) and the *Oxford English Dictionary* also refer to consciousness as a personal unity. In this sense, consciousness is "the totality of the impressions, thoughts, and feelings which make up a person's conscious being." Therefore, all of one's mental episodes might constitute one's consciousness.

The sixth definition refers to consciousness as a normal waking state. This may be the most common usage of the concept. The *Oxford English Dictionary* says that consciousness is a "general state or condition of the person." Thus, a state of consciousness is a state of wakefulness with attentiveness to stimuli or to events in one's environment. Since this is a widely used definition of consciousness, we will address it throughout the book. We will often use it as a comparison for altered states (Tart, 1972, 1975) or with what Zinberg (1977) refers to as *alternate* states.

The seventh definition of consciousness refers to multistates of information processing, or what Natsoulas has called *double consciousness*. Since we do not assume a priori that individuals have only a single state of consciousness, we can discuss different levels of consciousness. An individual may be aware of the presence of some stimulus at one level, while at another level he or she may not be aware of its presence. The concept of threshold in perception is a good illustration of how an individual can react to a stimulus situation at different levels of awareness. For instance, if a light source at a very low level of intensity is present and a subject is requested to indicate when he or she is first able to see the light, we notice that they do not give their indication immediately. There are several reasons for this delay in response. The receptor system (retinal photoreceptors) may not be physically capable of detecting light at this low level. Or the subject thinks he or she saw the light but is not quite certain. Thus the subject chooses to be conservative and delays the response. Or it may be a combination of these two reasons.

However, light *is* being emitted from a source and photons are impinging on the retinal photoreceptors of the subject's eyes; he or she simply is not able to detect the light. Does this mean the light is really not present? This question is basically a philosophical one, just like the question, What noise does a tree make when it falls if no one is around to hear the crash? Obviously a crash and resultant noise occur physically but are not perceived.

In the case of the light, we might simply say that, for a given individual at the normal state of awareness and processing, the light was not present since the subject did not perceive it. However, we know it is physically present and, therefore, it could have been perceived, if not by the subject, by someone else. Thus, the normal waking state of awareness or consciousness may differ from one individual to the next.

At the same time, it is also possible that an individual may perceive the light at one level of consciousness and not at another level. An excellent example of the existence of such multilevels of consciousness or awareness is illustrated in the work of Hilgard (1973, 1976, 1977a, 1977b, 1979). This work is discussed in Chapter 4. Briefly, he has shown experimentally that, with the aid of hypnosis, it is possible literally to separate out at least two different levels of consciousness. At one level a subject perceives an event, while at another level he or she is totally unaware of the event.

The final definition of consciousness as delineated by Natsoulas comes closest to ours. We believe that consciousness is the *processing of information at various levels of awareness.* (As you can readily see, we are equating the term *consciousness* with states of awareness.) In fact, we will go one step farther than Natsoulas and Hilgard: consciousness exists at *many* levels. We define a *level* as one state of awareness that is distinguishable, either empirically or experientially, from another state. Hilgard has demonstrated nicely two of these levels. However, there is evidence to indicate that more than two levels of consciousness or awareness may exist. For example, we can count the several stages of sleep as different levels of awareness. Many more levels may exist during other states of consciousness, whether altered or wakeful. One of our goals is to deal with consciousness from the perspective of a multilevel approach. Another goal is to show that we have only begun to touch the surface in our understanding of consciousness, especially of the different levels of consciousness and what takes place in them.

CONTEMPORARY THEORIES OF CONSCIOUSNESS

It is generally not difficult to communicate what consciousness in the normal waking state means. We are well aware of what it feels like to be awake. We also can describe what we are minimally capable of doing while awake. However, what does it feel like to not be awake or to be in an altered state of consciousness? What are we capable of doing in an altered state? Does performance in such a state differ from performance in the waking state?

To begin to answer these types of questions it is necessary to enumerate what we believe to be altered states of consciousness or awareness. Then we must decipher existing experimental evidence to determine whether behavior changes or is different in such states. Finally, if behavior does differ, it is necessary to summarize the evidence to formulate laws and theories of cognition, information processing, or neurophysiology that will help to explain the psychology of consciousness.

Several years ago, Weil (1972) attempted to theorize about the concept of consciousness. Although his theory was not formal in any sense of the word, he did elaborate on many observations and hypotheses that ultimately could lead to a formal and comprehensive theory of consciousness. His observations and hypotheses were based primarily on his own personal experiences as well as on laboratory experimentation. The major points Weil made were:

1. The drive to experience modes of awareness other than the normal waking state is innate.
2. Individuals experiment with methods or techniques of changing consciousness.
3. Altered-state experiences are normal, and individuals spend a certain amount of time each day in such experiences.
4. Individuals may not always be aware that they are experiencing or have experienced behavior in an altered state.
5. Altered states form a continuous spectrum from ordinary waking consciousness.
6. Artificial agents (e.g., drugs) may elicit altered states but do not cause them.
7. It is important to learn how to enter an altered state, because experiences in this state may lead to a more comprehensive understanding of the workings of our central and peripheral nervous systems, to the realization of untapped human potentials, and to a better understanding of the functioning of our ordinary waking state of consciousness.

As we shall see throughout this book, many of Weil's observations are indeed valid premises for a potential theory of consciousness. However, a great deal more experimentation to test his hypotheses is necessary before these points can constitute an estabished theory.

In a more formal sense, Tart (1975, 1977a) also proposed a theory of consciousness. He asserts that our states of consciousness are the product of a highly complex construction. As a result, such states are learned. He also proposed the existence of such phenomena as basic awareness and a more refined self-awareness. Basic awareness is cognizance of one's surroundings or environment. Self-awareness is cognizance of one's thoughts and feelings about the environment. Tart also recognizes that individual differences exist within the concept of consciousness. These differences limit and shape the manner in which we respond to our environment, and ultimately affect our understanding and control of human potentialities.

Tart discusses the terms *discrete state of consciousness* (d-SoC) and *discrete altered state of consciousness* (d-ASC). The former concept refers to such phenomena as sleep, dreams, hypnosis, drug intoxication, and various forms of meditation. The latter concept refers to the difference in observable, and perhaps measurable, behavior between some baseline state of consciousness (waking state) and a d-SoC. Therefore, Tart's views of consciousness are very much in line with a multilevel concept that we advocate in this book. It is true that Tart discusses only two levels of consciousness but it is certainly a good start toward a theory of consciousness.

Perhaps the most controversial theory of consciousness was proposed by Jaynes (1976). On the basis of many laboratory experiments involving the brain (e.g., Gazzniga, Bogen, and Sperry, 1965; Gazzaniga and Sperry, 1967; Gordon and Sperry, 1968; Milner, 1965; Galin and Ornstein, 1972) and a close reading of existing archaeological evidence, Jaynes proposed that ancient civilizations could not independently process information or "think" as we do today. As a result, people from these cultures were not conscious. Unable to introspect, they experienced many sensory anomalies, including auditory and visual hallucinations (many examples of these are witnessed in both the Old and New Testaments). Such sensations, coming from the brain's right hemisphere, told a person how to behave in circumstances of stress or uncertainty.

Because of the catastrophes and cataclysms of many centuries, civilizations (and individuals within those civilizations) were forced to become more independent in their thinking and to learn, perhaps in order to survive, consciousness. Therefore, consciousness did not evolve in the strict biological sense but was produced via our experiences with history and with different cultures and races. Furthermore, according to Jaynes, consciousness is grounded in the physiology of the brain's right and left hemispheres (we discuss brain laterality in Chapter 2).

Within Jaynes's theory exist three forms of human awareness. He refers to these as the bicameral or god-run man, the modern or problem-solving man, and the contemporary forms of throwbacks to bicamerality. These throwbacks include such states as hypnotism, schizophrenia, and poetic and religious frenzy. As part of these throwbacks, modern man relegates his consciousness to a "back burner" in order to obey the commands of an individual, group, or higher power who gains control for a period of time (specified, as in hypnosis, or unspecified, as in schizophrenia).

An examination of Jaynes's theory suggests that all altered states of consciousness are throwbacks to bicamerality. This suggests further that such states temporarily produce a loss of wakeful and controllable awareness in an individual. This idea may be true to some extent and, of course, will be addressed in the course of this book.

In summarizing our sampling of three contemporary theories of consciousness we can find many commonalities. Consciousness appears to develop through a learning process (defined broadly). There are many individual differences to be found in states of consciousness, and many of these differences help us to learn about the process. Many human potentials can be tapped through knowledge of consciousness and experiencing of altered states of consciousness. Finally, consciousness is a virtue to be considered positive in the development of humankind and civilizations and, as such, can help improve the quality of life and its accomplishments.

Within the areas of consciousness to be considered here, we will attempt to determine (1) how an altered state of awareness comes about; (2) how various levels of consciousness or awareness are believed to be operating for a given phenomenon; (3) how these levels can be identified; and (4) how behavior exhibited at each level can be assessed. Thus, we are not abandoning entirely the positive aspects of science given to us by the behaviorists. In order to deal with these areas of concern, we need to establish methods of measurement that can be generalized. As such, we are not advocating a return to the looseness of introspectionism.

However, the study of consciousness requires that we release enough of our rigidity in collecting data to permit the assessment of responses that may not be considered scientifically pure by the radical behaviorist. Thus, verbal responses are permissible and are important in the study of consciousness. Furthermore, many of these responses may not be of such a nature as to be mutually shareable. Because so many individual differences exist, it will be difficult to establish laws and theories of behavior. Yet this must be accomplished, and Weil (1972), Tart (1975), and Jaynes (1976) are leading the way to doing just that. Not to do so is to relegate the study of consciousness to nonscience. This cannot be permitted if psychology is seriously to consider behavior that occurs during altered states of awareness.

Therefore, the psychology of consciousness as it is presented here is a beginning step in the advancement of a study of levels of awareness. It is not the first step, since many have preceded us from as far back as James (1904) to as recently as Ornstein (1977). However, it is an attempt to integrate the many diverse areas that define the psychology of consciousness. Many refer to these areas as the peripheral areas of psychology. Yet they are popular areas for discussion by scientists and nonscientists alike. They are also very important areas of study in their own right.

AREAS OF CONSCIOUSNESS

Although consciousness as a concept may not have a universally acceptable definition, the area of study is generally definable by a set of phenomena. Most of these are enumerated by Goleman and Davidson (1979), Ornstein (1977), Tart (1972), and Zinberg (1977). What unites all of these phenomena under a single rubric is the notion that each is a tool for demonstrating the possible existence of various levels of consciousness or awareness. Specifically, each phenomenon can potentially show us that humans are capable of processing various types of information at different levels of control. These levels can differ in both their exhibited behavior and in resultant consequences from the normal waking state. Therefore, it may be said that we are capable of exhibiting different levels of consciousness and that behavior may differ at each level.

In the remaining chapters we will examine the variety of subject matter that we refer to as the psychology of consciousness. These include such diverse topics as drug-altered states of behavior, hypnosis, meditation, biofeedback, sleep, dreams, sensory deprivation, extrasensory perception (ESP), and mysticism. In examining each topic we shall look at states and levels of consciousness to determine whether they truly exist and what, if anything, can be accomplished by recognizing their existence. You will see that this endeavor is diverse, difficult, and complicated, but exciting at the very least.

FOR FURTHER READING

Goleman, D., and Davidson, R. J. *Consciousness: brain, states of awareness, and mysticism.* New York: Harper & Row, 1979.

Jaynes, J. *The origin of consciousness in the breakdown of the bicameral mind.* Boston: Houghton Mifflin, 1976.

Ornstein, R. *The psychology of consciousness.* New York: Harcourt, Brace, Jovanovich, 1977.

Tart, C. T. *Altered states of consciousness.* Garden City, NY: Doubleday, 1972.
—— · *States of consciousness.* New York: Dutton, 1975.

Weil, A. T. *The natural mind: a new way of looking at drugs and the higher consciousness.* Boston: Houghton Mifflin, 1972.

Zinberg, N. E. *Alternate states of consciousness.* New York: Free Press, 1977.

chapter two ═══════════════════

The Physiology of Consciousness

In discussing the concept of consciousness, psychologists typically avoid references to its physiological basis. Instead they concentrate on behavioral changes
as well as means for achieving these changes (often referred to as *altered states*).
However, our understanding of how these changes in consciousness come about
and are maintained may be increased by an awareness of their underlying physiological concomitants. In part, at least, the apparent lack of interest on the part
of many psychologists in the development of a physiological explanation of
conscious states can be attributed to historical accident. In Chapter 1 you saw
that the early interest in the psychology of consciousness faded quickly in
response to the scientific rigors of behaviorism (ca. 1913). This, of course,
occurred long before the tremendous technological advancements of the 1950s
and 1960s, which provided modern physiological psychology with a much
better understanding of brain function than previously had been possible. Only
in the past decade has there been a rekindling of interest in the study of consciousness on the part of psychologists (Ornstein, 1972). Simply not enough
time has passed for these psychologists to mount a concerted research effort
aimed at the development of a physiological explanation of conscious states.
However, some studies have considered possible loci for consciousness in the
cerebral hemispheres. It is to this research that we now turn our attention.

CEREBRAL SPECIALIZATION

It has long been recognized that states of awareness or consciousness are products of the brain. Most people who have watched boxing matches, for example, are cognizant of the fact that a single blow delivered to the head may be sufficient to render the recipient unconscious for several minutes. Medical professionals have observed that severe brain damage, such as that which might result from an accident or major illness, may reduce the individual to little more than a "vegetable"—an organism with a series of simple reflexes but with no awareness or consciousness. Finally, more focal damage to specific regions of the brain have been shown to produce a loss of particular functions, abilities, and even some aspects of awareness or consciousness.

In all likelihood, you probably are already aware of the fact that humans have essentially a bilaterally symmetrical body plan. Put another way, if we could pass a very sharp instrument through and down your body along the median plane we would then have two equivalent halves, a left side and a right side. You already knew you had two arms, two legs, two feet, and so on, and that, in each case, one was located on the left side of the body and one on the right side. The human brain also gives the appearance of following this general body plan. Hence the right and left cerebral hemispheres (i.e., halves of the brain) which communicate via several bands of transverse nerve fibers that cross the median plane (commissures). The most prominent of these fibers is the *corpus callosum* (see Fig. 2-1). It is clear that the left cerebral hemisphere

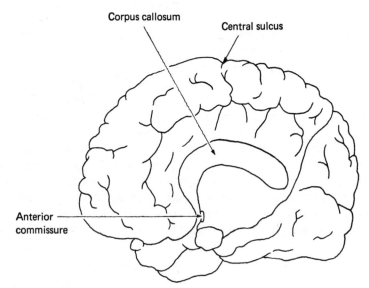

FIGURE 2-1.   *Sagittal section of hemisphere.*

controls the right side of the body, while the right cerebral hemisphere controls the left side of the body. This arrangement comes about because as the afferent (input) and efferent (output) fibers course up and down the brain and spinal cord, they decussate—that is, they cross over the median plane to the opposite side.

Bruner, as early as 1965, and later Ornstein (1972, 1977) both of whom have contributed significantly to our understanding of individual consciousness, suggested that two major modes of consciousness coexist within a single person. The data base for such a notion comes in part from research such as that of Domhoff (1969–1970), who asked a number of right-handed subjects to rate the concepts "left" and "right" on several dimensions. The subjects regarded left as "bad," "dark," "profane," and "female," while they considered right to be just the opposite of these descriptions. The investigators also suggested that the notion of two major modes of consciousness existing in one individual is apparently a cross-cultural phenomenon. Most of us are familiar with the notion of two warring factions within a single person. It is very possible that you also are familiar with Freud's notion of the conscious and the unconscious, and most adults are familiar with Robert Louis Stevenson's Dr. Jekyll and Mr. Hyde. Eastern culture counterparts include the I Ching's receptive (yin) and creative (yang) and the Buddhi and Manas of the Vedanta.

Finally, Ornstein (1977) has gone one step further and argued that "both the structure and function of these two 'half-brains' underly in some part the two modes of consciousness that coexist within each one of us" (p. 20). The obvious question is whether such a statement is wild speculation or whether there is sufficient evidence to warrant such a position. Some support for Ornstein's statement has come from the studies of individuals whose brains have been damaged by accident or illness who have undergone brain surgery. Our first understanding of cortical function was obtained from the systematic study of cases of focal epilepsy by Hughlings Jackson, first in 1863 and again in 1870. On the basis of these observations, Jackson was able to predict that an area existed in the cerebral cortex that governed isolated movements of the contralateral (opposite-sided) extremities (Marcus, 1972).

Since Jackson's study, many other clinical neurologists and psychologists have obtained data that support differential specialization of the two hemispheres. For example, Milner (1965), studying patients who had portions of the left or right cerebral cortex removed surgically as a treatment for severe epilepsy, obtained clear-cut results. Her findings suggest that verbal abilities and speech require an intact region of the left parietal lobe of the cortex (see Fig. 2-2), while spatial and complex perceptual abilities appear to depend on a comparable region of the right cerebral cortex. Also noted was the finding that musical ability seemed to depend more on the right hemisphere. The ability to handle mathematics and symbols, however, depends more on the left hemisphere. Also, studies such as those by Geschwind and Levitsky (1968) suggest that there is clearly a differential specialization of the two hemispheres. This was particularly

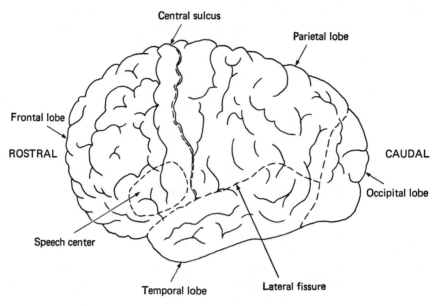

FIGURE 2-2.   *Dominant lateral cortical surface with lobes and speech center identified.*

true in the case of the parietal lobes. These investigators found that destructive lesions in the parietal lobe of the dominant hemisphere produces one or more of a complex of symptoms, including dysgraphia (a deficit in writing in the presence of intact motor and sensory functions in the upper extremities), dyscalculia (deficits in the performance of calculations), left–right confusion, and errors in finger recognition in the presence of intact sensation. Patients with involvement of the nondominant parietal lobe, however, often demonstrated abnormalities in their concepts of body image, in their perception of external space, and in their capacity to construct drawings. The Russian physiologist Luria (1966) has suggested that mathematical functioning is also disturbed by lesions in the left hemisphere.

Clinical neurological research correlating the different functions of the hemispheres impaired by brain damage is interesting, of course. However, one must keep in mind that these studies are correlational at best and thus they lack the experimental controls necessary to make conclusions about cause and effect. Equally interesting and certainly far more persuasive is the neurological research exemplified by Milner, Branch, and Rasmussen (1966), who studied 212 patients with use of the Wada technique. This procedure involves injecting a barbiturate, usually sodium amytal, into one of the carotid arteries (Wada, 1949). The effect of such an injection is to bring about an immediate contralateral paralysis (a paralysis on the side opposite the point of injection) by depression of neuronal activity. The investigators found that, when the injection depressed the hemisphere that is dominant for speech, the subject evidenced several language difficulties (e.g., difficulty in repeating a well-known series, such as the days of the week). They also observed that depression of the non-dominant hemisphere still produced the contralateral paralysis but did not produce language problems. This study clearly suggests that language functions are strongly lateralized in the human brain.

Actually, it had been known for some time that language abilities reside mainly in the left side of the brain. However, until fairly recently very few anatomical differences between the two hemispheres had been observed. With the development of more sophisticated techniques it has become clear that a number of these structural differences do exist, some of which may account for the hemispheric lateralization of functions. The most striking asymmetry in the cortex is to be found in the upper surface of the temporal lobe, the planum temporale, most of which is hidden in the lateral fissure (see Fig. 2-2). Geschwind and Levitsky (1968) observed that this area varied in both size and form. Of the 100 brains they studied, they noted that the planum temporale was larger on the left side in 65 percent, approximately equal in 24 percent, and larger in the right hemisphere in only 11 percent. Additionally, the investigators found that the posterior margin of the planum is angled backward rather than forward in the left cerebral hemisphere. Galaburda, LeMay, Kemper, and Geschwind (1978) report that the two hemispheres also evidence some cytoarchitectural (i.e., cell structure) differences. They observed that certain cell areas in this region are much larger in the left than in the right hemisphere. Such findings support both the general notion of hemispheric differentiation and specialization and the more specific fact that the speech function and related language functions appear to be centered in the left hemisphere in a large majority of people.

SPLIT-BRAIN AND CONSCIOUSNESS

Earlier in this chapter we observed that the two cerebral hemispheres appear to communicate with each other through the transverse bundles of fibers called commissures. In the early 1950s, Myers and Sperry, working with a cat, observed that when they cut the largest of these commissures, the corpus callosum, each hemisphere functioned independently as if it were a complete brain. It was only natural that this initial finding was to open up an entirely new set of research questions concerning the extent of the independence of the two hemispheres and the role of the corpus callosum in the integration of the cerebral hemisphere functions in the intact brain. Many of the questions first initiated by the split-brain preparation were subsequently pursued by Sperry and his colleagues using research animals. These findings were reviewed by Sperry (1961, 1974).

In the split-brain procedure the brain is literally divided into two halves—a left and a right hemisphere. The transverse bundles of fibers that connect the cerebral hemispheres—the anterior commissure and the corpus callosum—are surgically severed. This procedure can be carried out easily on laboratory animals. However, commissurotomy in humans is a radical surgical technique employed only as an end-of-the-line effort to control life-threatening epileptic seizures. Perhaps the most surprising observation made by Sperry and his colleagues as they followed and made extensive studies on the behavior of patients who had undergone this kind of surgery is that, despite the drastic nature of this surgical intervention, it did not produce noticeable changes in the patients' temperament, personality, or general intelligence. In fact, these patients appeared to behave quite normally.

However, closer observation of these patients' everyday behavior, combined with their performance on specialized tests devised by the experimenters, revealed some very distinct behavioral changes. For example, these patients showed a strong tendency to favor the right side of the body, which, as you will recall, is controlled by the dominant left half of the brain. While spontaneous activity was frequently observed on the right side of the body, it appeared to be lacking on the left side. Additionally, responsiveness to sensory stimulation of the left half of the body was diminished.

More specific tests of sensory function initially suggested that, while the dominant left cerebral hemisphere appeared functionally normal with respect to vision and tactile perception, the right side was severely limited. However, when patients were provided with a nonverbal means of reporting their experiences, their visual and tactile perception controlled by the right hemisphere was practically as good as that controlled by the dominant left hemisphere. Clearly the initial sensory differences observed were due to the fact that the speech centers of the brain are located in the left hemisphere.

Specific tests of motor function in these patients showed that, while the hemispheres exercised normal control over the contralateral (opposite-sided) hand, they had less than normal control over the ipsilateral (same-sided) hand. When a conflict develops between the two cerebral hemispheres, their individual inputs dictating distinctly different movements for the same hand, the hemisphere opposite the hand generally takes charge and overrides any input from the ipsilateral hemisphere.

In examining the effects of such surgery on intelligence, perception, and emotion, Sperry (1961) noted that all observations indicate that the surgery left each patient with two separate minds—that is, with two separate spheres of consciousness. As we already have seen, the dominant left hemisphere showed a clear advantage in both verbal and mathematical tasks. However, the right cerebral hemisphere did not prove to be inferior to the left in all respects. On certain spatial tasks, for example, the right hemisphere showed a clear superiority. Such patients were able to arrange blocks to match a pictured design or draw a three-dimensional cube better with their left hand than their right, which had been deprived of input from the right hemisphere. Additionally, both hemispheres appeared to be equally capable of independently generating an emotional reaction.

Clearly there is evidence to support Ornstein's suggestion (described earlier) that the structure and function of the two cerebral hemispheres underlie two distinct modes of consciousness that coexist within each of us (Puccetti, 1981). We would be going well beyond the research data available, however, were we to proclaim or leave you with the impression that Ornstein's hypothesis is now a proven fact. Basic to Ornstein's view is that consciousness exists as a dichotomy; this, however, is but one way of looking at the phenomenon. For example, Bradshaw and Nettleton (1981), citing other kinds of neurological data, argue that consciousness exists as a continuum, not as a dichotomy. Additionally, much of the supportive research we have described involved the use of patients with neurological problems or who have undergone drastic neurosurgical procedures. Certainly, at the very least, the use of such a population could introduce uncontrolled variables that might confound the research results.

In summary, very little can be said about the physiology of consciousness at this time, except what we have described as the split-brain and laterality phenomena. Some investigators argue that humans have a double, physiological consciousness; others believe that, physiologically, consciousness is not a dichotomy but rather is a continuum. Unfortunately, the state of the science does not permit us to resolve this controversy. We also would have been more than pleased to delineate physiological seats of consciousness, or places in the brain that influence or control some of the altered states of consciousness and awareness that we will discuss. However, except for some consciousness-altering drugs (see Chapter 3) and the altered state of sleep (see Chapter 7), this is not possible. Hopefully, as the study of consciousness grows as an area of interest within psychology, more will be learned about the physiology of consciousness. We look forward to the discoveries.

FOR FURTHER READING

Bennett, T. L. *Brain and behavior.* Belmont, CA: Wadsworth, 1977.

Brown, T. S., and Wallace, P. M. *Physiological psychology.* New York: Academic Press, 1980.

Bruner, J. *On knowing: essays for the left hand.* New York: Atheneum, 1965.

Carlson, N. R. *Physiology of behavior.* Boston: Allyn and Bacon, 1977.

Ornstein, R. E. *The psychology of consciousness.* New York: Harcourt, Brace, Jovanovich, 1977.

chapter three ══════════════

Consciousness-Altering Drugs

Go to your family medicine cabinet and count the number of different drugs that have been stored away. You will probably be as surprised as I was when I recently engaged in this exercise. Of course, there was the usual family-sized bottle of aspirin for that occasional headache, but that was not all that I found. To begin my count, there was my own medication for high blood pressure, a barbiturate and a diuretic. Two bottles of decongestants and several cough syrups (all prescription medications) that had been used last winter in the family's annual bout with the flu were also stored there. A three-year-old bottle of codeine pills prescribed for pain relief following oral surgery, a bottle of muscle relaxants, two containers of antihistamines, and one bottle of ear drops concluded my count. What was your list like? This exercise should drive home the notion that we are fast becoming a culture of drug users and, quite possibly, drug abusers. If, however, there is still any doubt in your mind, consider the following statistics:

1. Despite the warnings issued by the Surgeon General of the United States, approximately 54 million Americans consumed about 620 billion cigarettes in 1980 (Schlaadt and Shannon, 1982).
2. Consumption of coffee in the United States is around 12 pounds per individual (Ray, 1978).
3. In 1980 it was estimated that 10–15 percent of all Americans took diazepam (Valium) sometime during the year (Schlaadt and Shannon, 1982).

4. 31 percent of youths (12–17 years of age), 68 percent of young adults (18–25 years of age), and 20 percent of older adults (26 years of age and older) in the United States have tried marijuana (Fishburne, Abelson, and Cisin, 1979).
5. 27.5 percent of young adults (18–25 years of age) have tried cocaine (Fishburne, Abelson, and Cisin, 1979).

Clearly, drugs are quickly becoming a part of the American culture. Thus, the hypothetical American businessman, after a weekend of business and social entertaining involving the consumption of many cigarettes and alcoholic beverages, may find that he needs a couple of strong cups of coffee and several aspirin tablets to beat the Monday morning hangover. On his way to the office the traffic is terrible. He arrives too late for an important appointment, his boss is upset with his performance, and his desk is piled high with paperwork requiring his immediate attention. It is little wonder, then, that our junior executive may find himself needing something to calm himself down, perhaps a tranquilizer. After a businessman's lunch that includes at least a couple of drinks, some more work, and a battle with the homeward bound traffic, our businessman arrives home, greets his family, and collapses into his easy chair with the newspaper and a before-dinner drink. How will he ever get through an evening of bridge with the neighbors? Obviously he will take something to "pick him up," perhaps an amphetamine. The evening over, our friend gets ready for bed, only to find that the amphetamine he took earlier is now preventing him from falling asleep. Finally, in desperation, he goes to the medicine cabinet to get a sleeping pill. Unfortunately, the next morning he wakes with a splitting headache and feeling as tired as he was before he went to sleep. Thus, the vicious cycle begins again.

Traditionally, a *drug* is defined as a compound that, by virtue of its chemical structure, interacts with a specific biological system, perhaps a cell, in ways that change the structure or functions of that system (Ray, 1978). The problem with this definition is that it is much too broad and all-inclusive for our purposes. For example, food and water interact with biological systems so as to produce such changes. Under this definition, then, food and water would have to be considered drugs. However, unless one is on the verge of starvation or dehydration, it would be extremely difficult to argue that food and water have much to do with one's state of consciousness. The definitional problem is not an insurmountable one, however; all that is needed is greater specificity about the type of drugs. In the present context we are interested only in those drugs that bring about changes in consciousness or affect mood when they are swallowed, inhaled, or injected. These are the *psychoactive* drugs. Although these drugs vary considerably both in chemical structure and in their effects on awareness and mood, Ray (1978) suggests that several basic principles apply to all of them.

First, every psychoactive drug has multiple effects. Thus, while the barbiturate user may seek only one of the drug's effects, such as the euphoria or high, clearly other aspects of consciousness, such as thinking, solving problems, and remembering, are also altered.

Second, the effects of a psychoactive drug depend on the amount of drug the individual has taken. Changes in the dosage level may alter the drug's effects in two ways. Increasing the amount of the drug taken may result in a heightening of the effects obtained at lower drug levels. Also, different dosage levels may change the kind of effect. Many of us are familiar with the fact that, while a few bottles of beer may relax the drinker and produce euphoria, a pint of whiskey may well be sufficient to cause the drinker to pass out.

Third, in part, the effects of a psychoactive drug depend on the user's history and expectations. It seems logical to assume that, since these drugs change the level of awareness and thought processes, any effect they may produce in an individual would depend on preexisting conditions. Thus, such factors as attitudes, emotional state, previous drug experiences, and physical setting may interact with the drug to alter the user's level of awareness. Smith (1964) wrote: "If there is one point about which every student of the drugs agrees, it is that there is no such thing as the drug experience per se—no experience which the drugs, as it were, merely secrete. Every experience is a mix of three ingredients: drug, set (the psychological make-up of the individual), and setting (the social and physical environment in which it is taken)." In brief, to attempt to describe the effects of a particular drug without specifying these factors is an extremely difficult, if not an impossible, task.

Finally, the drug itself is neither "good" nor "bad." For example, morphine when used to alleviate the pain of a terminal cancer patient is considered good, but the same drug when used by an addict to feed a drug habit is labeled bad by most of our society. Note, however, that in actuality it is not the drug, but rather the use to which it is put, that is labeled.

BASIC PSYCHOPHARMACOLOGICAL CONCEPTS

In reading the following detailed descriptions of the physiological and consciousness-altering effects produced by a sample of psychoactive drugs, it is necessary that you familiarize yourself with a number of common psychopharmacological concepts.

Drug abuse refers primarily to the recreational, as opposed to the medical or psychiatric, use of the drug. Drug abuse is classified as a disorder by the American Psychiatric Association and is defined in terms of the resultant behaviors that are maladaptive in that they impair social functioning. Also recognized as a disorder by the American Psychiatric Association is *drug dependence,* which results from the repeated use of a drug taken in sufficient dosages such that a strong desire to continue to take the drug develops. Two kinds of drug dependence are recognized: physiological and psychological. The former is frequently referred to as *drug addiction.* This type of dependence is partially or completely organically based. Thus, through the continued use of the drug the body eventually becomes physiologically dependent on it. Physiological dependence is characteristics of users of such drugs as alcohol, barbiturates, morphine, heroin, and chlordiazepoxide (Librium.) Psychological dependence, sometimes called habituation, is a strong and sometimes overwhelming desire to continue using a drug. Such dependence is typically based on the drug's effects on consciousness levels and moods. The use of such drugs as amphetamines, barbiturates, cocaine, marijuana, and phencyclidine, which relieve anxiety or lead to euphoria, may lead to psychological dependence.

Finally, a pharmacological concept of some importance is that of *drug tolerance.* This is a physiological reaction to the prolonged use of a drug such that the body begins to require increasingly greater amounts of the agent in order to experience the same effects. Drug tolerance has been observed in the use of alcohol, barbiturates, amphetamines, and opiate derivatives, such as morphine and heroin. Sometimes the development of tolerance for one drug occurs after the repeated use of another drug. This is known as *cross-tolerance.* Thus, a heroin user may develop a tolerance not only for heroin, but also for morphine.

A cursory review of the literature from the many disciplines that are concerned with drugs (chemistry, pharmacology, law, social work, psychology) clearly demonstrates the existence of a number of drug classification schemes. To simplify matters, we have divided the psychoactive drugs into four major groups: (1) hallucinogens, (2) narcotics, (3) stimulants, and (4) depressants. From each of these categories, we have selected one or more representative agents for detailed discussion. We will examine these drugs and their effects on behavior because it is generally accepted that such drugs may bring about changes in levels or states of consciousness.

HALLUCINOGENS

The term *hallucinogen* has been reserved to describe a group of drugs that are believed to induce hallucinations, a sense perception for which there is no appropriate external stimulus. In point of fact, however, the drugs included in this category most frequently distort rather than produce sensory images. Thus, the hallucinogen user sees and hears what is going on in his or her world in very strange and different ways. The major drugs included under this heading are marijuana, lysergic acid diethylamide (LSD), psilocybin (PCP), mescaline, and peyote. In this section we will discuss marijuana and LSD as examples of the hallucinogens.

Marijuana

The earliest known record of marijuana use dates back to 2737 B.C. A description of the drug was found in a book of medicines belonging to the Chinese emperor Shen Nung. Its use as an intoxicant spread to India, where it became a favorite ingredient in Indian cookery. During the nineteenth century, English ladies visiting India enjoyed their afternoon tea, which was often served with teacakes containing marijuana. From India the use of this drug spread to North America and then to Europe. It is believed that one of the major factors involved in this later extension was the return of Napoleon's troops to France after the Egyptian campaign. Although it had been known in South and Central America for centuries, marijuana did not appear to any significant extent in the United States until about 1920 (Grinspoon, 1969). Snyder (1971) observed that a century ago, cannabis (the common hemp plant from which marijuana comes) was used for medical reasons much like aspirin is today. It could be found in almost any drug store, purchased without prescription, and was commonly prescribed by physicians for many common medical problems such as ulcers, headaches, cramps, and tooth decay. It was in 1937 that cannabis became illegal in the United States.

The leaves and flowers of the hemp plant (Cannabis sativa; see Fig. 3-1), which grows mostly in Jamaica, Mexico, Africa, India, the Middle East, and parts of the United States, when harvested and dried are what we know as marijuana. The major psychoactive constituent of the drug is the compound $1-\Delta^9$-tetrahydrocannabinol, most commonly called THC. This compound was first synthesized chemically in Israel in the 1960s, and is very expensive to manufacture. In its naturally occurring form it is concentrated in the sticky resin of the flowers and seeds of the female plant and, to a much lesser extent, in the leaves and branches of both male and female plants. Because THC resembles

FIGURE 3-1. *Cannabis sativa leaf.*

other psychoactive compounds or neurotransmitter molecules that we presently know about, we have very little idea how marijuana actually produces the changes in consciousness reported by its users.

The physiological effects of marijuana closely resemble those produced by the sympathetic nervous system when it is mildly stimulated. Cardiovascular effects include an elevated systolic blood pressure and an increased pulse rate. The respiration rate is increased, pupils may be dilated, and the eyes may be bloodshot. Certain spinal reflexes may be elicited more easily than normally, suggesting a lower sensory threshold. Additionally, gastrointestinal symptoms, such as diarrhea and nausea, may occur (Brown, 1971, 1972).

How does the inhalation of marijuana alter the awareness of the user? First, it should be noted that the subjective experiences reported by "pot" smokers vary considerably from individual to individual, and it now seems clear that an expectancy effect does operate in this situation. In fact, an expectancy effect appears to operate for subjective reports of all consciousness-altering drugs (Barber, 1970). This means simply that the smoker often describes what he or she thinks the experience ought to be. As compared with some of the other drugs we will discuss in this chapter, marijuana takes effect fairly slowly, and the subjective experiences may take as long as ten minutes to occur after the user has inhaled the smoke and even longer when the drug is ingested. It is quite possible, however, that these experiences may persist for considerable periods of time. This is because marijuana is metabolized slowly and its half-life in humans has been estimated to be as long as 48 hours (Ray, 1978).

According to Tart (1972), perhaps the most striking experiences reported by subjects were changes in perception. They observed physical objects to be clearer than before using marijuana. They examined shapes and colors very carefully. Their auditory perception underwent a similar change, with sounds being more vivid and musical notes being more pure. Some subjects reported that listening to music becomes a "total experience." Touch, taste, and smell also appeared to be similarly enhanced. Subjects reported increased appetite and appreciation for the flavor of food. Sexual pleasure seemed to be increased, although this apparently is due in large part to generally heightened perceptual awareness. In any event, there is little concrete evidence that sexual performance is improved and, indeed with large doses, it is likely to be significantly impaired. Marijuana users also report perceptual distortion of space and time fairly regularly. They may judge distances inaccurately and overestimate the passage of time.

It is these perceptual changes that may account, at least in part, for the findings reported by Petersen (1977, 1980) and Klonoff (1974). These investigators suggest that smoking the amounts of marijuana commonly used is detrimental to performance in automobile driving, whether it is measured in the laboratory or on the road. Whatever the cause, this decrement in driving skill has been firmly established as a contributor to automobile fatalities (Sterling-Smith, 1976). Janowsky, Meacham, Blaine, Shorr, and Bozzetti (1976) have also demonstrated that airplane pilots evidence a marked decrease in performance in flight simulators after getting high on marijuana.

Drowsiness and sleep may occur if the marijuana user gets high alone. However, in the presence of others the drug is more likely to induce a euphoric mood. Feelings of detachment and happiness and a preoccupation with simple and familiar objects are likely to dominate the conscious awareness of the individual. Sometimes the user experiences a paranoid state in which he or she is keenly aware of others watching. If the surrounding company seems unpleasant, the user typically withdraws rather than resorting to antisocial behavior. Marijuana users exhibit the latter behavior only rarely. While prolonged and regular use of the drug does not bring about the development of a physical dependency, it may result in a feeling of apathy, especially in adolescence; this is often referred to as the "amotivational syndrome." Such a phenomenon has not been observed in the general population, however.

Finally, smoking cannabis appears to impair memory function, particularly short-term memory. It is generally believed that such effects are short-lived and tend to disappear in a matter of only a few hours. More recently Entin has obtained results which suggest that marijuana may well have a long-term effect on memory impairment in the marijuana smoker (E. Entin, personal communication).

LSD

"Last Friday, April 16, 1943, I was forced to stop my work in the laboratory in the middle of the afternoon and to go home, as I was seized by a particular restlessness associated with a sensation of mild dizziness. On arriving home, I lay down and sank into a kind of drunkenness which was not unpleasant and which was characterized by extreme activity of imagination. As I lay in a dazed condition with my eyes closed (I experienced daylight as disagreeably bright) there surged upon me an uninterrupted stream of fantastic images of extraordinary plasticity and vividness and accompanied by an intense kaleidoscope-like play of colors. This condition gradually passed off after two hours" (Hofmann, 1971, p. 23).

Thus wrote Albert Hofmann (1906–   ), the Swiss chemist who in 1938 first extracted d-lysergic acid diethylamide (LSD-25). He was describing his experiences following the accidental ingestion of a small amount of this substance. As we noted earlier, "acid," "sugar," "big D," "trips," or "microdots," as LSD-25 is called in the language of the streets, is an extremely potent hallucinogen. The average dosage that produces changes in the individual's state of awareness or consciousness—what Barron, Jarvik, and Bunnell (1964) called the *psychomimetic effects*—is approximately 0.5-1.0 micrograms of LSD per kilogram of body weight. What is even more amazing is the fact that, if such a dosage is taken orally, only about 1 percent of it will ever reach the brain. While it is generally agreed that the use of LSD probably does not produce either physica. or psychological dependency, it is known that the user develops a ιoierance for the drug very quickly. After three or four days of use, previously effective dosage levels become ineffectual. However, this tolerance appears to be lost after an equal period of abstinence.

Chemical analysis of this white, tasteless, odorless powder reveals that structurally LSD-25 is composed of a lysergic acid and a diethylamide portion. The former is a natural product of the ergot fungus than can be found growing on grains, especially rye. The latter component is related structurally to certain other drugs that are commonly employed as smooth-muscle relaxants. Perhaps the most interesting chemical feature of the LSD molecule, however, is the existence of what chemists refer to as an indole ring. As you can see in Figure 3-2, the indole ring is characteristic not only of LSD and PCP (both hallucinogenic drugs), but also of the neurotransmitter substance serotonin.

At present, exactly how the LSD-25 molecule exerts its effect on an individual's state of consciousness is not completely understood. However, current theory, based in large part on the work of Aghajanian, Haigler, and Bloom (1972) and Haigler and Aghajanian (1974), suggests that the LSD molecule acts to inhibit the firing of those serotonin-rich cells of the raphe nucleus, which are located in the brain stem. The investigators found that delivery of very small

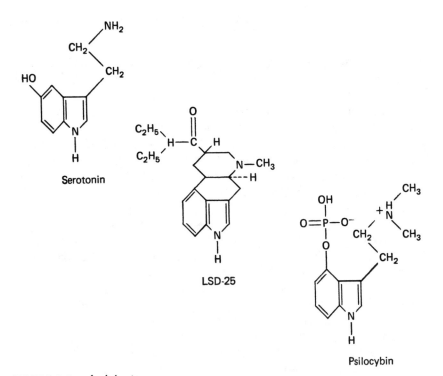

Serotonin

LSD-25

Psilocybin

FIGURE 3-2.   *Indole ring.*

amounts of LSD-25 directly to the neurons of the raphe could inhibit its firing. Most of the raphe can be classified as inhibitory; thus, the net effect of LSD, according to their theory, is removal of the inhibition from the neural sites to which the raphe nucleus projects, such as the hypothalamus, the septum, the hippocampus, the cortex, the basal ganglia, the amygdala, and the cerebellum (Dahlström and Fuxe, 1964; Fuxe and Jonsson, 1974; Ungerstedt, 1971).

What types of changes in consciousness might one expect to experience after the ingestion of an average dose of LSD? The following paragraphs describe some of the most typical experiences reported by LSD users. It is necessary, however, to keep in mind that such effects may vary considerably as a function of the interaction of the user's mental set, environmental setting, and the drug.

After the oral ingestion of a sugar cube (upon which LSD is typically applied for ingestion), there is generally a period of 30–45 minutes during which no effects occur. This is followed by a period of 8–10 hours, during which the individual goes through changes in sensory perception, lability of emotional experiences, and feelings of depersonalization and detachment. These changes in awareness typically peak between the second and the fourth hour of the LSD experience.

Chief among these experiences are the changes reported in sensory perception. Katz, Waskow, and Olsson (1968) observed that, while there is a feeling of perceptual sharpness, perceptions of the outer world take on an unreal quality. Vision appears to be the sense affected most profoundly (Levine, 1969). Illusions develop initially as both objects and people in the environment appear to change color, shape, and perspective (Ebin, 1961). Walls and other objects may become wavy and appear to move; colors seem brighter and more intense. Bizarre shapes and designs that have no basis in reality may also be seen. Generally, awareness of time is also affected such that the individual cannot distinguish past, present, and future. Often the LSD user reports the visual perception of music or the "warmth" of red and the "icy" feeling of blue. This curious phenomenon, which involves the translation of one type of sensory experience into another, is called *synesthesia.*

Such distortions in consciousness, when combined with an emotional state of euphoria, are descriptive of what was labeled a "mind expanding" trip during the LSD craze of the 1960s. Many of the early, prominent proponents of the drug, such as author Aldous Huxley (1894-1963), as cited by Ray (1978), suggested that its use allowed them to achieve a degree of personal insight, increased their sensitivity, produced mystical experiences, and helped them to develop an understanding of their place in the universe that they could not have achieved in any other way. Lilly (1972) observed that the LSD experience may lead not only to mystical or transcendental adventures, but also to profound insights. While it has been suggested that LSD experiences can bring about an enhancement of creative activity, studies by the American Medical Association (1968) and by independent investigators (Rinkel, 1966) have failed to provide supportive evidence for such a claim.

Not all LSD experiences can be described as pleasant, mind expanding trips. In fact, some experiences, referred to as "bad trips," can be extremely harrowing and traumatic. Although the problem has been addressed experimentally (Blacker, Jones, Stone, and Pfefferbaum, 1968), exactly what determines whether a trip will be pleasurable or nightmarish remains unknown. As is the case with the pleasurable trip, hallucinations constitute a dominant feature of the bad LSD experience. Objects and people in the environment, as well as one's own body image, may become distorted so that they are perceived as grotesque and threatening. These perceptions may seem so unreal as to produce a feeling of detachment from the real world. Strange and bizarre thoughts and emotions may creep into consciousness, and the user may have mental experiences that may cause him or her to feel completely out of control. Such thoughts may represent a major break with reality—a belief that one can fly, walk on water, or perform some other amazing feat. Depression and feelings of acute anxiety or panic are often a part of the bad trip. Occasionally these feelings may lead to extremely dangerous self-directed behavior, including suicide. Smith and Rose (1967-68) have observed that a feeling of paranoia may also develop, in which the individual fears not only strangers but friends and relatives as well.

Finally, some individuals experience the phenomenon of "flashbacks." The flashback is a spontaneous, involuntary recurrence of perceptual distortions or hallucinations that may follow LSD use weeks or even months later. Flashbacks may produce changes that are every bit as vivid as those experienced during the original trip. However, since the individual is completely unprepared for such an experience, he or she is likely to react to it with fear, anxiety, and, in some cases, psychotic behavior (Smith and Rose, 1967-68; Horowitz, 1969; Brecher, 1972).

In addition to alteration of the state of awareness, LSD produces a number of other effects. Ataxia, or loss of muscle coordination, and spastic paralysis are frequently observed. Autonomic effects include an elevated heart rate (tachycardia) and blood pressure, faster and more erratic breathing, excessive amounts of sugar in the blood (hyperglycemia), elevation in body temperature, and pupillary dilation.

NARCOTICS

The opium derivatives morphine, heroin, codeine, and methadone, along with their antagonists (e.g., nalorphine) make up the class of consciousness-altering drugs referred to as narcotics. Of course, these agents do have a medical use—the alleviation of pain. At low concentrations narcotics serve this function without causing drowsiness or sleep. At higher concentrations, however, they inevitably lead to sleep. Heroin, the most frequently abused narcotic, is discussed in this section.

"Horse," "Harry," "smack," "stuff," "junk," or just plain "H" are but a few of the many street names by which heroin is known. A derivative of the opium poppy plant, Papaver somniferum (Fig. 3-3), heroin is usually introduced into the body by smoking, "snorting," eating, "skin popping," and "mainlining." The last two are techniques that use a hypodermic syringe. In the case of skin popping, the liquefied heroin is injected just beneath the surface of the skin. Mainlining involves the introduction of the drug directly into the bloodstream by intravenous injection.

The name of the drug is derived from the Greek god Heros, who was the "savior of mankind." In a real sense, that is probably how many initially viewed heroin after its discovery in 1874 by Heinrich Dreser. Another opium derivative, morphine, had been used before Dreser's work, both as an analgesic and in the treatment of alcoholism. However, it proved to have one serious side effect: its use often led to addiction. Dreser, searching for a nonaddictive opiate, found that by treating morphine with an inexpensive and readily available chemical called acetic anhydride, he could produce a drug much more potent

FIGURE 3-3. *Opium poppy plant.*

than morphine without the addictive properties, or so he thought. Rapidly the new drug replaced morphine as a painkiller, and later, by the early 1900s, heroin was being used in the treatment of alcoholism and morphine addiction. Soon it was found, however, that heroin was not only more powerful than morphine but also more addictive. Since 1912 the Harrison Act and subsequent laws and court decisions have progressively restricted the legal use of heroin until today, when its use for any purpose is considered illegal.

In addition to restricting the level of awareness of the user, the effect of heroin reported most frequently is an immediate and intense feeling of pleasure, lasting about one to five minutes and often described as resembling a whole-body orgasm (Mathis, 1970). This brief euphoric spasm, called a "rush," "bang," or "kick," is followed by a sense of euphoria and contentment that may last from four to six hours. During this high period, the heroin user is able to escape reality and experience the predominantly pleasant feelings of relaxation, euphoria, and reverie. Since the heroin user no longer cares about much of anything, he or she does not seem to be bothered by tensions and anxieties. Everything looks rosy and harmonious, at least until the drug effects wear off. Lethargy, withdrawal, and a marked diminution of bodily needs, including those for food and sex, are typically experienced during this phase. As one might predict, heroin has a dramatic effect on pain perception and the response to it. The major effect on pain, however, is not so much to raise the pain threshold as to simply change the response to pain. Heroin makes the pain bearable.

Heroin also produces some physiological reactions, including pupillary constriction, changes in body temperature, constipation, nausea, and vomiting. Clearly not all of these reactions are pleasant. However, the negative physiological effects seem to be overridden by the euphoria and the escape from reality. Continued use of heroin results in the development of both a psychological dependence and a tolerance and physiological craving for the drug. After frequent and repeated administration of smack for two or three weeks, a tenfold tolerance can easily develop. Although the actual time necessary to establish the drug habit varies considerably from individual to individual, it has been estimated that continued use over one month or longer is sufficient to develop a physiological addiction. The addict finds that the high is followed by a negative phase that produces a desire for more of the drug. If for some reason the supply of the drug is cut off for even a short time, the heroin addict enters into a phase of withdrawal, during which he or she becomes physically ill. Finally, as one might anticipate, individuals vary widely in their reactions to the drug. Thus, for some, the introduction to heroin is anything but pleasant. Such experimenters may experience only the nausea, vomiting, and other discomforts associated with heroin use (Isabell and White, 1953).

In altering the state of consciousness, opiate drugs such as heroin apparently act upon the central nervous system (CNS). For some years it had been hypothesized that these drugs might in fact be acting on specific receptor sites in the brain. The way the opiate drug acts on these sites is suggested to resemble a lock-and-key mechanism. Thus, the receptors are specific nerve cells that serve as locks into which the appropriate opiate drug fits.

Pert and Snyder (1973) from The Johns Hopkins University were the first to provide experimental evidence that such receptor sites actually exist. They first injected radioactively tagged naloxone into each of their animal subjects. (Naloxone is a drug whose chemical substance so closely resembles morphine that its molecules fit the same receptor locks. Thus it acts as an opiate antagonist and competes for the same receptor sites.) This afforded the investigators the opportunity to observe the distribution of radioactivity and thus the distribution of opiate receptors. Their findings suggest that the opiate receptor sites are to be found in especially large numbers in the amygdala, the caudate nucleus, the substantia nigra, the medial nuclei of the thalamus, and the periventricular and periacqueductal gray matter that immediately surrounds the ventricles in the lower portion of the brain. Other investigators, Simantov, Goodman, Aposhian, and Snyder (1976), discovered that only vertebrates possess receptors of this type. However, the degree to which opiate receptors appear seems to be constant among all vertebrates, from the most primitive to the most advanced.

Another reason for suspecting that the opiates may operate on specific receptor sites in the brain was best expressed by Restak (1977). Restak suggested that the existence of a lock strongly suggests the existence of a key or keys in the brain. Stated differently, if there are opiate receptor sites in the brain, then there should also be opiumlike substances that are manufactured in the brain. In 1975, Hughes and associates at the University of Aberdeen (Scotland) announced their discovery of two short-chained peptides called enkephalins, which are produced in the brain and distributed in the same locations as the receptor sites (Hughes, Smith, Kosterlitz, Fothergill, Morgan, and Morris, 1975). These results have been confirmed in other laboratories (Akil, Watson, Sullivan, and Barchas, 1978).

Such advancements in the understanding of the physiological mechanisms that underly opiumlike drug activity led Snyder (1977) to offer a theory of opiate addiction. According to Snyder, under normal conditions opiate receptors are exposed to a certain basal level of enkephalin. If an opiate drug is administered to the individual at this time, the drug molecules will proceed to bind the usually unoccupied receptor sites. The net effect is a potentiation of the analgesic effects of the enkephalin system. If the administration of opiates is continued, the opiate receptor sites are soon overloaded with opiatelike material, causing them to transmit a message, probably by some hypothetical neuronal feedback loop, to the enkephalin neurons to cease firing and releasing enkephalin. Once this occurs, the receptor cells are exposed only to the opiate, and they can now tolerate more of it in order to make up for the enkephalin they are no longer receiving. When the administration of the opiate is terminated, the opiate receptors find themselves with neither the opiate nor the enkephalin. Snyder believes that it is this lack that initiates a sequence of events resulting in withdrawal.

STIMULANTS

Drugs such as caffeine, strychnine, pentylenthetrazol (Metrazol), amphetamines, and cocaine share at least one common property: they all excite the CNS. This stimulation or speeding up of CNS activity is accomplished in a variety of ways, but the end effect on the individual's state of consciousness is the same—the production of a heightened level of arousal. In this section we have chosen to discuss cocaine, a definite consciousness-altering drug, as one of the major abused stimulants.

Cocaine is a natural plant product which is derived from the leaves of Erythoxylon coca, a plant that thrives on the Amazon slopes of the Andes Mountains of Bolivia and Peru, where there is an annual rainfall of more than 100 inches (Ray, 1978). Research indicates that as early as 500 A.D., the native inhabitants of these areas chewed on the leaves of this tree to increase their physical stamina (Guerra, 1971).

Before the invasion led by Juan Pizarro (1470-1541) in the 1500s, the Incas had built a well-developed civilization in Peru. The coca leaves played an important role in Inca culture, functioning initially as a part of the religious ceremonies and later, by the time the Spanish under Pizarro had arrived, as a medium of exchange. The conquistadors also adopted this custom and paid the native laborers in coca leaves for mining and transporting gold and silver. The leaves probably gave the workers an increased sense of strength and endurance and at the same time decreased their appetites (Ray, 1978).

While historians, through their writings on Inca civilization, had made available to Europeans the knowledge of the unique properties of the coca leaves much earlier, no real interest in the plant was manifested on the Continent until the later part of the nineteenth century (Taylor, 1949).

Ray (1978) suggests that there were three individuals who played very prominent roles in the introduction of cocaine to Europe. One was the French chemist Angelo Mariani, who first made the coca leaves available to the general public by using their extract in the production of a series of products, including coca tea, coca lozenges, and his famous Mariani coca wine. Uplifted spirits, freedom from fatigue, and an overall good feeling were the major benefits derived by consumers of Mariani's coca leaf extract products. The second member of this trio was Sigmund Freud (1856-1939), the father of psychoanalysis. In the early 1800s, while suffering from a bout of depression and fatigue, Freud read an account of the isolation of cocaine and was determined to experiment with this "new" drug. He found that it not only relieved his own depression and fatigue, but it also seemed to provide him with new-found energy to continue his work. It is clear that his personal experiences with the drug, combined with the results he achieved using it in his practice, made Freud an early advocate of cocaine. Thus in his *Cocaine Papers*, written in 1885, Freud recited a litany of the drug's supposed therapeutic benefits, which included:

(1) effectiveness as a local anesthetic, (2) production of exhilaration and aphrodisiac properties, (3) usefulness in treating asthma and digestive disorders of the stomach, and (4) its role in the treatment of alcohol and morphine addiction. It was in regard to the last benefit that Freud wrote:

> It was first discovered in America that cocaine is capable of alleviating the serious withdrawal symptoms observed in subjects who are abstaining from morphine and of suppressing their craving for morphine . . . On the basis of my experiences with the effects of cocaine, I have no hesitation in recommending the administration of cocaine for such withdrawal cures in subcutaneous injections of 0.03 to 0.05 grams per dose, without any fear of increasing the dose. On several occasions, I have even seen cocaine quickly eliminate the manifestations of intolerance that appeared after a rather large dose of morphine, as if it had a specific ability to counteract morphine (Freud, 1885).

So convinced was Freud of the effectiveness of cocaine in this connection that he used it in the treatment of the morphine addiction of a close friend, Dr. Fleischel. What transpired clearly was not anticipated. Freud found that, as treatment progressed, increasingly larger doses of the drug were needed, until finally a cocaine-induced psychosis was precipitated. This experience was more than adequate to change Freud's initial attitudes toward cocaine (Jones, 1953).

Finally, in 1890, it was made public that the world's foremost, fictitious detective, Sherlock Holmes, advocated the use of cocaine as a means of relieving the boredom of a day-to-day existence (Grilly, 1978). In *The Sign of the Four* (Doyle, 1938), the fictitious Dr. Watson describes the effects of cocaine use on the master detective:

> 'Three times a day for many months I had witnessed this performance, but custom had not reconciled my mind to it. . .
>
> 'Which is it today,' I asked, 'morphine or cocaine?'
>
> 'He raised his eyes languidly from the old black-letter volume which he had opened.
>
> 'It is cocaine,' he said, 'a seven-percent solution. Would you care to try it?'
>
> 'No, indeed,' I answered brusquely. 'My constitution has not got over the Afghan campaign yet. I cannot afford to throw any extra strain upon it.'
>
> He smiled at my behemence. 'Perhaps you are right, Watson,' he said. 'I suppose that its influence is physically a bad one. I find it, however, so transcendently stimulating and clarifying to the mind that its secondary action is a matter of small moment.'

'But consider!' I said earnestly. 'Count the cost! Your brain may, as you say, be roused and excited, but it is a pathological and morbid process which involves increased tissue-change and may at least have a permanent weakness. You know, too, what a black reaction comes upon you. Surely the game is hardly worth candle. Why should you, for a mere passing pleasure, risk the loss of those great powers with which you have been endowed?' . . .

He did not seem offended. On the contrary, he put his finger-tips together, and leaned his elbows on the arm of his chair, like one who has a relish for conversation.

'My mind,' he said, 'rebels at stagnation. Give me problems, give me work, give me the most abstruse cryptogram, or the most intricate analysis and I am in my own proper atmosphere. I can dispense then with artificial stimulants. But I abhor the dull routine of existence. I crave for mental exaltation.' (pp. 91-92).

In the United States, use of cocaine for both medical and quasimedical purposes was widespread around the turn of the century. Drummers sold their "snake oils," "elixirs of life," and patent medicines, all of which supposedly contained a secret ingredient to bring long life, a sense of exhilaration, and well-being to all its users. Very often the so-called secret ingredient was cocaine. In fact, cocaine was also at one time an ingredient in cola soft drinks. With the passage of the Harrison Act of 1914, use of cocaine was forced underground, where it was to remain virtually until the emergence of the drug subculture in the late 1960s. Since 1969 use of cocaine in the United States has shown a substantial increase.

Cocaine acts both as a local anesthetic and as a CNS stimulant. The ability of cocaine to numb the area to which it has been applied topically was first discovered in 1860 by a Viennese doctor, Carl Koller. Low concentrations of cocaine used in this manner appear to block neural conduction when brought into direct contact with sensory nerve fibers. The drug's ability to increase the awareness level of the user represents the CNS function of cocaine. All available evidence would suggest that the initial central effect occurs at the level of the cerebral cortex, although it is possible that this effect may be mediated by subcortical activity.

The increase in CNS arousal is closely associated with the action of cocaine at noradrenergic synapses—that is, synapses at which norepinephrine serves as the transmitter substance. It is generally accepted that cocaine inhibits norepinephrine. This means that the transmitter will be in contact with postsynaptic receptor sites at higher concentrations and for longer periods than would normally be the case.

The gross physiological responses to cocaine are essentially sympathomimetic. Both heart rate and respiration rate are increased, and blood pressure is elevated. Peripherally, the drug increases the user's body temperature and brings about a constriction of the peripheral blood vessels. Despite these functional changes, it is currently not clear whether cocaine produces physiological dependence (Jaffe, 1980; Petersen, 1979).

Cocaine, also referred to as "coke," "flake," "snow," and "gold dust," is a white, translucent, flaky substance that is usually mixed with a sugar substance to cut its strength. Coke is very convenient to use (Ashley, 1976). In the United States, cocaine is most frequently inhaled, or snorted, into each nostril. The drug is absorbed from the mucous lining into the bloodstream, reaching the brain almost instantaneously. Another, more dangerous method of ingestion is intravenous injection, or mainlining. Additionally, cocaine can be prepared so that it can be smoked, a technique that is common in Latin America. Clearly, factors such as how cocaine is ingested and what dosage is used will play a major role in the determination of both the physiological and the psychological effects of the drug (Resnick, Kestenbaum, and Schwartz, 1977).

A typical single dose of cocaine, (approximately 30 milligrams), ingested in the usual manner (i.e., snorting) usually precipitates a state of euphoria that peaks in a matter of a few minutes. The high typically lasts between 20 and 40 minutes, generally with little or no discernable aftereffects (Ray, 1978). This altered state of consciousness, however, may be preceded by headache, dizziness, and restlessness. Feelings of fatigue and sleepiness vanish and are replaced by those of exhilaration, new-found energy, and excitement. The individual may exude a sense of increased self-confidence, which may be a product of the feelings of enhanced mental abilities. Cocaine has been viewed as a social drug, one that has recreational properties; that is, instead of turning inward, the user becomes talkative and seeks the company of others. Finally, it has been reported that cocaine may enhance the user's sex drive and sexual experience. At least one study (Resnick, Kestenbaum, and Schwartz, 1977) has produced results that suggest a biphasic effect of cocaine—that is, an initial state of euphoria followed by dysphoria. Six of the subjects in this study reported that, following an initial high, they experienced "postcoke blues" or "crashing," which was characterized by feelings of anxiety, depression, fatigue, and a desire for more cocaine.

Most users do not habitually take high dosages (Post, 1975). However, when coke is chronically abused it produces a toxic syndrome that is typified by an enhanced sense of physical and mental capacity; loss of appetite; grinding of teeth; stereotyped, repetitious behavior; and paranoia. One interesting common symptom is the appearance of the "cocaine bugs," technically called formication (Post, 1975). The user feels a sensation like bugs crawling under his or her skin, and the sensation may become so great that he or she may resort to using a knife to cut them out. Drug-induced stimulation of free nerve endings in the skin probably is the physiological basis for this phenomenon (Ellinwood, 1969). Recent studies (e.g., Wetii and Wright, 1979) suggest that only in rare cases does chronic abuse of cocaine prove fatal.

DEPRESSANTS

Included in this class of drugs are alcohol, chloral hydrate, paraldehyde, the bromides, methaqualone (Quaalude), and barbiturates. Depressants bring about a reduction in both behavioral output and level of consciousness. This is accomplished primarily by decreasing the activity of the recticular activating system and other areas of the brain (Ray, 1978). In this section we will discuss the use and abuse of alcohol and barbiturates.

Alcohol

Although few of us probably view alcoholic beverages as drugs in the same way that we do heroin, barbiturates, amphetamines, and tranquilizers, the fact remains that alcohol does fit our initial definition of a drug in that its chemical structure interacts with a specific biological system so as to produce a change in the structure or function of that system. What is even more important here is that alcohol alters both the mood and the conscious state of the user. Thus, it is also a psychoactive drug.

From a historical standpoint it would appear that alcohol has been with us for a very long time. Mead, which was made from honey, is probably the oldest of the alcoholic beverages, and some authorities (Ray, 1978) suggest that it first appeared as early as about 8000 B.C. Beer and berry wine were known and used about 6400 B.C., while grape wine first made its appearance about 300–400 B.C. Cambyses, king of Persia in the sixth century B.C., holds the dubious distinction of being one of the first alcoholics on record. His drunken episodes apparently were associated with periods of uncontrollable rage. He behaved much like "a madman not in possession of his senses" (Whitwell, 1936, p. 38). On one occasion it is reported that Cambyses, without making any plans for the feeding of his troops, set out to thrash the Ethiopians, who had angered the king by referring to the Persians as "dung eaters." Because of his lack of preplanning, King Cambyses and his troops were forced to retreat to Memphis, where, much to his anger, he found his people celebrating the feast of Apis. In his drunken state and perceiving that the people were rejoicing at his failure, he ordered that the entire citizenry taking part in the feast be executed. The list of other celebrities, poets, painters, authors, musicians, and leaders who are known to have used alcohol excessively in their lifetimes would be endless—Samuel Butler, Lord Byron, Edgar Allan Poe, Ulysses Grant, John Barrymore, and Ernest Hemingway, to name a few.

The basis for all alcoholic beverages is a process called *fermentation.* Certain yeasts act on sugar (glucose) in the presence of water so that the yeast recombines the carbon (C), hydrogen (H), and oxygen (O) of the sugar and water into ethyl alcohol and carbon dioxide ($C_6H_{12}O_6 + H_2O \xrightarrow{\text{yeast}} C_2H_6O + CO_2$). Glucose is readily available in most fruits, including grapes. The limitation of this process lies in the fact that yeast generally has only a limited tolerance for alcohol. Thus, when the alcohol concentration reaches approximately 15 percent, the yeast cells die and the fermentation process is terminated.

Cereal grains are also used in the production of alcoholic drinks, but here the process is somewhat different. To begin with, grains contain starches, not sugars. Thus, before fermentation can take place it is necessary to convert the starches to sugars by the use of enzymes during a process called *malting*. The grain is placed in water and allowed to sprout; afterward it is dried slowly to kill off the sprouts while preserving the enzymes that were formed during the growth. This dried, sprouted grain is then crushed, and, when mixed with water, the enzymes convert the starch to sugar. Once yeast is added, fermentation can begin.

However, what if concentrations of alcohol stronger than the 15 percent that can be obtained by fermentation are desired? In this case it would be necessary to resort to a second process, called *distillation*. During this process an alcohol-containing solution is heated; the resulting vapors are then collected and condensed into a liquid form once more. Because of the difference in the boiling points of alcohol and water, (alcohol has a lower boiling point), the distillation process produces a much higher concentration of alcohol in the distillate (the condensed liquid) than was present in the original solution. While there are any number of variations in the processes leading to the end product (e.g., charcoal fire brewing, storing and aging in special barrels), it is the processes of fermentation and distillation that determine the beverage's alcoholic content. In the United States the alcoholic content of a distilled beverage is indicated on the label by the term *proof*. Thus, when a friend gives you a gift bottle of 90-proof rum you should know that you are really getting a distillate from the fermentation of sugar cane molasses, which now contains 45 percent ethyl alcohol. In brief, the percentage of alcohol by volume is one-half the proof number indicated on the label.

Because of its widespread use and, often, abuse, it is safe to assume that many of you have had some personal contact with one or more of the many alcoholic beverages available during the course of your life. These experiences may range from a curiosity-motivated sip of beer or wine "just to see what it tastes like" to a more dangerous "lost weekend" to (most probably) something in between these two extremes. You may have discovered already, by comparing your experiences with those of your friends, that alcohol, like most other drugs, produces a variety of behavioral effects. Some of these effects are general and are experienced by most people, while others are peculiar to the individual and may well be the result of an interaction of the individual's mental set, the setting, and the alcohol.

Alcohol is a consciousness-limiting drug that appears to attack and numb the higher brain centers. See what happens to our fictitious friend, Joe College, whose fraternity pledge class has decided to hold its annual weekend "house-cleaning-and-keg" party. By Friday evening the fraternity house is spanking clean, the older members have gone their various ways, and now the kegs and other assorted bottles are brought from their hiding places: the party has officially begun. Depending on how tired he is, when he ate last, his body size, his mood, and a host of other factors, the first drink or two may have little effect on Joe's state of awareness. However, with a couple of more drinks Joe's alertness is decreased and he begins to experience good feelings—feelings of expansiveness, warmth, and well-being. All the unpleasantness, tensions, and worries of the real world begin to melt away. His feelings of self-worth are greatly increased and everybody is Joe's friend. With a few more drinks our friend's judgment and other rational processes become impaired and his self-control diminishes. With the diminution of restraints more primitive emotional responses are very likely to occur, (e.g., the lamp shade on the head, crying, and even aggression), responses that under more normal circumstances he would have kept under control. Most of us are familiar with the "crying" or "belligerent" drunk. By now the alcoholic content in Joe's bloodstream has reached or exceeded 0.1 percent, and he is officially intoxicated. Joe's motor coordination is now beginning to show some signs of impairment. This, combined with slowed reaction times and impaired judgment, means that it is time for one of Joe's sober friends to hide the keys to his new car. Should Joe decide to go for a ride at this point he would be a menace, not only to himself, but also to anyone else on the road. As the drinking continues and the alcoholic content of Joe's blood increases, his ability to sense pain, cold, and other discomforts is also severely diminished. Perhaps you know someone who took a flask of the spirits to a football game or on a winter hunting expedition to help keep warm, only to suffer frostbite or worse because of an inability to sense accurately the severity of the cold weather.

Certainly by this point the clumsiness, staggering, the unsteadiness in standing and walking, all symptomatic of impaired motor coordination and vision, are very apparent. Joe's speech is now badly slurred, and his judgment of his own condition and ability is extremely disturbed. When Joe's blood alcohol reaches approximately 0.5 percent, his entire neural balance is upset and he slowly slides out of his chair and under the table. He has passed out. As blood alcohol concentrations above 0.55 percent are considered lethal, it is generally agreed that this lapsing into a state of unconsciousness is simply the body's way of protecting itself. An unconscious drinker is not likely to take another drink, at least for a while. Had Joe College's bout with the "demon spirits" gone this far he probably would awaken the next day with an upset stomach, fatigue, headache, thirst, depression, anxiety, and an overall bad feeling—the classic hangover. It is also quite probable that he will not be able to remember many of the previous night's events (the "blackout").

Exactly how alcohol produces these effects is not yet clear. However, at a cellular level, the best evidence to date would suggest that it acts directly on the membrane of the neuron rather than on the synapse. It is generally accepted that alcohol acts on the nerve cell's ability to produce electrical impulses so that it is unable to process information normally. Specifically affected, at least initially, are nerve cells that comprise the ascending reticular activating system (ARAS). Depression of the activity of this system leads in turn to a disruption of cortical activity and the changes in behavior and arousal observed in the drinker.

Barbiturates

In the 1850s a group of new chemical compounds called *bromides* was introduced. These agents gained almost immediate popularity as a sleep preparation. However, with this popularity came abuse and the realization that such excessive use of bromides results in consciousness-altering effects such as delusions, hallucinations, and a variety of neurological disturbances. The toxic psychosis caused by bromide abuse proved to be a major cause of admissions to mental hospitals for some time (Jarvik, 1967). Participating in the search for a sleep-inducing drug with fewer dangerous side effects, Adolf von Bayer (1835-1917) in Munich, Germany, succeeded in combining urea with malonic acid to produce a new compound called barbituric acid (Sharpless, 1970). Bayer's 1862 creation was not a CNS depressant; however, the many barbiturates that came to be derived from barbituric acid proved to be excellent CNS depressants. The first barbiturate to be used clinically, barbital (Veronal), was introduced in 1903.

Although barbiturates have legitimate medical uses (e.g., tension reduction, relaxation, sleep induction), they have proved to be extremely dangerous and are commonly associated with both physiological and psychological dependence as well as fatalities from overdose. Barbiturates are usually classified on the basis of the duration of their activity (Martindale, 1967). It is the short-acting agents, such as pentobarbital (Nembutal) and secobarbital (Seconal), that are abused. These are the barbiturates that are likely to produce the initial euphoric high within 15 minutes after they have been ingested. The duration of their action is typically between two and three hours. Tolerance to barbiturates develops gradually, and the dosage must be increased periodically in order to maintain a constant effect. Unfortunately, as the dosage required to produce the same effect increases, the lethal dosage remains the same. Thus, as tolerance develops, the difference between these two dosage levels becomes dangerously small.

When the daily dosage required by the individual reaches about 400 milligrams, the individual will probably experience some withdrawal symptoms if barbiturate use is temporarily interrupted. Traditionally, barbiturate dependence has been associated with an emotionally maladjusted individual seeking relief from the stresses and strains of life. More recently the introduction of the "all new and greatly improved" diet pill has provided a new cause of barbiturate addiction. The old diet pills helped the user shed unwanted pounds of fat but produced a bad case of "jumpy nerves." This was because the old diet pills contained only amphetamines. To counteract this unwanted side effect, the new pills contain fixed-ratio combinations of amphetamines and barbiturates.

Unfortunately, both types of drugs are highly addictive, either separately or in combination. In addition, since the addition of barbiturates may make the amphetamines more tolerable, addiction-prone persons may increase their pill intake rapidly, thus increasing the possibility of addiction to both drugs (Kunnes, 1973).

While this fact may help to account for the increase in barbiturate abuse among middle-aged persons, it does little to explain such an increase among teenagers. Cohen (1971), testifying before a U.S. Senate subcommittee to investigate juvenile delinquency, noted that, "For the youngster barbiturates are a more reliable 'high' and less detectable than 'pot.' They are less strenuous than LSD, less 'freaky' than amphetamines, and less expensive than heroin. A school boy can 'drop a red' and spend the day in a dreamy, floating state of awayness untroubled by reality. It is drunkenness without the odor of alcohol. It is escape for the price of one's lunch money."

Teenagers have also discovered a distinctly different effect that is obtained by combining barbiturates, amphetamines, and alcohol; this effect has been described as a controlled hypersensitivity. Because barbiturates and alcohol potentiate one another, one very real possible effect of such a combination is barbiturate overdose and death.

It is generally agreed that barbiturates have their primary effect on chemical transmission at the synapse rather than on neuron conduction. Exactly how this is accomplished remains unknown. However, the best hypothesis to date suggests that barbiturates decrease the release of excitatory neurotransmitters from the terminal vesicles of the presynaptic element. At clinical dosages, barbiturates have little or no effect on peripheral nervous system activity. However, at the CNS level they produce a general diminution of brain excitability (Sharpless, 1970). This decrease in brain activity probably can be best accounted for by the fact that the multisynaptic pathways of the ARAS are among the first of the major brain centers to be affected by barbiturates.

Shortly after dropping some "rainbows" (Tuinal) or "red devils" (Seconal), the individual experiences feelings of relaxation, some behavioral stimulation, and a euphoric high. It is also possible that the individual will exhibit some aggressive behavior, as if he or she were fighting the inevitable drowsiness and sleep. This is especially the case if the barbiturate used is secobarbital (Tinklenberg and Woodrow, 1974). These effects on the consciousness level of the user are then replaced by a sense of confusion and cognitive impairment such that solving problems and making decisions seem to require a great deal of effort; the individual is usually aware that his or her thinking is, at best, "fuzzy." Memory and concentration may also be impaired. Emotionally, the user is likely to be extremely labile, ranging from the euphoric high to severe depression. Finally, loss of motor coordination is reflected in the person's slurred speech, depressed motor activity, and staggering gait (Wesson and Smith, 1971). At dosages of between 100 and 200 milligrams, secobarbital and pentobarbital have a hypnotic or sleep-producing effect; thus they are often employed in the treatment of certain sleep disorders, including insomnia. This will be discussed in some detail in Chapter 7. It is sufficient here to note only that these drugs do not bring about a normal sleep in that rapid eye movement sleep is suppressed (Dement, 1972).

In addition to the behavioral effects described, barbiturates also produce psychophysiological effects suggestive of parasympathetic arousal, including pupillary constriction, decreased heart rate and blood pressure, and depressed respiratory rate. Excessive dosages are lethal because they result in a paralysis of the respiratory centers of the brain.

To summarize, many drugs have been or are being abused by adults as well as by children as young as four or five years. Whenever a "new" drug becomes available, there undoubtedly are individuals who will try it and find that it produces a new consciousness-altering experience. This person will tell his or her friends of the experience and they may proceed to try it. Thus we have the makings of a new drug of abuse. Very little can be done to protect society from such abuse except to prohibit the use of the drug totally, even for beneficial medical purposes. This is impractical, however; besides, it would not halt the abuse of drugs any more than prohibition stopped the use of alcohol in the United States. As was mentioned in Weil's (1972) theory in Chapter 1, many humans have a drive to experience altered states of consciousness. Unfortunately, this drive may exhibit itself in the abuse of certain drugs, such as the ones we have described here. Our list is by no means comprehensive or all-inclusive. We have chosen to discuss what we consider the most abused drugs. Hopefully, this list will not grow with the continued development of the study of consciousness in the 1980s and the 1990s. However, in all likelihood, it will, since people inevitably choose these drugs to express their drive to experience different states or levels of consciousness.

As we have seen, drugs affect behavior and have dramatic and immediate effects on consciousness. As human beings ingest drugs, they alter their states of consciousness in profound ways. Sometimes the changes are mild and produce only states of relaxation. Other times the changes are profound, long-lasting, and produce anywhere from mild to serious changes in mood, temper, personality, and behavior. When psychologists study such changes in behavior, they are studying the effects of how drugs alter consciousness. They have studied particularly carefully both how various dosages of various drugs affect consciousness and the relationship between drug dosage and changes in states or levels of consciousness. If we consider consciousness as a state of awareness, drugs clearly alter that state in significant ways.

FOR FURTHER READING

Aaronson, B., and Osmond, H. *Psychedelics: the use and implications of hallucinogenic drugs.* Garden City, NY: Anchor Press, 1970.

Hofmann, F. G. *A handbook on drug and alcohol abuse: the biomedical aspects.*
     New York: Oxford University Press, 1975.
Julien, R. M. *A primer of drug action.* San Francisco: Freeman, 1978.
Ray, O. *Drugs, society, and human behavior.* St. Louis: C. V. Mosby, 1978.

chapter four ════════════════════

Hypnosis

Hypnosis has long been a popular topic for discussion by both scientists and nonpsychologists. For many individuals, their only exposure to hypnosis has been the most stereotyped version, namely, stage hypnosis. In this form of entertainment participants from an audience are hypnotized and then asked to perform all sorts of strange acts. Some are made to sing the "Star-Spangled Banner," while others are asked to act like a turkey and gobble about on stage. It appears to the audience that the hypnotist has complete control over the behavior of the participant.

As a result of the popularity of stage hypnosis, the fear of loss of control by potential hypnosis subjects, and the many misconceptions that have been created concerning the reality of hypnosis and its usefulness off stage, hypnosis has received an inordinate share of bad press. Furthermore, many people often ask whether hypnosis is a real manipulation or simply an act performed by entertainers. If it is a real bona fide phenomenon, what is it? Why is it that some people can be hypnotized readily, while others cannot? What does it feel like to experience hypnosis? Is hypnosis an altered state of consciousness? These questions and many others will be addressed in this chapter as we consider hypnosis as an area of study in the psychology of consciousness.

In the scientific investigation of hypnosis, the manipulation is as much a mystery today as it has always been. This is primarily because there is no clear definition of it. However, several attempts have been made to describe the phenomenon to some extent. Some have identified hypnosis as a trance state or as an altered state of consciousness (Hilgard, 1965, 1979). Others have described hypnosis as a normal state of awareness or consciousness involving the holding of positive attitudes, strong motivations, and positive expectancies of the hypnosis situation (Barber, Spanos, and Chaves, 1974). Regardless of how hypnosis is defined, we do know that it is a manipulation that can often affect or alter behavior.

Before discussing the contemporary applications of hypnosis in science and behavior, we need to elucidate the role of hypnosis in the study of consciousness. A brief historical overview of this manipulation will then be presented, along with a discussion of the various theoretical explanations of what hypnosis is and is not in light of existing experimental evidence.

HYPNOSIS AND CONSCIOUSNESS

As was stated in Chapter 1, our definition of consciousness is synonymous with the concept of awareness. To be aware of an event is to be fully conscious or cognizant of its occurrence. When we are not aware of an event, this generally indicates that the information from its occurrence either is not processed or is being processed at a level below consciousness.

It appears that a different level of awareness is in operation during hypnosis, as compared with the nonhypnotic state. When individuals are hypnotized they may or may not feel sleepy, although they usually do feel a bit more relaxed than usual. They report experiencing behavior that differs from their normal state of consciousness or awareness (Hilgard, 1977b). While hypnotized, individuals have an increased susceptibility to suggestions. They also experience enhanced imagery and imagination, including the availability of visual memories from the past. Hypnotized individuals also experience a loss of initiative and lack the desire to make and carry out plans of their own. This change from their normal state of consciousness is only relative, for the hypnotic subject retains the ability to initiate or terminate actions. In other words, the popular belief that there is total loss of control when an individual is hypnotized is simply not true. There also is a reduction in reality testing for hypnotized subjects. For example, they accept falsified memories, they may show a change in their own personality, they may modify the rate at which they process time, and they may experience the presence of an object that is physically not present or not perceive an object that is present.

Because of the nature of the behavior exhibited by hypnotized subjects, hypnosis is considered to be an integral part of the study of consciousness. To study the phenomenon of hypnosis may help unravel many of the mysteries of how and at what level information is processed. Furthermore, we will see how hypnosis can be employed as a tool to help focus or refocus the processing of information for modifying behavior that is not as easily shaped or changed in the normal state of awareness or consciousness.

HISTORICAL DEVELOPMENT

The earliest reference to the use of a manipulation resembling hypnosis most probably can be traced (Shor, 1979) to a Viennese physician, Franz Anton Mesmer (1734–1815). In the latter part of the eighteenth century, Mesmer demonstrated that behavior could be affected with the use of magnetic plates that would induce so-called cosmic fluids to react in individuals. He called this reaction "animal magnetism." Animal magnetism was demonstrated by placing magnetized metal bottles of water in a large wooden tub called a baquet. Beneath the bottles in the tub was a surface of powdered glass and iron filings. The tub was subsequently filled with water and covered with a top containing openings through which iron rods were passed. The rods were then applied to a subject's body. Since the tub was, in reality, a crude form of a battery, the application of such rods produced a mild electrical charge. The mesmerist

FIGURE 4-1.   *Lithograph reproduction of Franz Anton Mesmer.*

(as early hypnotists were called) would then apply his hands to the subject's body. The result of this mesmeric process was the induction of convulsions and seizures, which in all likelihood were produced by the electrical current. Afterward, the subject often reported an alleviation of minor aches and pains. In some instances more severe afflications such as blindness and deafness were reported to have been successfully treated.

As you can imagine, the treatments provided by Mesmer were highly controversial and met with considerable disfavor from the medical and scientific communities. (In 1784 the Franklin Commission, organized to pass judgment on the value of animal magnetism, disaffirmed the existence and value of it.) However, the Marquis de Puysegur (1751-1825) did see some promise in the mesmeric demonstrations. Unlike Mesmer and in agreement with the Franklin Commission, he did not believe that the results reported and observed were due to the production of seizures and convulsions. Rather, he felt that the presence of a trancelike state was the major reason for the ability to treat afflictions with mesmerism. In such a state the subject could respond to suggestions made by the mesmerist. As such, animal magnetism was superfluous in the treatment of Mesmer's patients.

With the focus of mesmerism shifted toward a trancelike manipulation and away from the mystical concept of animal magnetism, John Elliotson (1791-1868), a British physician, tried to gain consent to teach mesmerism at University College Medical School in London. Unfortunately he was not successful. As a matter of fact, this suggestion met with such furor that he was subsequently forbidden to practice his trade within the confines of his affiliated medical school hospital. As a result of his futile effort, Elliotson resigned his position at the medical school and established the first journal devoted to the study of mesmerism, the *Zoist.*

During Elliotson's period, James Esdaile (1808-1859) was making considerable use of mesmerism in India. Fortunately, mesmerism did not receive the scorn in India that it had in England. As a result, mesmerism became an acceptable manipulation in hospitals during the time of Esdaile, especially as a means for inducing anesthesia during surgery. Also during Elliotson's time, James Braid (1795-1860) introduced a very important theory that advanced the historical development of hypnosis (mesmerism). He recognized that certain mesmeric phenomena were genuine, but he rejected, as did the Marquis de Puysegur, the influences of external or cosmic forces. In lieu of Mesmer's mystical explanation of animal magnetism, Braid advanced a naturalistic, physiological theory to account for the results of mesmerism. This theory was based on the production of eye-muscle fatigue during a mesmeric induction. Since Braid observed that subjects who fixated on a bright object for a given period demonstrated a gradual lowering of the eyelids or a closing of the eyes, he postulated that this closure was the result of a general exhaustion of the nerve centers. In other words, an important characteristic of mesmerism was an induced state of relaxation or "near sleep." In addition to demonstrating this important characteristic of behavior during the process of mesmerism, Braid also wanted to remove as much of the stigma associated with the concept as was possible. To help with this, he changed the name of mesmerism to *neur-hypnotism.* The prefix was later dropped. Thus, Braid is credited with coining the term *hypnotism* (1826).

A few years before Braid changed the name of mesmerism to hypnotism, José Custodi di Faria (1756-1819) advocated a psychological explanation of the phenomenon. Basically, he stressed that "lucid sleep," as he referred to hypnosis, was produced solely by the subject's heightened expectations and receptive attitudes. Since the subject wanted to be hypnotized and expected something to result from this manipulation, the expectations were in fact realized. With the emphasis on psychological factors during the hypnosis process, Faria developed what might be called a standard procedure for inducing lucid sleep. He used a series of soothing and commanding verbal suggestions while the subject was in the receptive hypnotic state. Faria then realized, as did others many years later (e.g., Ambroise Auguste Liébeault [1823-1904], Hippolyte Marie Bernheim [1837-1919]), that verbal suggestion played a major role in hypnosis.

After Faria's discoveries became known and well-publicized, Braid extended Faria's ideas and developed a concept he called *monoideism.* Basically, this term refers to a process of focused attention or concentration on a single idea or image during a state of relaxation. Thus, during hypnosis, a subject's attention is focused only on this thought while all other thoughts are attenuated or "put on the back burner." This concept is comparable to what is referred to today as *selective attention* (Treisman and Geffen, 1967; Haber and Hershenson, 1980). According to Braid, the ability to readily attend to a single idea or thought was limited to about 10 percent of his subjects.

Thirty years later, Jean Martin Charcot (1825-1893) described hypnotism as a process involving physiological reflex actions, including eye-muscle relaxation. Although there was and still is no evidence that hypnosis has a physiological basis in origin, the eminence of Charcot as a leading authority on neurology gave considerable credence to the phenomenon of hypnosis.

Sigmund Freud (1856-1939) also must be mentioned as having played an important role in the historical development of hypnosis. Actually, some of his early theoretical conceptualizations of psychoanalysis were formalized with information he obtained from his patients while they were hypnotized. For example, he observed that, on awakening, patients did not recall many suggestions given to them during hypnosis. As a result of this demonstration of hypnotic amnesia, Freud believed that many human behaviors were the result of unconscious thoughts or motivations. Freud also discovered that many pent-up emotions and feelings could be uncovered with the aid of hypnosis. With hypnosis it was possible to tap information from the so-called unconscious or subconscious. Freud eventually abandoned the use of hypnosis because he believed it allowed access to repressed feelings too quickly, suppressed symptoms too easily, and swayed individual responses toward what he perceived the hypnotist wanted (Shor, 1979).

As you can see, hypnosis has had a controversial historical development (Shor, 1979). However, without the brave experiments and applications of hypnosis by Elliotson, Braid, and others, hypnosis would only be a quaint relic of the past and not an important manipulation in science and medicine.

ASSESSING HYPNOTIC SUSCEPTIBILITY

Knowing that hypnosis is a scientifically valid and reliable tool, it has become possible to determine how susceptible given individuals are to this manipulation. In determining whether a subject can be readily hypnotized or is readily susceptible to hypnotic suggestions, three standard tests and several nonstandard procedures have been employed. Each of these tests is administered to subjects in a wakeful state, and each is used primarily to measure susceptibility for future clinical or experimental hypnosis. The standard tests include the Stanford Hypnotic Susceptibility Scale (Weitzenhoffer and Hilgard, 1959, 1962), the Barber Suggestibility Scale (Barber and Glass, 1962), and the Harvard Group Scale of Hypnotic Susceptibility (Shor and Orne, 1962).

The Stanford scale consists of twelve parts and is administered to subjects on an individual basis. That is, only one person at a time is tested for susceptibility to hypnotic suggestion. The twelve parts of the test are arranged in order of difficulty, so that the first few parts or tasks are easier and the last parts are the most difficult in terms of subject compliance. Thus, most subjects are capable of performing the first few tasks easily, while only a small number of subjects are capable of performing the last ones.

The first and easiest task on the Stanford scale is referred to as *postural sway*. In this portion of the test, the individual is first asked to close his eyes, after which he is given the suggestion that he is slowly falling backward.

The second item is called *eye closure*. In performing this task the subject has his eyes wide open and is given the suggestion that his eyelids are becoming very heavy, so heavy that he can no longer keep them open.

Hand lowering is the third item on the scale. In this situation the individual is asked to extend one of his arms out in front of his body. He is then given the suggestion that his hand is becoming very heavy, so heavy that he can no longer keep it from falling.

The next item is referred to as *arm immobilization*. This task is, in essence, the opposite of the third task. Instead of the administrator suggesting to the subject that his arm is falling, the person is told that his arm is becoming so heavy that he cannot lift it from the original position.

The fifth task on the Stanford scale is the *finger lock*. To perform this task the subject is instructed to interlock the fingers of both hands. He is then told that his fingers have become a solid mass and he will not be able to separate them from one another. The individual is then challenged to separate his hands.

Arm rigidity is the next item on the scale. In this task the subject is asked to extend his arm out straight in front of his body. He is then requested to make his arm as rigid as possible. Following this procedure he is challenged to bend his arm.

The seventh task is concerned with *hand movement.* Here, the subject is required to move his hands together. To perform this task, the individual is required first to separate his hands, palms facing inward, about twelve inches apart. He is then requested to imagine that a strong, magnetic force is attracting his hands, pulling them together.

Verbal inhibition is the eighth task on the scale. For this situation the individual is given a suggestion that, when he is asked his name, he will be unable to verbalize it.

The next task is perhaps one of the most difficult on the Stanford scale. It is called the *fly hallucination* suggestion. In the performance of this suggestion the individual is asked to imagine a fly buzzing about his body. He is further told that the fly is becoming more and more annoying and he will want to shoo it away. The test administrator tells the subject to get rid of the fly so it will no longer be a disturbance.

The tenth scale item is called *eye catalepsy.* While the individual's eyes are closed, he is given the suggestion that he will feel as though his eyes have been glued shut and he will not be able to open them. He is then challenged to open his eyes.

The next-to-last item is a *posthypnotic suggestion.* Here, the subject is told that after the testing session is over, to determine his hypnotic susceptibility level, he will for some reason feel like changing chairs upon hearing a tapping noise. After the test administration a tapping noise is sounded.

The final task item on the Stanford scale is the testing for *hypnotic amnesia.* After completing the susceptibility scale items, the subject is first required to enumerate the tasks in which he does remember participating. Failure to recall more than three such tasks is considered adequate evidence that hypnotic amnesia was successful.

After completion of the Stanford scale, a subject's hypnotic susceptibility level can be determined by adding the total number of task items with which a subject successfully complied. Generally, if a subject complied with nine to twelve suggestions, he is considered highly susceptible to hypnotic suggestion. If he complies with three or fewer suggestions, this is taken as evidence that he will be difficult to hypnotize and, as such, is considered low in the attribute of hypnotic susceptibility. A score of between five and eight is considered to indicate moderate hypnotic susceptibility. Most individuals taking the test fall within this range. It should be mentioned that which items a subject successfully completes is not as important as the total test score. However, it is rare to find a subject who successfully completes the most difficult scale items and not the easiest ones.

As with the Stanford test, the Barber Suggestibility Scale is also administered on an individual basis. However, unlike the Stanford scale, the

Barber scale consists of only eight tasks. Three of the eight items are comparable to items on the Stanford scale. These include arm lowering, hand clasp, and verbal inhibition. The remaining five items are arm levitation, extreme thirst suggestion, body immobility, posthypnotic response, and a selective amnesia.

The third standardized test to determine the level of hypnotic susceptibility is the Harvard Group Scale of Hypnotic Susceptibility. Unlike the Stanford and Barber scales, this test is administered in a group setting. Also, subjects taking this test score themselves for their level of hypnotic susceptibility. This is not the case for the Stanford scale or the Barber scale, in which the test administrator does the scoring. Scoring for hypnotic susceptibility on the Harvard scale is comparable to that on the Stanford scale. A score of between nine and twelve is considered high susceptibility to hypnotic suggestion; a score below three is considered low susceptibility.

In addition to the standardized techniques for assessing hypnotic susceptibility, investigators have reported several "quick" methods of assessment. One such technique, albeit a highly controversial one, is referred to as the eye-roll test (Spiegel, 1970a). In this test (see Fig. 4–2) the subject is requested to open his eyes as wide as possible. He is then instructed to roll his eyes to the top of his eyelids and to lower his eyelids very slowly over his eyes without moving his eyes from the upward position. The subject's ability to perform this simple task is considered to be evidence of his susceptibility to hypnotic suggestion.

Although the eye-roll test appears to be a test of hypnotic susceptibility for some subjects, it is far from being a reliable and valid measure. For example, Wheeler, Reis, Wolff, Grupsmith, and Mordkoff (1974) found a very weak relationship between hypnotic susceptibility as assessed by the scales described previously and the ability of a subject to perform the eye-roll procedure. Therefore, the eye-roll test cannot be considered a reliable or valid substitute for the standard testing procedures.

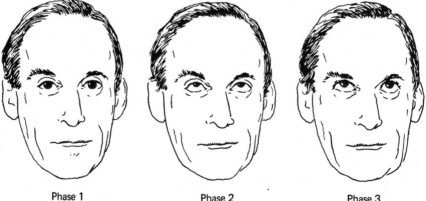

Phase 1   Phase 2   Phase 3

FIGURE 4-2. *Eye-roll test.*

Other investigators have also reported fast methods for determining hypnotic susceptibility. For example, Wallace and colleagues (Wallace and Garrett, 1973; Wallace, Garrett, and Anstadt, 1974; Wallace, Knight, and Garrett, 1976; Wallace, 1979) found a relationship between level of hypnotic susceptibility as assessed by the Harvard scale and frequency of perceiving various visual illusions (see Fig. 4-3). Generally, the more susceptible a subject is to hypnotic suggestions, the greater is the susceptibility to visual illusions, especially those involving a frequency report such as in viewing the Necker cube, the Schroeder staircase, and the autokinetic effect (the illusory movement of a stationary light source). Although this frequency procedure is not employed currently as a tool for assessing hypnotic susceptibility, tentative evidence seems to suggest that it could be used for this purpose.

In addition to determining whether certain variables are related to hypnotic susceptibility, an important question to ask at this point is whether hypnosis is related to any physiological activity or characteristic of the individual. In other words, can hypnosis be measured physiologically in a manner similar to its behavioral assessment? There appears to be some evidence that there is a difference in recorded brain-wave activity for different individuals as a function of hypnotic susceptibility. London, Hart, and Leibovitz (1968) found that subjects judged to be highly responsive to hypnotic suggestions tended to show more alpha-wave activity during the waking state than subjects with low responsiveness to hypnotic suggestions. However, for the most part, this finding has not been replicated (Evans, 1979). In addition, there appear to be no other reliable physiological correlates of hypnotic responsiveness. When brain-wave activity, heart rate, blood pressure, and body temperature of hypnotized subjects or highly hypnotizable subjects are measured in the waking state, the physiological values appear to be identical to those taken from the general population. Some investigators have used the failure to find a physiological correlate of hypnosis as an argument that hypnosis is not an altered state of consciousness. However, this is not a widely held view and to make such a judgment at this time may be a bit premature.

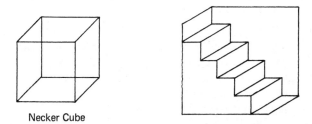

Necker Cube

Schroeder Staircase

FIGURE 4-3. *Reversible illusion figures (From: B. Wallace, T. A. Knight and Garrett, J. B. Hypnotic susceptibility and frequency reports to illusory stimuli.* Journal of Abnormal Psychology *85: 1976. 558-563. Copyright © 1976 by the American Psychological Association. Reprinted with permission.)*

HABIT CONTROL

Regardless of what hypnosis is or is not and what variables are associated with hypnotic susceptibility, hypnosis can be a useful tool in dealing with certain behavioral problems, such as the control of an unwanted habit. Hypnosis has been used extensively in dealing with obesity, smoking, stress, and the control of other types of potentially debilitating habits. This application is possible most likely because hypnosis enables individuals to deal with their habit at a level of awareness or consciousness that varies from their normal state of consciousness. In the normal waking state, an individual's habit is in full force and is difficult to alter or reshape. However, at a different level of awareness, where subjects are more susceptible to suggestions of changing their habit, and thus perhaps are more inclined to do so, reshaping or altering becomes easier. Hypnosis, then, is a useful tool for reshaping behavior that can be generalized beyond the altered state to the normal waking state of awareness.

With regard to weight control, Stanton (1975) has found hypnosis to be a useful technique in the treatment of obesity. Specifically, he employed five procedures to help patients with weight-control problems, all with the aid of hypnosis. These included direct suggestions relating to amount and type of food to be eaten in the future; ego-enhancing suggestions to help patients live their lives more pleasantly; mental imagery to establish a desired goal; self-hypnosis to reinforce the therapist's suggestions; and audiotapes to provide additional support after the completion of formal treatment. Stanton reported that the combined use of these techniques had a marked effect on weight loss as reported by patients who completed the entire process. In other words, hypnosis was a successful procedure in the treatment of obesity.

Hypnosis has also been a successful manipulation in the treatment of smoking. Spiegel (1970b) employed a competing-response technique using hypnosis to help individuals stop smoking. After a subject had been hypnotized he or she was asked to concentrate on three points: (1) that cigarette smoking is a poison to the body; (2) that life is not possible without the body; and (3) that life is possible only if one respects and protects one's body (i.e., by not smoking). These suggestions, administered under hypnosis, were then put in a type of competition with the life process, since Spiegel made it clear that a subject could not maintain both life and the smoking habit. As such, life could only be reinforced if the individual was willing to stop smoking. Thus, smoking became a destructive force in maintaining life.

When subjects were confronted with the life-versus-smoking dilemma, it was up to them to make a choice. They could choose smoking and thereby decrease life, or they could choose life by abandoning the smoking habit. With the aid of hypnosis and the suggestions, Spiegel reported a 20 percent success rate in the termination of the smoking habit. Although this is not a high percentage, one must keep in mind that subjects received only a single treatment session. With an increase in the number of hypnosis sessions, Hall and Crasilneck

(1970) reported a 75 percent cure rate. Recently, Powell (1980) also showed that individuals who had stopped smoking through hypnosis and who subsequently returned to smoking were helped to become more permanent non-smokers with a flooding of hypnosis and systematic desensitization sessions. It appears, then, that the smoking habit can be controlled with the help of hypnotic suggestions.

In a more recent study, Barkley, Hastings, and Jackson (1977) compared hypnosis to rapid smoking as a method for treating the smoking habit. In rapid smoking an individual is made to smoke a large number of cigarettes in a short time. Again, hypnosis was found to be an effective treatment method, although the rapid-smoking technique proved slightly more effective. However, one must question this advantage because rapid smoking produces severe effects, such as explosive nausea (vomiting) and a loss of appetite.

Thus it appears that hypnosis can play an important role in the treatment of overeating and smoking. However, one must ask whether the cure is long lasting. The follow-up data on the treated subjects indicate that some individuals return to their old eating or smoking habits. This was true especially in cases where relatively few hypnosis sessions were employed to treat the habit; that is, hypnosis ceased to serve as a strong motivator to control the habit. Thus, although it has been a successful method of treatment for some individuals, hypnosis alone probably is not a likely method of treatment for habit control. However, when it is used as an adjunct to behavior modification techniques, it appears to be fairly successful (Dengrove, 1976).

HYPNOTHERAPY

Hypnosis has also been used in the treatment of other behavioral problems, such as phobias and various types of sexual dysfunctions. With regard to phobia control, if an individual shows an irrational fear of some type of object, event, or environment, a popular method of treating this fear is to use hypnosis along with a process called *systematic desensitization* (Wolpe, 1969). This process creates a hierarchy of stimuli that provoke different levels of fear of the event. For example, if someone is fearful of nonpoisonous snakes, the hierarchy might consist of a series of fear levels ranging from fright on hearing the word "snake" to severe fear of direct contact with a snake. If the hierarchy consists of several steps, desensitization would involve a process of giving the subject muscle relaxation therapy at each step of the hierarchy and to continue this therapy until the subject no longer is fearful of the snake at that level. Thus, the therapist would first try to reduce the fear of hearing the word "snake." Once this was accomplished, the therapist would continue to reduce fear at more increasingly intense levels until fear at all levels of the hierarchy had disappeared.

Although systematic desensitization is a successful treatment therapy by itself (Wolpe, 1969; Coleman, Butcher, and Carson, 1980), it can be even more successful when used in conjunction with hypnosis (e.g., Lang and Lazovik, 1963). This is because once a level of fear has been established for a phobic individual, hypnotization prior to the start of actual desensitization therapy increases the efficacy of the therapy. The irrational fear probably developed at a subconscious level of awareness; hypnosis may help to reinstate this level of consciousness and allow the fear to be treated at the same level of awareness at which it was created.

An example of the joint use of hypnosis and desensitization in the treatment of a phobia is illustrated in an experiment by Lang and Lazovik (1963). The investigators were interested in the success of systematic desensitization in treating persons with a phobia of nonpoisonous snakes. Using the technique illustrated earlier, they found that asking subjects to imagine the fear situation at various levels of the established hierarchy under hypnosis was conducive to producing relaxation and vivid imagery. Therefore, the individual could overcome the fear of snakes through imagery. Thus, the dual use of hypnosis and desensitization can be a potent means of treating phobias.

This treatment procedure sounds fairly impressive, and the results reported are equally impressive. However, what is even more important is that the success reported with imagery held true in actual situations. That is, individuals who overcame fear of snakes under laboratory conditions using this procedure also showed a diminution or elimination of the fear when they actually encountered a snake. Lang and Lazovik reported that the therapy maintained its effectiveness after six months.

Another successful use of hypnosis teamed with systematic desensitization is in the treatment of sexual dysfunctions. One such dysfunction that has successfully been treated in this way is vaginismus (Fuchs, Hoch, and Kleinhauz, 1976; Fuchs, Hoch, Paldi, Abromovici, Brandes, Timor-Tritsch, and Kleinhauz, 1973). Vaginismus is a disorder in which the vaginal opening is constricted so as not to permit entry of the penis. One case involved a 23-year-old woman who had never had sexual intercourse with her husband because her vagina was too constricted to allow his penis to enter. After it was determined that the woman's problem was not physiological in origin, the investigators treated the vaginismus as a fear of pain associated with sexual intercourse. They employed a treatment similar to that used by Lang and Lazovik in the treatment of snake phobia. That is, the woman was taught to relax and to produce vivid imagery under hypnosis. In addition, a fear hierarchy of pain was developed for her. She subsequently was given the hierarchy of events to imagine under hypnosis in order of the least to the most anxiety provoking. The hierarchy ranged from imagining herself going home with her husband and resting with him (least anxiety provoking) to imagining herself having sexual intercourse with him (most anxiety provoking situation). The therapy continued until the woman felt relaxed imagining the final level of the fear hierarchy.

When the patient no longer felt fearful of having intercourse with her husband (as witnessed by overt signs of relaxation, such as muscle relaxation and the patient stating that she felt relaxed), she was requested to try to have intercourse with him. The patient reported that the treatment had been successful and that, for the first time in two years, her husband had been able to penetrate her vagina. Thus, as with snake phobia, the fear of sex can also be successfully treated with the dual use of hypnosis and systematic desensitization.

It appears, then, that hypnosis is a useful manipulation in the treatment of many psychological problems. In addition, hypnosis has been used by surgeons and dentists as an analgesic or an anesthetic. The next section of this chapter considers the use of hypnosis in the relief of pain during surgery.

HYPNOSIS AND PAIN CONTROL

As we mentioned earlier in this chapter, in the 1800s, Esdaile successfully employed hypnosis to create an anesthetic effect during surgery. As a matter of fact, hypnosis was used as a means of eliminating pain before chemical anesthetics were discovered. Before Esdaile's important work in this field, surgery without anesthesia was so painful that 40 percent of all patients who underwent surgery for the removal of tumors eventually died. However, with the advent of hypnotic anesthesia, this rate was reduced to about 5 percent (Fromm and Shor, 1979).

When chemical anesthetics, such as chloroform and sodium thiopental (Pentothal), appeared for use in surgery, hypnosis was effectively eliminated as a procedure to reduce experienced pain, since chemical agents were faster at inducing an anesthetic effect. This development was most unfortunate for several reasons. First, although time-consuming to administer, hypnosis was a successful procedure for reducing pain. Second, hypnotic anesthesia was far safer to use than chemical anesthetics, since the latter were associated with several side effects, including respiratory depression, myocardial depression, cardiac arrhythmias, and prolonged somnolence.

Why does hypnosis play an important role in reducing pain? Mostly because hypnosis helps to dissociate the experience of pain into two levels of awareness (Hilgard, 1973). At one level the patient is aware of feeling the pain. During an altered state of awareness such as hypnosis, however, the patient does not experience the pain (Hilgard and Hilgard, 1975).

For surgeons who employ hypnosis in their practice today, this manipulation is used primarily when a patient shows allergic reactions to chemical anesthetics or when the surgeon wishes to reduce the dosage of the chemical agent (Fredericks, 1980). Regarding the latter concern, many surgeons believe that there really is no need to rely totally on chemical agents as anesthetics during surgery. Therefore, they might reduce the dosage of the anesthetic by employing hypnotic anesthesia as an adjunct. The more effective the hypnotic anesthesia, the lower the dosage of chemical anesthetic. The dual use of chemical and hypnotic anesthesia effectively reduces many of the drug-related risks mentioned earlier.

Unfortunately, not all patients can benefit from the use of hypnotic anesthesia. Many are not highly susceptible to hypnotic suggestions and, as such, are not readily capable of dissociating various levels of experienced pain. For such patients there is usually no choice but to use a chemical anesthetic. Although hypnotic susceptibility may improve with practice (Diamond, 1974), the time required to train individuals to be more hypnotically susceptible becomes a great obstacle to normal operating procedures, both before and during surgery. As a result, relatively few surgeons employ hypnotic anesthesia as either an alternative or an adjunct to chemical agents.

Besides the use of hypnotic anesthesia in surgery, this pain-reducing procedure has been employed in the field of obstetrics. The use of hypnotic anesthesia and analgesia in childbirth is not new; it was used as a means of reducing childbirth pain more than 100 years ago (Kroger, 1977). As with hypnotic anesthesia in surgery, it is necessary first to determine whether the patient is sufficiently susceptible to hypnotic suggestions. If the expectant mother is susceptible, she can be trained to accept suggestions for hypnotic anesthesia before and during parturition. However, only a small percentage of patients (about 20 percent) can be taught to reduce pain effectively without the aid of some chemical anesthetic or analgesic.

There are some obvious advantages for patients who can profit by the use of hypnotic anesthesia during childbirth. These include a reduction in post-operative side effects that would be present with chemical anesthetics, a reduction in postchildbirth pain, and the elimination of danger to the baby from the administration of a chemical agent to the mother (Kroger, 1977). However, while hypnotic techniques are beneficial during childbirth, we should point out that procedures for natural childbirth (e.g., the Lamaze method) are as beneficial as hypnosis (Davenport-Slack, 1975). Perhaps this is because both procedures enable women to alter their state of awareness temporarily and thus escape the level of pain they would normally experience during the waking state. Additionally, natural childbirth procedures are not much different from self-hypnosis procedures. During self-hypnosis, an individual can temporarily induce an altered state of consciousness. Thus, both hypnotically induced pain relief and natural childbirth procedures are equally effective in helping a mother to alter her state of consciousness during childbirth.

Hypnosis has also been employed as a means of dealing with pain during dental procedures. However, in dentistry, hypnosis is rarely used as an anesthetic or analgesic. Rather, it is used as a tool to help reduce tension and fear of pain and to allow the patient to become more relaxed. The result of this, of course, is to reduce the magnitude of experienced pain. In general, as with the use of hypnosis in surgery, its use in dentistry is not common. It is time consuming to administer, and only a limited number of patients can profit by its use. Thus, surgery and dentistry do not make considerable use of hypnosis in dealing with experienced pain.

As an analgesic, hypnosis has been used in the treatment of headaches. Generally, two procedures have been tried in treating this type of pain: glove anesthesia and the hand-warming technique. Glove anesthesia (Kroger, 1977) is a procedure whereby the patient's hand is anesthetized hypnotically. The person is then taught to apply the anesthetized hand to the portion of the head that is hurting. The result is to transfer the anesthetic effect to the head. In this manner, individuals can be taught to eliminate or control headaches. Naturally, for this procedure to be maximally beneficial, the individual must be taught self-hypnosis so that he or she can learn to anesthetize the hand in order to apply it to the head. The second procedure, hand warming, was developed by Sargent, Green, and Walters (1973) and utilizes hypnosis as well as biofeedback (see Chapter 5). In this technique patients are taught to achieve passive concentration and to relax their entire body with hypnotic procedures. Then they receive instructions concerning the use of temperature in the control of pain. Patients are instructed to visualize temperature changes in their hands while watching a temperature trainer, a feedback mechanism by which they can determine whether their hand temperature really has changed. Thus they think about making their hand warm and, in fact, it becomes warm. Then they apply the warm hand to the head; in this way the severity of the headache is reduced or the headache is totally eliminated. The principles underlying this phenomenon are discussed in the next chapter.

Success has been reported in the treatment of headaches with the use of both glove anesthesia and hand warming (Graham, 1975; Andreychuck and Skriver, 1975). Therefore, hypnosis can be a beneficial substitute for chemical agents (e.g., aspirin, buffered aspirin, acetaminophen) commonly used to relieve headache pain. Another method for treating headaches is the sole use of biofeedback in a manner similar to the hand-warming technique.

MEMORY, PERCEPTION, AND HYPNOSIS

Hypnosis has been used to study the processes of memory and perception. Several experiments conducted for this purpose include those by True (1949) and by Walker, Garrett, and Wallace (1976). In each of these studies, hypnotically induced age regression was used to help individuals recall or reconstruct information no longer available to conscious retrieval.

True (1949) used hypnosis to enable subjects to regress to the ages of eleven, seven, and four. At these points in time, he asked them on which day of the week their birthday occurred. True reported that 81 percent of his subjects named the day correctly. This appears to be a remarkable use of hypnotic age regression, since the results of True's study have implications far beyond his interesting finding. For instance, if this technique is used for practical purposes, subjects could be made to recall many types of information that they felt were erased from memory and conscious awareness long ago.

Unfortunately, several attempts at replicating True's findings have met with failure (Barber, 1961; Fisher, 1962; O'Connell, Shor, and Orne, 1970). Barber, Spanos, and Chaves (1974) have enumerated possible reasons for this failure. They believed that True may have known before the experiment on which day a given subject's birthday occurred. If this was the case, True's procedure for assessing the validity of hypnotic age regression was a poor one. For example, in his study subjects were to name their birthday via the use of a progression technique. In this procedure True simply would ask, "Was it Sunday?" "Was it Monday?" "Was it Tuesday?", and so on. Subjects would then reply. Unfortunately, it is possible that True may have conveyed information to his subjects that might have given them clues as to the correct response. For example, True may have changed his tone of voice or his voice inflection when he asked the questions, especially if he knew the correct date. Thus, such biases may have provided subjects with the correct response. If this was the case, the information True obtained obviously was not miraculously uncovered with the aid of hypnotic age regression.

However, the hypnotic age regression manipulation used in a study by Walker, Garrett, and Wallace (1976) did not appear to be vulnerable to the same criticisms. Walker and associates were studying eidetic imagery, which they noted was very rare for adults to exhibit. The investigators reasoned that a good test of hypnotic age regression would be to recreate the process of eidetic imagery in adults who regressed to the age at which this process is most visible (around the age of seven or eight). They also reasoned that if age-regressed adults displayed eidetic imagery (popularly known as photographic memory) in an experimental paradigm in which results could not be faked, they would find evidence to suggest that hypnotic age regression is a valuable tool for investigating the processes involved in memory. As we mentioned previously, adult subjects in a non-age-regressed state were not capable of performing the extremely difficult task of recombining in memory the two halves of a stereogram. However, when the same subjects were hypnotically age regressed to the period when eidetic imagery is most prevalent, two out of twenty were capable of identifying the "hidden" figures (a triangle, a square, and a cube) correctly.

Hypnotic age regression has also been employed extensively in recent years by law enforcement agencies. Specifically, it has been used to help people remember information about a crime they witnessed and about which they could not otherwise recall specific facts. For example, with the aid of hypnotic age regression, witnesses have been able to remember numbers or letters from license plates of cars in the vicinity of a crime. Similarly, rape victims have been able to recall details about their rape and about the rapist that were not otherwise available to their conscious recall. Needless to say, this interesting area of research has not been thoroughly investigated in the real world, nor have laboratory experiments in this area met with total success. For these reasons, extreme caution is often advocated for the use of hypnosis in courtroom testimony or in similar circumstances (Worthington, 1979). However, Raikov (1980) believes that some experiments with hypnotic age regression have failed because of the nature of the hypnotist's suggestion and the subjects' depth of hypnosis. Hopefully, in the years to come we will learn more about how and why hypnotic age regression works. However, we can speculate that the reason witnesses to a crime often fail to recall important information about the event is that the information becomes relegated to the subconscious and, as such, is retrievable most easily with hypnosis.

From the perspective of either a scientist or a student, one can appreciate the usefulness of hypnosis in the study of behavior. Although there is and will continue to be controversy concerning the phenomenon of hypnosis, it has proven itself to be a useful tool for scientific research. Hypnosis can be used in a variety of experiments and professional therapies for habit control, phobias, obsessions, compulsions, and sexual dysfunctions. It can also be employed beneficially in the control of pain and in the recall of information that cannot be extracted in the normal waking state of consciousness.

Now that we have seen how hypnosis is measured and used, how has this phenomenon been explained? In other words, what theories exist to describe the phenomenon of hypnosis?

CONTEMPORARY THEORIES OF HYPNOSIS

Today, basically two theoretical approaches predominate in explaining the phenomenon of hypnosis. These were mentioned very briefly at the beginning of this chapter. They include the trance theory of hypnosis (Hilgard, 1965; Conn and Conn, 1967; Fromm and Shor, 1979) and the nontrance theory (Barber, 1969, Barber, Spanos, and Chaves, 1974).

The trance theory postulates that hypnosis is a process that involves an altered state of consciousness, or a trance, during which a subject is in a heightened state of susceptibility or responsiveness to suggestions or commands. Therefore, in hypnosis, an individual must either be temporarily dissociated from the normal waking state of awareness or consciousness or be minimally capable of performing some task(s) with hypnosis which are not as easily accomplished or accomplishable at all without hypnosis.

A sampling of several experiments that appear to support the trance theory are those by Krauss, Katzell, and Krauss (1974) and Walker, Garrett, and Wallace (1976). Krauss and associates were concerned with testing the effects of hypnotic time distortion on free-recall learning. In this situation subjects received instructions under hypnosis that were designed to stretch three physical minutes of time into ten psychological minutes. The investigators postulated that if subjects were capable of performing this task, they should also be capable of learning a task in three minutes that would normally require ten minutes to learn. The results of their experiment demonstrated that subjects were able to do this. That is, tasks that took nonhypnotized subjects ten minutes to learn took hypnotized subjects only three minutes to learn.

A recent experiment by Walker and colleagues (1976) also tends to support the existence of a trance phenomenon in hypnosis. Their study was concerned with the possible restoration of eidetic imagery (akin to photographic memory) with the aid of hypnotic age regression. The major basis for the Walker study was the reliable finding in the literature that approximately 8 percent of all children are capable of some form of eidetic imagery (Haber and Haber, 1964), whereas the phenomenon is almost nonexistent in adults (Stromeyer and Psotka, 1970). The investigators believed it might be possible, with the aid of hypnotic age regression, to determine whether eidetic imagery, a primitive form of processing information, could be temporarily restored in an adult population.

The task employed was a difficult one and not easily faked. Subjects were asked to perceive, in a binocular fashion, half of a 10,000-dot stereogram (Julesz, 1971) for 60 seconds. Immediately after the removal of the first half, they were asked to perceive the second half. Presentation of either half produced a meaningless, unidentifiable composite of dots. Subjects then were asked to combine the memory of the first half with the observed dot composite of the second half and to identify the object formed by such a combination. From a sample of twenty hypnotically age-regressed subjects, two (10 percent) were capable of demonstrating eidetic imagery.

One might ask at this point whether subjects who were asked to perform the same task under high task-motivating instructions might be capable of performing the same feat. This possibility was considered in a study by Wallace (1978). Replicating the Walker study, Wallace asked a group of subjects to perform the Walker task with high task-motivating instructions. The results of this experiment were similar to those reported by Walker and colleagues. Only subjects who were hypnotically age regressed were capable of performing the task; high task-motivating instructions did not produce the results. Therefore, with results that cannot be faked, it appears that hypnosis may involve an altered state of consciousness.

Hilgard (1973, 1979) also presents evidence that a subject is in a special state of consciousness during the reception of hypnotic instructions. In dealing with the perception of pain, Hilgard produced pain by applying extreme cold to a subject's arm. Such application produces what is referred to as *cold-pressor* pain. Hilgard found that hypnotically suggested analgesia can reduce considerably the felt pain sensation associated with the cold pressor. However, if a subject reports feeling no pain and is then asked to write down his or her felt experiences; he or she does indeed report experiencing pain. Therefore, though the subject did not orally report pain, automatic writing reveals that he or she did experience pain. Therefore, according to Hilgard, a subject experiences pain at two levels. One level is consciously cognitive; at that level hypnotic analgesia clearly affects the severity of experienced pain. The subject indicates a cessation or diminution in the level of pain. However, at the second level, the subject does experience pain and reports this via automatic writing. On the basis of these results, Hilgard developed a neodissociation theory of pain reduction in hypnosis. This theory specifies that, at some cognitive level, the subject has experienced the cold and can report its intensity even though the suffering may be reduced. Since Hilgard's theory obviously implies cognitive control of a stimulus event, it suggests that a trance or altered state of consciousness appears to be operating during hypnosis.

However, Barber (1969) has suggested that hypnosis does not require a trance or a trance state in order for the phenomenon to be demonstrated. In other words, according to his theory, hypnosis is not an altered state of consciousness. Rather, it is a predisposition in a normal state of awareness to attend to commands and suggestions from a hypnotist. Barber believes that most of the phenomena purported to come about as a result of hypnosis can be demonstrated in a nonhypnotic, wakeful situation as well. Thus, non-hypnotized subjects are capable of performing tasks that supposedly are possible only under hypnosis. A subject who has positive attitudes about hypnosis, who is sufficiently motivated to perform a given task, and who expects that a given task is possible with hypnosis, can perform hypnotic feats without being in an altered state of consciousness.

Some examples of experiments in support of Barber's theory include those by Spanos, Ham, and Barber (1973) and Johnson, Maher, and Barber (1972). In the experiment by Spanos and associates, subjects were asked to hallucinate the presence of an object that in reality was not present. Three conditions were employed in this study. In the first condition, subjects were asked to hallucinate the presence of an object without any special instructions. In the second condition, subjects received task-motivational instructions in which they were told to try as hard as they could to imagine the object. The third condition involved the standardized induction of hypnosis, in which the hallucination of an object was suggested via so-called hypnotic instructions. The results of the study showed that 98 percent of the control subjects (i.e., those given the first condition) reported imagining the object either vaguely or vividly, but they really did not *see* it. However, 8 percent of subjects who were given either a hypnotic-induction procedure or task-motivational instructions reported actually seeing the object. This percentage did not differ as a function of receiving hypnotic-induction procedures or task-motivational instructions. Therefore, the investigators concluded that task-motivational instructions were as effective as actual hypnotic-induction procedures in producing a visual hallucination. This finding appears to indicate that a trance or an altered state is not necessary for the production of a phenomenon that theoretically is possible only under a hypnotic trance.

Johnson and associates (1972) reached a similar conclusion. In their experiment, they investigated a phenomenon referred to as *trance logic*. Trance logic (Orne, 1959) refers to the use of a special form of reasoning in which it is totally plausible for an individual to report seeing a hallucinated image in a room and at the same time see the same object in another room. Or a person may see a person in one part of the environment and at the same time see a hallucinated image of that person in another part of the environment. This supposed ability of objects or people to be in two places at the same time does not appear illogical to hypnotized subjects; hence the term trance logic. Accordingly, it appears, as Orne postulates, that a special trance state exists in order for a subject to be able to perform trance logic. However, Johnson and associates found that nonhypnotized subjects gave the same kind of reports with the same frequency as subjects who were judged to be deeply hypnotized. Therefore, it appears that the phenomenon of trance logic is possible both for subjects who appear to be in a hypnotic trance and for subjects who are not hypnotized but who are asked to imagine this form of hallucination under task-motivational instructions. Again, this type of experimental evidence led Barber to postulate that hypnosis is not a trance state but rather is the result of positive attitudes, positive motivations, and positive expectancies toward the hypnosis-related task.

It appears that, at least for some situations, Barber has found sufficient evidence to support his theory. However, many experiments exist that support the trance theory so that Barber's theory cannot be considered the sole explanation of hypnosis (see Bowers, 1976, and Fromm and Shor, 1979, for reviews of this literature). Also, many experiments have shown that positive attitudes, motivations, and expectancies toward hypnosis may not always be sufficient to produce hypnosislike results (see Krauss et al., 1974; Walker et al., 1976).

It is without question that Barber's research has added considerable information to the study of hypnosis. However, in order for the nontrance approach to be more acceptable, results such as those obtained by Wallace (1978) also will have to be explained in terms of positive attitudes, motivations, and expectancies. At present this has not been accomplished.

As you can see, the definition or theory of hypnosis is as controversial as the phenomenon itself. Each theory has its advocates and its opponents. In addition, there is usually experimental evidence available that appears to support, at least to some extent, each side of the argument. In order to help resolve the controversy, it may be necessary to accept a position similar to that expressed in Hilgard's description of the two levels in hypnotically controlled pain. That is, with regard to the phenomenon of hypnosis, at one level individuals become cognizant of hypnosis, and at another level they experience hypnosis. Thus, it is possible that, at one level, individuals have positive attitudes, motivations, and expectancies concerning their ability to be hypnotized. At this level hypnosis becomes possible even though the individual is still in a normal waking state of consciousness. At the second level, however, a subject must assume an altered state of consciousness in order for a hypnotic feat (e.g., hypnotic analgesia) to become effective. With this dual approach to hypnosis, perhaps we can come a bit closer to defining the phenomenon. Ultimately, we may discover that hypnosis involves many more levels of consciousness than even Hilgard describes. For example, we know that some hypnotized subjects can be in a so-called light trance at one point and in a deep trance at another. Whether these trance states are actually different levels of awareness or incremental differences in the same level is not known. However, such speculation can be fruitful only if scientists are encouraged to pursue an answer to this possibility.

One unfortunate aspect of the study of hypnosis is our failure to understand fully what it is. We also do not know why some individuals are readily hypnotizable while others are not. Furthermore, we do not know what triggers a state of hypnosis. We think we know that hypnosis is not controlled physiologically, but that idea does not tell us what *does* control hypnosis. Despite the theories that purport to explain the phenomenon, hypnosis is as controversial now as it was during the days of Mesmer. Only the passage of time, a proliferation of experiments, and an understanding of the general role of hypnosis as an altered state of consciousness will help place this important scientific tool in the forefront of investigations in the behavioral sciences and medicine.

FOR FURTHER READING

Barber, T. X., Spanos, N. P., and Chaves, J. F. *Hypnotism, imagination, and human potentialities.* New York: Pergamon Press, 1974.

Bowers, K. S. *Hypnosis for the seriously curious.* Monterey, CA: Brooks/Cole Publishing, 1976.

Hilgard, E. R. *The experience of hypnosis.* New York: Harcourt, Brace, and World, 1968.

Wallace, B. *Applied hypnosis: an overview.* Chicago: Nelson-Hall, 1979.

chapter five ═══════════════

Biofeedback

Our bodies have many physiological responses of which we normally are not aware. Some of these include our heart rate, muscle tonus, blood pressure, skin-surface temperature, and brain-wave activity. However, through a process called *biofeedback*, it may be possible to train ourselves to become aware of such involuntary responses. In other words, through biofeedback we may be capable of learning to attend to responses that normally we cannot control consciously.

Very simply defined, biofeedback is a behavioral technique that, by use of instrumentation, is meant to increase an individual's level of awareness of his or her biological condition. Such awareness may help people to bring a physiological response under conscious control. The increased level of awareness or consciousness is brought about as the biofeedback instrument detects the physiological activity of the response(s) in question and simultaneously provides this information to the subject in the form of visual or auditory feedback. Using this feedback, the subject can then manipulate and control the physiological response.

In this chapter we will attempt to explain the relatively simple and basic principles underlying biofeedback. We will also describe the historical development of the manipulation and the basic components of the technique as it functions to help us gain access to bodily information of which we normally are not aware. Finally, we will assess the importance and validity of biofeedback as a means of helping us bring to consciousness physiological information that we can use in dealing with behavioral and medical problems.

BIOFEEDBACK AND CONSCIOUSNESS

To explain the process of biofeedback, we will first illustrate a basic principle of learning through general feedback. Try to recall the very first time you experienced the sport of bowling. Remember when you picked up the ball and discovered how heavy it seemed? Remember how far away the pins appeared, and how awkward you felt as you approached the foul line and released the ball for the first time? Finally, remember the embarrassment of watching the ball roll down the gutter or, at best, of leaving all but one or two pins completely unscathed?

If, after all this, you were still determined to continue bowling, you probably found that, with the passage of time and experience, the ball seemed a bit lighter than before, your feelings of awkwardness as you approached the foul line diminished substantially, and rather than drop your ball two or three feet to the alley or hurl it into the gutter, you actually released it correctly. As a consequence of these improvements, gutter-ball frames became a much less frequent occurrence as more and more pins fell victim to the onslaught of your ball.

In large part, these improvements in performance were made possible by learning through sensory feedback. Imagine what your improvement would have been had you been forced to wear very effective earplugs and a blindfold each time you went bowling. Lacking such sensory input you would have been completely unaware of your successes and failures, your need or lack of need for correction. For any given frame your score would be pretty much a function of blind luck. In short, without such feedback, learning to bowl, as measured by improvements in pin count, would be virtually impossible.

Instead of bowling, suppose that you wanted to learn to increase or decrease your heart rate at will. An obvious similarity between the bowling task and the heart-rate task is that both involve bringing certain muscles or muscle groups under conscious control. On the basis of the bowling example, you might predict that any improvement in performance (i.e., increasing or decreasing heart rate as desired) will be dependent in large part on your reception of adequate sensory feedback. Herein lies the problem. The human body simply is not designed to provide any but the most rudimentary feedback concerning internal physiological states. As you read this page, you probably are not conscious or aware of the fact that your heart is beating at a rate of between 65 and 75 beats per minute.

At this point make a guess as to what your heart rate is, note it in the margin, and then take your pulse. The simplest procedure for accomplishing this is to count pulse beats for a fifteen-second period, multiply this value by four, and express your answer in terms of beats per minute. Note your actual pulse rate in the margin and circle it. How accurate was your guess?

Suppose for a moment that our systems were constructed so that we did not receive constant feedback concerning their level of physiological activity,

drug curare (d-tubocurarine). The injection of curare at
blocks the action of acetylcholine at the skeletal neuro-
gas, 1959) while leaving the autonomic nervous system
(Miller and Dworkin, 1974). Such a preparation is left
must be respirated artificially.

the studies of operant conditioning reviewed by Katkin
ed curare with a human subject. After a baseline period
sessions, an immobilizing but subparalytic dose of curare
senior author and only subject in an electrodermal study
r, Shapiro, and Tursky (1966). Although Birk was to
duce more skin-potential responses during the curarized
ring the baseline control period, the results were con-
use he was conscious and only partially paralyzed.

9) curarized rats in an attempt to determine whether
o change their heart rate, blood pressure, vasomotor
ity, and renal blood flow (Miller and Banuzzizi, 1968;
; Trowill, 1967). With experimental success achieved,
nditioning of specific autonomic responses could occur
r cognitive mediation gained wide acceptance from the
en Katkin and Murray (1968) were willing to accept
tely controlled examples of operant conditioning of
wever, they were not willing to take the necessary next
imilar processes were involved in human autonomic
tly, Miller and Dworkin (1974) and other investigators
969; Slaughter, Hahn, and Rinaldi, 1970) have reported
ating the large response changes reported in the earlier

nse to the mediation position, Crider, Schwartz, and
ed that Katkin and Murray should identify some of
so frequently invoked to discount the earlier examples
rant conditioning. It soon became clear, even to Kat-
n (1969), that the controversy they had begun was of
l importance. From any applied or therapeutic stand-
duces an increase or decrease in response magnitude,
f occurrence is not nearly as important as the fact that

y early training experiments with alpha brain waves
ecame widely known despite the fact that they were
amiya (1968, 1969) turned his attention to a deter-
cts could exercise control over their alpha brain-wave
r this work many credit Kamiya with initiating the
o in 1969, the Biofeedback Research Society, now
ciety of America, was formed at a scientific meeting

and that each system was under voluntary control. If this were the case, our
consciousness would be bombarded constantly with information concerning the
physiological state of each organ of the body. All our conscious efforts would
have to be directed toward making certain that each system functioned properly
simply to stay alive. Imagine the sensory overload that would occur. With our
attention so focused, we would have little or no awareness of our external
environment and little or no time to respond to changes in it. As we have already
noted, however, under normal conditions our bodily systems continue to function well despite our lack of awareness of such functioning.

Does this mean that we are never aware of the biological state of an organ
system? The answer to this, obviously, is no. From previous experiences at the
doctor's office, almost everyone is familiar with the fact that hopping up and
down on one foot for one minute produces a perceptible increase in heart rate.
However, we are aware of an increase in heart rate under these conditions
because the number of beats per minute has almost doubled.

Now stop reading for a minute and check your pulse rate in the same
manner as before. When you compare this new value with the one circled earlier,
you will probably observe a change of several beats per minute, even though in
all likelihood you were not aware of any such change because it was so small.
Unfortunately for us, at least in terms of the heart-rate task, it is these minute
changes that are the most valuable as feedback in permitting us to achieve
conscious control over the response.

The process of biofeedback training places the individual in a closed
feedback loop with an instrument that continually provides him or her with
information about subtle changes in one or more bodily processes. This information, which increases the individual's awareness of the biological condition
of the system in question, is responded to; in turn, the individual or subject
undergoing biofeedback continually adjusts, corrects, and modifies responses as
more and more information is received. The training is continued until it is
determined that some final, generally predetermined, goal has been achieved
(Hart, 1967).

The biofeedback procedure as it exists today is a relatively new technique
but one that has substantial historical roots. In order to place biofeedback in
its proper historical perspective, we will now examine some of the most important factors that have led to its present state of development.

HISTORICAL DEVELOPMENT

Many centuries ago, Plato (427–347 B.C.) observed that humans possessed
a "superior rational soul" located in the head, and an "inferior soul" located
in the heart and liver. Plato believed that the superior rational soul, which
he equated with reason, controlled the voluntary responses of the striated
musculature, while the inferior soul controlled the responses of the nonstriated

muscles and glands. Plato equated the inferior soul with emotions. This dichotomy between reason and emotion, between voluntary and involuntary, was to prove both troublesome to later theorists in the area of learning, and extremely persistent in psychological thought.

In the seventeenth century this dichotomy once again gained prominence when M. F. Bichat (1771–1802), a French neuroanatomist, distinguished between the cerebrospinal nervous system, which he labeled the "great brain," and the spinal cord and sympathetic ganglionic chains, which he referred to as the "little brain." To the former he attributed control of the voluntary skeletal responses, while to the latter he attributed control of the emotional and involuntary visceral or autonomic responses.

The twentieth-century manifestation of this dichotomy was expressed by the European investigators Miller and Konorski (1928). They distinguished between what they called Type I (classical) and Type II (instrumental) conditioning. More important for our discussion, however, is that they proposed for the first time that autonomically mediated responses were not subject to instrumental conditioning. The subsequent acceptance of this stance by some of the most prominent psychologists of the day (e.g., Schlosberg [1937], Mowrer [1938], and, eventually, Skinner [1953]) turned the exclusion of autonomic responses into psychological dogma (Kimmel, 1974).

This is not to suggest that there were no dissenters. Several independent groups of investigators had begun research programs designed to demonstrate that human autonomic responses could be operantly modified. In the Soviet Union, for example, Lisina (1965) attempted to condition operantly the dilation and constriction of the blood vessel in a single finger. Initially, this investigator employed electric shock as a negative reinforcer, but such training failed to produce operant modification of blood-vessel activity in either direction (constriction or dilation). When Lisina combined electric shock with a visual feedback display of the subject's vasomotor activity, however, she was able to demonstrate operant conditioning of dilation in the blood vessel.

Meanwhile, in the United States, Harwood (1962) and Shearn (1960) were engaged in attempts to modify heart-rate responses using operant learning techniques. Harwood, using rats as subjects, obtained what essentially were negative findings for both acceleration and deceleration of the heart rate. Shearn was somewhat more successful in that he was able to condition increases in the heart rate of human subjects to whom such an increase postponed the delivery of an electric shock.

Finally, Mandler and colleagues at the University of Toronto and Kimmel and colleagues at the University of Florida were interested in determining whether the galvanic skin response (GSR) or sweat-gland activity could be operantly conditioned. The results obtained by Mandler, Preven, and Kuhlman (1962) forced these investigators to report negative findings with respect to the possibility of operant autonomic conditioning. These results could be considered suggestive, however, in that when the workers reviewed the results, subject by

---

subject, they found
greater number of C
extinction period.

Kimmel and H
unpleasant odors as
ological problems
obtained results th
the conscious abilit
used in the initial
white light). Fowl
of instrumental co
of the study.

Having dem
instrumental techr
the next logical s
search. Kimmel (
that a number o
general, they ha
the operant mod
quately demonstr

Kimmel's
Murray (1969) a
the question of
tion we can ret
One of the way
adopt a strateg
first taking you
taking your pu
the Katkin and
heart rate, ove
strategy. Inste
of breathing)
to produce or
it could be arg
had demonstr
to produce t
voluntary-mu
they contend
would have
that these r
their subjec
the subjects
by manipula

A wa

---

mediation is to use th
relatively low dosages
muscular synapse (Cha
essentially unaffected
limp and motionless an

Actually, one of
and Murray had emplo
and six normal training
was administered to the
reported by Birk, Crid
successfully able to pro
seventh session than d
sidered inconclusive bec

Later, Miller (196
they could be taught
response, intestinal acti
Miller and DiCara, 1969
the idea that operant co
independent of skeletal
scientific community. E
these findings as adqua
autonomic responses. H
step to conclude that
conditioning. More recer
(Hothersall and Brener, 1
great difficulty in replica
curare studies.

In a critical respor
Shnidman (1969) suggest
the "mediators" they had
of human autonomic ope
kin, Murray, and Lachma
little more than theoretic
point, how a subject pro
frequency, or likelihood o
it has been accomplished.

Following some ver
in the late 1950s, which b
not formally published, K
mination of whether subje
patterns on command. Fo
study of biofeedback. Als
called the Biofeedback So
held in California.

THE BIOFEEDBACK TRAINING PROCESS

Today, biofeedback training is the procedure by which a subject is made aware of what previously was an unconscious physiological activity and learns to use this information to gain control over an involuntary process. Because biofeedback training often differs from one laboratory or clinic to another, we need to examine the actual procedure more closely. This variability is probably due to a number of factors, not the least of which is the comparative newness of the technique and the consequent lack of much-needed methodological research. Another factor that contributes to the differences in the biofeedback procedure is the many different applications that have been found for the procedure. Despite the great variability in biofeedback training, however, at least four common elements can be extracted: (1) the trainee, (2) the trainer, (3) the instrument, and (4) the training sessions. To help answer some of the questions you may have about the biofeedback process itself, we will consider each of these elements.

The Trainee

The trainee is the subject of a biofeedback experiment or the client who seeks biofeedback therapy. In brief, the trainee is the individual who will actually experience the biofeedback process. The selection of a volunteer to serve as a subject in biofeedback research is based primarily on the match between the individual's characteristics and the subject characteristics demanded by the nature and design of the study. The biofeedback client is someone who has concluded, either through their own reading or study or after consultation with a physician or other primary-care source, that biofeedback may be helpful in dealing with a particular symptom.

Typically, both the biofeedback therapy client and the research subject are requested to submit current health information about themselves. The reasons for this become clear when we recall that the eventual goal of biofeedback training is to increase the trainee's awareness of an involuntary physiologic activity so that he or she can learn to bring the physiological response under voluntary control. Does the trainee have any health problems that might contraindicate the use of biofeedback? Obviously, one would not want to include a patient with hypertension (high blood pressure) in an experimental group being trained to increase blood pressure. Perhaps less obvious is the need to consider the trainee's mental health as well. Sterman (1973) and Fuller (1978), however, have observed that the use of biofeedback is contraindicated if the client suffers from a mental illness in which the biofeedback instrument may become a component of a delusional framework or in which existing feelings of dissociation may be increased by biofeedback-induced relaxation. Biofeedback is also contraindicated for individuals who suffer from depression.

Another reason for obtaining health information is to determine whether the trainee is currently taking drugs, either prescribed or nonprescribed, that might affect performance in biofeedback training. Finally, the biofeedback therapist must be aware of the client's current state of health if he or she is to select the biofeedback technique that will be most effective in dealing with the client's presenting symptom.

In Chapter 4 we described several standardized tests for determining whether a subject could be readily hypnotized. Although such tests would be of great value in biofeedback, their development remains a task for future investigators. Clearly, however, a highly motivated individual with a positive attitude toward biofeedback has at least two personality characteristics of a potentially successful trainee. Assessment of these factors ought to be considered a necessary feature in any such test designed to predict success or failure in biofeedback training.

The Trainer

The trainer is the individual responsible for the administration of the biofeedback training process. In addition to being well trained in his or her area of expertise (e.g., medicine, psychology, physical therapy), it is essential that the trainer have a firm understanding of the nature of the physiological processes as they are related to biofeedback training. He or she also should have a working knowledge of biofeedback instrumentation and techniques.

In the biofeedback training process, the trainer and the trainee form the elements of a social dyad. We might expect, therefore, that the characteristics of one member of the dyad (the trainer) may affect the performance of the other (the trainee). Unfortunately, biofeedback research has failed to address this problem. Findings in related areas, such as social psychology (Deutsch, Canavan, and Rubin, 1971; Rosenthal, 1966; Sattler, 1970; Winkel and Sarason, 1964) and psychophysiology (Christie and Todd, 1975; Fisher and Kotses, 1973), clearly suggest that trainer-trainee characteristics and interaction are important topics for future biofeedback research, since they may well have effects on trainee performance. In the absence of such direct evidence, Gaarder and Montgomery (1977) suggest that the trainer who brings to the training process a cheerful, positive, friendly, and encouraging attitude should have a positive influence on the performance of the trainee.

The Instrument

We noted earlier that the human body is not designed to provide its owner with the subtle information concerning internal states that would be necessary in order to develop conscious control over a physiological response. To make the trainee aware of these changes in activity, the biofeedback instrument mirrors the response and feeds the information back to the subject in the form of a tone, lights, meter display, and the like.

Three basic types of instruments are used in biofeedback training (Paskewitz, 1975). The first of these is the biomedical polygraph or electroencephalograph (EEG) combined with certain logic modules and some type of feedback display. These instruments are highly accurate and reliable and have the capacity to monitor more than a single response at one time. They also provide the trainer with a permanent record of the monitored response system(s). The only disadvantages other than cost of such instruments are their size and complexity. Many investigators engaged in basic research in the field of biofeedback still rely on such equipment.

Major advancements in electronic technology have made possible the development of another class of instruments designed to meet the needs of the clinical therapist and the applied researchers. These instruments are what we generally think of when we hear the term "biofeedback machine." In addition to being considerably less expensive than the first class of instruments, the biofeedback machines are more compact and simpler to operate. Additionally, today's machine sacrifices little, if any, reliability or accuracy. The major drawback of such instruments is that only one signal from one site can be monitored at any given time. This problem has been answered recently, in part at least, by the development of the multichannel data-acquisition system. Such systems are composed of several biofeedback instruments monitored simultaneously by an automatic printout device. As you might expect, however, such systems are much more expensive than the single biofeedback machine.

As researchers began to find more and more applications for biofeedback, and as these applications began to receive popular media coverage, the public demand for a private, home-use model increased. The machines developed to meet this demand constitute the third class of instruments. The use of these devices ranges from home practice of therapy to exploration of self-awareness and meditation. In the production and development of these machines, accuracy and reliability are often sacrificed to reduce their cost.

Despite the great differences in outward appearance, all instruments operate on similar basic principles. First, the physiological activity must be picked up by electrodes or a transducer attached to the surface of the body. When this activity is a bioelectric signal, electrodes are employed. Examples of such responses include muscle tonus, brain waves, and skin response. In instances where the signal takes some other form of energy (e.g., mechanical, thermal, photoelectric), a transducer is employed to translate the signal into an electrical event. Monitoring of responses such as blood pressure, respiration, and skin surface temperature call for the use of a transducer.

In either case, the signal detected is very small and may contain not only the signal of interest but other electrical activity (noise) as well. Thus, signal refinement is the next step necessary in the biofeedback loop. Signal refinement involves boosting or amplifying the raw signal and then filtering it. This is accomplished with a series of complex electronic circuits that make up a pre-amplifier and amplifier. Finally, the energy of the refined signal is converted by the signal display into some type of varying stimulus that is made available to the subject; this is the feedback.

The Training Sessions

Because the physiological changes that occur during biofeedback training usually are beyond the level of conscious experience, it is necessary that, in the initial stages of training, the trainee work with a biofeedback machine designed to monitor subtle physiological changes in a system, refine the biological signal, and make the trainee aware of this activity using some type of feedback display. This is the external feedback loop illustrated in Fig. 5-1. It is anticipated that this increased awareness will enable the trainee to accomplish two major tasks. The more immediate of these is to respond to the feedback in such a way as to alter the physiologic activity of the system in a desired direction. Often the trainee is instructed to develop, or develops independently, a kind of strategy (e.g., imagining feelings of warmth, calm, peace) to bring about these changes. Early in the training process, performance may be extremely variable as the trainee attempts first one strategy and then another. A more constant, desirable performance is achieved as the trainee receives more and more positive feedback (i.e., feedback that indicates to the subject that the physiologic changes are in the desired direction) and settles on the particular technique that works best. As the trainee practices the strategy, it is hoped that he or she will become aware of the relationship that exists between the psychological activity and the physiological changes that occur.

    The second task that the trainee must accomplish during these sessions is to learn to produce the desired response change without the aid of the machine. Until this point in the training process, the trainee has depended almost ex-

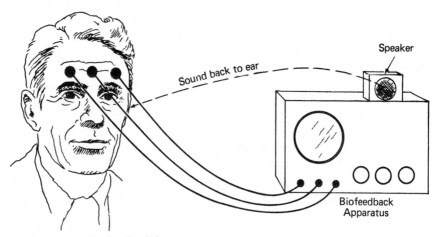

FIGURE 5-1. *Biofeedback loop.*

clusively on external feedback. Now, he or she must become aware of internal sensory cues that provide information about the overall physiological state and the relationship between this state and external feedback. Once these links have been established, the information from the internal sensors can replace the external feedback, thus establishing an internal loop.

The actual biofeedback training process can be broken down into a series of training sessions, the number and nature of which vary considerably depending on the goal of the investigator or therapist. There are four major types of training sessions. These are (1) the baseline sessions, (2) the shaping and reinforcement sessions, (3) the test sessions, and (4) the follow-up sessions.

The goal of the initial baseline session(s) is to obtain a representative sample of the internal system's activity before training. Measurements obtained during these sessions are used to set training goals and to compare pretraining and posttraining levels of performance. If the sample is to be considered truly representative, it is desirable to take measurements during more than one baseline session.

The shaping and reinforcement sessions follow the initial baseline session(s). During the former, with the aid of feedback, the trainee will learn to bring about voluntarily a desired change in the physiologic activity of a system of which he or she was previously unaware and over which he or she had no control. Because the desired change usually occurs involuntarily and at an unconscious level, the probability of its occurrence is generally very low. Often the trainer must rely on small spontaneous changes in the response system that represent remote approximations of the desired change and reward their production when they occur. By rewarding progressively better approximations of the desired response, the response eventually can be shaped into occurring. Once the trainee has learned to produce the desired response, reinforcement in the form of feedback will increase its frequency of occurrence.

To determine whether the trainee has been able during these sessions to replace the external feedback loop with a newly developed internal loop, the trainee is subjected to a test session. During the test session, the trainee is required to produce the desired physiological changes without the aid of external feedback.

In many respects follow-up sessions are similar to the test session. The subject must again attempt to produce the desired change in activity without the aid of external feedback. Instead of being administered immediately after the final shaping and reinforcement session, however, follow-up sessions usually are executed some time later. The results of these sessions provide the trainer with information about how well such training holds up over time.

BIOFEEDBACK APPLICATIONS

How can we use increased awareness of the activity of an internal response system gained with the biofeedback training process? From almost the inception of this technique, applied research has focused on finding answers to this question. As an example, by altering people's levels of awareness and consciousness through the technique of biofeedback, they may be able to better their lives in some important ways. The applications to be considered in this section fall into three broad categories: (1) clinical therapy, (2) exploration of meditative processes, and (3) research.

The obvious potential of biofeedback training for use in alleviating symptoms produced a substantial flurry of research activity during the 1970s. Response systems, including brain-wave activity, muscle responses, cardiac activity, galvanic skin response, blood pressure, peripheral vascular activity, tissue temperature, and respiration, have been subjected to biofeedback training in an effort to deal with a variety of symptoms. Excellent reviews of the resultant research literature are available elsewhere (Gatchel and Price, 1979; Schwartz and Beatty, 1977). In this section we will only be able to give a sampling of the many applications identified by this research.

The chronic headache represents one of the first symptoms to be treated using biofeedback training. Approximately 90 percent of all chronic headaches are either muscle tension or vascular migraine headaches (Dalessio, 1972). Despite a dissenting point of view by Bakal (1975), who suggests that tension headaches, like migraine headaches, may be vascular in nature, it is generally agreed that chronic headaches result from the sustained contraction of one or more muscle groups located in the neck, scalp, or forehead.

Electromyographic (EMG) or muscle-potential feedback has been the major parameter employed in biofeedback therapy for tension headaches (Budzynski, Stoyva, and Adler, 1970, 1973; Wickramasekera, 1976). Rather than attempting to relax specific muscles or muscle groups thought to cause the symptom, however, most investigators have used a general relaxation process, which we will call EMG-feedback-assisted relaxation (Fridlund, Fowler, and Pritchard, 1980). In this process the trainee is made conscious of the activity level of a small pair of muscles located near the center of the forehead. These are the frontalis muscles. The subject's task is to reduce the activity level, and thus the tension, of these muscles. The rationale underlying this approach is that, by relaxing this muscle pair, biofeedback training will generalize the relaxation to the untrained muscles, and they, too, will show a decrease in tension.

In order to accomplish this task, investigators have focused on comparing EMG-feedback-assisted relaxation with other relaxation techniques. Although EMG-feedback-assisted relaxation is generally a successful technique, it is most successful when combined with other techniques, such as progressive muscle relaxation (Chesney and Shelton, 1976) or verbal relaxation instructions (Hutchings and Reinking, 1976). With the application of these relaxation techniques, EMG feedback has been found to be an effective tool in reducing chronic tension headache activity.

The second major type of chronic headache, migraine headache, is vascular in nature. Classic migraine has two phases: a preheadache or prodromal phase, and a headache phase. The prodrome is characterized by such symptoms as emotional changes, hunger, water retention, constipation, and temporary visual disturbances. This phase is thought to be caused by the constriction of blood vessels in the brain. In addition to the throbbing pain generally located on one side of the head, a migraine patient may experience loss of appetite, nausea, and vomiting during the headache phase, which is believed to be related to the dilation of certain extracranial blood vessels (Dalessio, 1972).

One of the parameters selected in the treatment of migraine headache is finger temperature feedback. The pattern of dilation and constriction of blood vessels of the scalp and brain that is assumed to cause the migraine is controlled by the sympathetic nervous sytem. The warmth of the hand is also controlled by this branch of the autonomic nervous system. Because the sympathetic nervous system tends to function as a whole, it has been hypothesized that, as the patient becomes conscious of his or her hand temperature and learns to control it, he or she is learning to cause indirectly a simultaneous normalization of the blood flow to the head.

The use of hand temperature biofeedback in the treatment of migraine was discovered by accident when a group of investigators at the Menninger Clinic, in an effort to improve the outcome of autogenic training (Schultz and Luthe, 1969), combined such training with EMG, alpha brain-wave, and temperature feedback. The encouraging results prompted Sargent, Green, and Walters (1973) to carry out a more extensive pilot project. In this project, they combined autogenic phases and temperature feedback in the treatment of nineteen patients with migraine headache. After their training, all the patients were evaluated clinically by an internist and two psychologists. Of the nineteen patients treated, all three researchers considered twelve to have improved and three not to have improved. The researchers did not agree on the clinical evaluation of the remaining four subjects. These successful findings have been confirmed by a number of other investigators (Johnson and Turin, 1975; Reading and Mohr, 1976; Stambaugh and House, 1977; Wickramasekera, 1973).

Biofeedback training has also been used to heighten the subject's awareness of a particular brain-wave pattern so that this pattern can be modified. Clinically, electroencephalographic (EEG) feedback training has been used successfully in the treatment of a number of symptoms, including hyperkinesis (overactivity) in children (Lubar and Shouse, 1976; Shouse and Lubar, 1977, 1979); insomnia (Bell, 1979; Besner, 1978; Feinstein and Sterman, 1974; Hauri, 1978; Stoyva, Budzynski, Sittenfield, and Yaroush, 1974); learning disabilities (Cunningham and Murphy, 1978; Murphy, Darwin, and Murphy, 1977); neurotic symptoms (Benjamins, 1978; Mills and Solyom, 1974; Weber and Fehmi, 1974); and epilepsy (Sterman and Friar, 1972; Sterman and MacDonald, 1978).

Finally, biofeedback training has been used in the treatment of certain cardiovascular disorders. One such disorder is essential hypertension, for which no physical cause is known. Three major factors appear to have contributed to an early interest by biofeedback researchers in essential hypertension. First, it is obvious that this disorder is a major health problem. In the United States, the incidence of essential hypertension in the general population has been estimated to be as high as 20 percent (Frohlich, 1977). Second, in addition to being a health problem unto itself, hypertension appears to be related to other major disorders, including blindness, congestive heart failure, hardening of the arteries, and kidney failure. Finally, because a physical cause for essential hypertension has not been identified, the disorder is considered to be related to and aggravated by behavioral, social, and environmental factors (Gutmann and Benson, 1971). Hyperactivity of the sympathetic nervous system has also been hypothesized to be a factor related to essential hypertension. With these assumptions, investigators have thought it logical to view biofeedback training as a possible nonmedical alternative for treating this symptom.

Before detailing some of the most important research in biofeedback training for hypertension, it is necessary to review some elementary concepts of blood pressure. Blood pressure reaches its peak during the contraction of the heart. This peak value is termed *systolic* blood pressure. As the cardiac muscle relaxes, blood pressure decreases until it reaches a minimum value, called *diastolic* blood pressure. Typically, these blood pressure values are measured in millimeters of mercury (mm Hg) and expressed together as a fraction, the systolic value over the diastolic value. A patient is said to be hypertensive when the resting blood pressure exceeds approximately 140/90.

Several studies have reported supportive evidence for the use of biofeedback in treating high blood pressure. Benson, Shapiro, Tursky, and Schwartz (1971) found significant decreases in systolic blood pressure ranging from 16 mm Hg to 34 mm Hg in several hypertensive subjects. Miller (1972) reported the case study of a 33-year-old female who had suffered a partial left-side paralysis as a result of brain-stem damage from a previous stroke. After a six-week baseline period, the patient was given blood-pressure feedback daily on an outpatient basis for three months. During each feedback session she was trained to decrease, then increase, and finally decrease again her diastolic blood pressure. After fifty sessions the patient had progressed so that she could increase her diastolic blood pressure from a baseline average of 76 mm Hg to an average of 94 mm Hg, and then reduce it to an average of 65 mm Hg. Her baseline blood pressure during the training period also decreased from 97 mm Hg to 76 mm Hg. Her improvement was good enough to withdraw her from antihypertensive medication during the last part of the training process. This study suggests that, to some extent, blood pressure can be controlled through biofeedback. Researchers still debate whether the results are simply a side effect of relaxation.

In one of the few studies designed to provide adequate follow-up data, Kristt and Engel (1975) selected five patients with histories of essential hypertension of at least ten years' duration for participation in a systolic blood pressure feedback study. Phase 1 was a seven-week period during which patients took their blood pressure at home and mailed the results to the researchers. During phase 2, a three-week period, patients were trained to increase, decrease, and alternately increase and decrease their systolic blood pressure. In phase 3, patients were required again to take their blood pressure daily and mail it to the investigators. This follow-up lasted three months. All five subjects were able to demonstrate control of systolic blood pressure. The average increase was 15 percent; the average decrease, 11 percent. Follow-up tests at one month and three months indicated that control had been maintained.

As is evident, biofeedback is a useful technique for permitting individuals to attend to psychophysiological responses of which they are normally and consciously not aware. Awareness and control of these responses can lead to many useful applications. However, in the case of biofeedback therapy, there has been a tendency to make enthusiastic claims that often exceed the published research data. It is quite possible, as Miller and Dworkin (1977) have noted, that such claims may actually be detrimental to the development and acceptance of biofeedback training as a therapeutic tool. They argue that overpessimistic rejection may result if time and additional research should demonstrate that biofeedback is not able to live up to all of these premature claims.

BIOFEEDBACK AND THE PRODUCTION OF ALTERED STATES

In addition to the use of biofeedback as a therapeutic technique, it has also been employed as a procedure to alter or change the conscious state indirectly through the manipulation of brain-wave patterns. For example, while the use of alpha biofeedback as a therapeutic technique has met with only limited success to date (Gannon and Sternbach, 1971; Glueck and Stroebel, 1975; Melzack and Perry, 1975), the "alpha state" has received a considerable amount of popular attention. Much of this enthusiasm can be attributed to the early studies of Nowlis and Kamiya (1970) and Brown (1970). These studies suggest that bringing the amount of alpha rhythm to a particular level can produce in the subject a state of meditativeness, serenity, and even happiness. This positive subjective state associated with alpha enhancement led to speculation that the "alpha experience" represented an altered state of consciousness. Interestingly, those who supported this view also pointed to findings of consistent physiological changes, including alpha-wave and occasional theta-wave activity, during the practice of certain meditation techniques, as reported by Anand, Chhina, and Singh (1961), Kasamatsu and Hirai (1969), and Wallace, Benson, and Wilson (1971). These observations are discussed more fully in Chapter 6. Finally, the fact that alpha-wave activity of the occipital lobe is seen to increase as the individual enters the sleep state (Dement and Kleitman, 1957) has been cited as further support for the notion that the alpha experience represents a state of consciousness that differs from wakefulness, sleep, or dream activity.

Despite these observations, many investigators were skeptical. To begin with, the alpha state simply does not exist. The use of such a term suggests that the brain is an undifferentiated mass of tissue that produces a single brain-wave pattern at a given time. This is not the case. Typically, alpha-feedback training involves becoming aware of and learning to increase the amplitude of 8–13 Hz activity reported from the back of the skull immediately superior to the occipital cortex. However, there are several ways of increasing the strength of occipital alpha waves without the aid of feedback training. These include relaxing, defocusing, or closing the eyes.

The oculomotor adjustment that is related to occipital alpha-wave production has been demonstrated in the research laboratory. In an extremely creative study, Dewan (1967) taught subjects to send Morse code using their brain waves, which they learned to modify simply by focusing or defocusing their eyes. Defocusing the eyes produced the occipital alpha rhythm, which in turn produced an audible tone. Whether a dot or dash was produced depended on how long the alpha signal was maintained. More recently, Plotkin and Cohen (1976) designed a study to ascertain the extent to which the strength of occipital alpha waves is related to five subjective dimensions most commonly associated with the alpha experience. The investigators found that visual processing and degree of sensory awareness were involved in control of occipital alpha waves, while the degree of body awareness, deliberateness of thought, and pleasantness of emotional state was not. These findings support the notion that the pleasant, quasimeditational state of consciousness known as the alpha experience is not associated directly with an increase of alpha-wave strength, and that the occipital alpha-wave strength is a direct function of oculomotor adjustment.

Findings such as these cast serious doubts on the findings of earlier alpha-feedback studies. First, a close reading of the early studies reveals that only about 50 percent of the subjects actually reported feelings of pleasantness and relaxation associated with alpha-wave production. Travis, Kondo, and Knott (1975) obtained similar percentages in a study designed to investigate the subjective aspects of increased alpha-wave production.

These findings suggest that factors other than alpha-wave manipulation may have been operating in these studies. Suggestion, in the form of instructional set, has been considered to be theoretically relevant to alpha feedback because of its demonstrated role in hypnosis and in other altered states of consciousness similar to the alpha state (Barber, 1970; Lynch and Paskewitz, 1971; Orne, 1959; Weil, Zinberg, and Nelson, 1968). In order to observe the individual and combined effects of alpha activity and instructional set, Walsh (1974) paired both alpha and no-alpha feedback with alpha-expectancy and neutral instructions. The alpha-expectancy instructions used in this study induced subjects to expect "a special state of consciousness known as the 'alpha state'; a calm, contemplative, dreamlike, or 'high' state. . ." The results showed that, in order for an alpha experience to occur, both alpha activity and alpha set are necessary and that neither alone is sufficient.

The findings of meditation studies often cited in support of the existence of an alpha experience are also equivocal. The EEG findings of the Kasamatsu and Hirai (1969) study of Zen monks suggest that these monks were in fact very much aware of the external environment. In short, although they were in a meditative state, the monks produced brain-wave rhythms that were not alpha.

Overall, the research results to date in support of a correspondence between an increase in alpha-rhythm production through alpha biofeedback and the alpha experience certainly have been less than convincing.

It is clear that much of the research in biofeedback and biofeedback therapy is of a pioneering nature. Many investigators appear to have been attracted by the exciting possibility of finding new applications for biofeedback and by the potential of biofeedback as a means of helping to understand our states or levels of consciousness. As with hypnosis, biofeedback requires subjects to attend to a stimulus event and to focus on this event in order to bring about an altered state of consciousness. Unlike hypnosis, however, biofeedback enables the subject to perceive directly and rather quickly the physiological consequences of the altered state. Because of this feature, biofeedback is deemed a very useful therapeutic technique as well. Hopefully, the future will lead to even more uses of biofeedback in the treatment of behavioral and physical problems. Biofeedback should also enable us to learn more about the capability of humans to control and manipulate involuntary and unconscious responses. Thus, biofeedback at present is one of the most interesting and research-oriented areas in the psychology of consciousness. In Chapter 11 we shall speculate on the possible uses of biofeedback in helping us to understand the control of consciousness.

FOR FURTHER READING

Brown, B. *New mind, new body—biofeedback: new directions for the mind.* New York: Harper & Row, 1974.

—— · *Stress and the art of biofeedback.* New York: Harper & Row, 1977.

Gatchel, R. J., and Price, K. P. *Clinical applications of biofeedback: appraisal and status.* New York: Pergamon Press, 1979.

Schwartz, G. E., and Beatty, J. *Biofeedback theory and research.* New York: Academic Press, 1977.

Wickramasekera, I. (ed.) *Biofeedback, behavior therapy, and hypnosis.* Chicago: Nelson-Hall, 1976.

chapter six ═══════════════════════

Meditation

Some individuals known as yogis, from Eastern countries such as India or Tibet, claim that they are able to perform some rather unusual feats. They say they are able to stop their heart from beating; they show how they can walk on fire or sleep on a bed of nails. They demonstrate these abilities and we watch with amazement and even with awe. Have these individuals really found the secret of controlling pain, like that which would be produced by walking on fire or sleeping on nails? Can they really stop their heart from beating? When asked how they can perform these seemingly impossible feats, yogis report that, as a result of meditating for many years, they have learned how to control pain so that they experience none during such activities. That is, meditation has taught them to concentrate on relaxation so that they do not experience the sensations that you and I might if we were to perform these foolhardy tasks. Or has it? Can meditation help to achieve such control over bodily functions and sensations? Or are these claims exaggerated? We shall consider this matter in this chapter.

In many respects, meditation, as a process for altering experiences of consciousness, is very similar to hypnosis. For example, in both processes subjects report being in a very relaxed state, far more relaxed than in their normal or waking state of consciousness. Also, meditation and hypnosis both require a form of concentration or attention to a stimulus event.

However, unlike hypnosis, which appears not to have reliable physiological correlates (Evans, 1979), meditators such as yogis claim that they can control physiological events, including brain-wave activity, electrical resistance of the skin, oxygen consumption, and blood lactate level. Some of these claims have experimental verification (Wallace and Benson, 1972). In this respect, meditation appears to be more similar to biofeedback in that it enables the subject to become aware of and to control behavior he or she is not capable of controlling during a normal, waking state of consciousness.

Also, unlike hypnosis, many have assumed meditation to be associated with religion or religious practices. Specifically, meditation is often believed to be something one does while praying. Because of this association, the lay community (and even some scientists) either have been influenced negatively concerning the process of meditation, or, at best, accept the process as an area of study in the psychology of consciousness but relegate it to nonscience. As a result, meditation is considered to be something one does in a church, synagogue, mosque, or home but not in the laboratory. This type of attitude has resulted in a serious lag in the scientific study of meditation.

At this point we need to elaborate on the role of meditation in the psychology of consciousness and to consider the historical roots of the practice. We also will examine the possibility of using meditation as a means of helping to control behavior and of tapping human potentials that usually are not accessible during the normal, waking state of consciousness or awareness.

MEDITATION AND CONSCIOUSNESS

As we mentioned, many forms of meditation are similar to hypnosis. In both situations, an individual must concentrate on a stimulus, thereby blocking external interference. In hypnosis, the stimulus to which an individual attends is typically the voice of the hypnotist. In meditation, the stimulus is either a visual object of regard, a physical motion of the body, or a chant.

However, it is possible to induce an altered state of consciousness by hypnotizing oneself. This process is called *autohypnosis* or self-hypnosis. The individual concentrates on a stimulus of his or her own choosing, and the net result is a very relaxed feeling. In fact, the behavior exhibited in self-hypnosis approximates the behavior observed in meditation, especially the Zen variety of meditation. Also, as in self-hypnosis, meditation is a procedure one must learn. The ability to hypnotize oneself or to meditate does not come either instantly or easily. One must practice for periods of time and on many occasions before one can concentrate effectively on a situation while attenuating potential sources of disturbance. Typically, initial attempts at self-hypnosis or meditation meet with failure because (1) it is difficult to concentrate on only one thing for a period of time, and (2) most people have never had to do this or anything like it before. Because the situation is novel to us, we resist at first. However, with time, the ability to concentrate on a stimulus situation and to isolate ourselves in our environment becomes easier and easier. Eventually, the task does not appear difficult at all. In fact, we start to enjoy it because it helps us to relax and to escape the world as we experience it in our normal, waking state of consciousness. These effects act as a reinforcer, and the result is that we have learned to meditate.

Where did meditation originate? What does one do to learn how to meditate? What are the different styles of meditation? What are the benefits one can achieve through meditation? These are some of the questions we will address in this chapter. In order to understand better how the process of meditation relates to altered states of consciousness, let us examine closely how meditation has developed over the decades and why psychologists view it the way they do.

HISTORICAL DEVELOPMENT

Meditation as an area of psychological study does not have a formal historical development comparable, for example, to hypnosis. There are no prominent figures in the history of psychology who have introduced important methodological or theoretical facets to the study of meditation. Therefore, in order to search for some of the roots of meditation, we must look to the various Eastern religions and religious practices. Since many such religions actively encourage the practice of meditation, it is not difficult to understand why many individuals automatically associate meditation with religion. In fact, for many, this association is so strong that to admit to meditating is akin to admitting membership in a strange religious cult. Obviously this need not be true, since many who meditate are neither members of such cults nor, for that matter, religious in any sense of the word. They simply practice meditation for its beneficial psychological effects (e.g., altering their state of consciousness) or its beneficial physiological effects (e.g., reducing tension, anxiety, blood pressure).

The popular forms of meditation in Western countries—Zen, yoga, transcendental meditation (TM), and Sufism—can trace their origins directly to Buddhism and Hinduism. The fifth-century Buddhist monk Buddhaghosa described meditation in his Visuddhimagga (a textbook of Buddhist philosophy and psychology) as a "path to purification" (Nanamoli, 1964, 1976; Goleman, 1977). Such purification eventually would lead to an altered state of consciousness he called *nibbana,* or *nirvana.* Because of the potential to achieve this state, and because the Visuddhimagga became incorporated into Buddhist tradition, meditation became a traditional practice for adherents of this religion.

The Visuddhimagga described the basic process of meditation, including the various exercises that must be performed to achieve a state of relaxation and eventually to achieve the state of nirvana. It describes in detail how one learns to focus attention on a specific object or thought and how to begin to attenuate possible sources of interference that can detract from or prevent achievement of nirvana. As such, the Visuddhimagga can be considered the first handbook or guide to the practice of meditation.

According to the Visuddhimagga, meditation consists of breaking with the normal state of awareness or consciousness through absorption, or *jhana.* The book describes eight jhanas, or levels of absorption, ranging from a simple attenuation of thoughts, which occurs during the normal state of consciousness, to total absorption away from normal consciousness and to a state of nirvana. Therefore, meditation is not a single altered state of awareness that differs from the normal state of consciousness. Rather, it is a multilevel process involving a continual and progressive change in awareness.

Hinduism also has played an important historical role in the development of contemporary meditation (Goleman, 1977). Its major contribution has been the emphasis on the mantram, or the chanting of a harmonious word or phrase on which one concentrates. Such concentration helps one to begin to become absorbed in the phrase and thus to meditate effectively. Although the mantram is not unique to Hindu meditative practices, it is stressed as a means of helping the meditator to become aware of his or her thoughts and to attenuate external sources of inference. Today the mantram is an important part of many meditative styles (this topic will be discussed in the next section).

Christianity and Judaism have also played a role in the historical development of meditation. In these religions, prayer often involves a process resembling meditation. During prayer it is not unusual to fixate one's thoughts upon an object or action to help one concentrate on the prayer and to attenuate possible sources of interference from the materialistic world and the normal state of consciousness. In Christianity one may fixate upon a cross (see Fig. 6-1) or an image (real or visualized) of the Christ figure. Catholics often use a rosary, or chain of beads, which they manipulate in their hand to help them fixate upon prayer and to attenuate thoughts which may interfere with prayer. In Judaism the star of David (see Fig. 6-1) and the Torah serve as objects of fixation during prayer. Also, orthodox Jews may perform a forward-and-backward swaying action during prayer to help them concentrate. The objects of fixation and the movements performed in Judaism and Christianity are very similar to actions performed in many Eastern religions and various meditative styles. Therefore, all major religions appear to have played an important role in the development of contemporary meditation.

The Star of David

The Cross

FIGURE 6-1.   *Religious objects of fixation.*

Probably the most important figure in the introduction of meditation to the Western world was the Maharishi Mahesh Yogi. He became known to the West as a result of visits to him in India by the British rock group the Beatles, who acclaimed the Maharishi to be a source of inspiration. This belief spread in popularity with the music of the Beatles. In fact, in many of their recordings they relied on Eastern instruments (e.g., the sitar) and chants (e.g., Hare Krishna). Other Eastern traditions, including meditation, became known to the West along with the introduction of Eastern music and chants. Soon the Maharishi was "on tour" in most Western countries, and many Westerners began to meditate and to join various meditation societies. These societies flourished, and many are still in existence with a following as strong as during the 1960s and the 1970s, the halcyon days of the Beatles.

MEDITATIVE STYLES

As we mentioned earlier, the four most popular forms of meditation are Zen, yoga, TM, and Sufism. Zen is the most classical form of meditation and is often referred to as Classical Buddhist Meditation (Ornstein, 1977). In this meditative style, an individual is given instructions to perform several acts. The first of these is a breath-counting exercise. The individual is requested to count his breaths from one to ten, over and over again. If the individual loses count as a result of inattentiveness, he must start all over. Once an individual has mastered this exercise in attention, indicating that he is now able to concentrate on a stimulus event (in this case, breaths), he is given a more advanced attention exercise. This time, instead of counting breaths, he concentrates on the breathing process itself. He is requested to concentrate on nothing but his breathing activity and to attend to the movement of air as it engulfs his lungs via the air passages through his nose and mouth. This exercise enables the individual to concentrate on his breathing rate. Such activity produces a monotonous, repetitious, rhythmic behavior pattern that enables the individual to begin meditating.

Some more advanced meditation exercises in Zen require the individual to remain motionless and to sit in the lotus position (Fig. 6-2). In this position the individual sits with legs crossed and back as straight and erect as possible. While in this position and while attending to his breathing, the individual is given a *koan*—a type of riddle or thought-provoking question on which the individual is to meditate. The koan is designed so as to be either very difficult or impossible to solve or respond to. A few examples of koans, as illustrated by Ornstein (1977), include, "Show me your face before your mother and father met" or "What is the sound of one hand clapping?" The basic idea behind a koan is to produce intense and deep concentration and thinking. This enables the meditator to focus his attention on the question and on nothing else. In other words, during Zen meditation an individual performs a type of

FIGURE 6-2.   *Example of the lotus position.*

selective attention (Treisman and Geffen, 1967). Such attending enables the individual to remove himself temporarily from his normal state of consciousness or awareness to an altered form.

Another popular form of meditation is referred to as yoga. This meditative style differs considerably from Zen or Buddhist meditation. In fact, yoga meditation is more closely related to biofeedback training (see Chapter 5), though it lacks the elaborate electrical/physiological equipment. Individuals who practice yoga attempt to alter their state of consciousness by regulating involuntary or autonomic physiological processes, such as heart rate, blood pressure, blood flow, digestion, and smooth muscle activity. During yoga meditation the practitioner usually assumes a lotus position and gazes on a visual stimulus known as a *mandala* (see Fig. 6-3). This object may take one of many forms, such as a circle, a square, a hexagon, or an octagon. The form of the mandala is not as important as its presence. The mandala serves a function very similar to that of the mantram: by focusing his or her thoughts on a single stimulus, the practitioner is better able to concentrate and to attenuate external forms of noise or interference. Such focusing becomes more and more elaborate throughout the concentration process. The meditator first focuses on the periphery of the object and gradually moves closer to the center. This technique is a more advanced method for helping the individual concentrate.

In terms of meditation exercises for yoga practitioners, a common usage is the *mantram*. A mantram is a word or a set of words that helps the meditator concentrate on a stimulus event. As a result, the meditator is able to attend to the mantram selectively while he attenuates all other forms of information, such as external noise. Thus, in yoga meditation the mantram serves the same function as does breath-counting in Zen meditation. Also, as with Zen breath-counting, the mantram must be repeated over and over again in order for the individual to attain a state of consciousness that differs from his normal, waking state.

FIGURE 6-3.   *Example of a mandala.*

Another visual technique for meditation used by yoga practitioners is the *tratakam* or steady gaze (Ornstein, 1977). This is very similar to the mandala, except that anything can serve as an object of a tratakam. For example, one may use a vase, a light from a candle, a star in the sky, the moon, or a flower in a garden. The exact form of the object is not as important as the act of concentrating and focusing on it. As we discussed earlier, Western religions rely on a tratakam during prayer (e.g., the cross or rosary in Christianity, the star of David and the Torah in Judaism).

In addition to the use of a mandala and a tratakam, yoga meditators may also practice *mudra*. Mudra consists of repetitive physical movements of the body. The body parts usually used are the arms, the legs, and the fingers. The individual performs some type of bodily movement on which he is to concentrate. This movement, then, serves the same function as the mandala, the mantram, and the tratakam: it enables the meditator to focus attention on some event and ignore all other sources of stimulation. Some yoga meditators even combine some concentrative stimuli during their practices. For example, one may combine a mudra with a mandala or with a tratakam. Again, the exact form of a concentrative stimulus is not as important as that it enables the practitioner to concentrate. It also must be sufficiently salient to prevent the practitioner from redirecting attention to another, interfering source of stimulation. When such interference occurs (as it usually does for most beginning meditators and even for some advanced ones), the task is to bring one's attention back to the original concentrative stimulus. Attentiveness to a concentrative stimulus and then to an interfering object or event indicates that, in fact, the individual is moving from one level of awareness or consciousness to another and back again. The goal is for such shifting of consciousness not to happen, and that is where meditation becomes a difficult task to master.

The third form of meditation is what is referred to as TM, or transcendental meditation. In reality, TM is a form of yoga meditation. As in all forms of yoga meditation, TM requires the practitioner to have a mantram on which to mediate silently over and over again. The meditator practices this for about a half hour twice a day, although he can meditate more often. Unlike the traditional form of yoga meditation, TM does not require a specific posture. The practitioner can assume any position that is most comfortable. While in this position the individual is to concentrate as hard as possible on the mantram, focusing his thoughts on this only. Should his thoughts wander to something else, he is to try as hard as possible to bring his thoughts back to the mantram. Thus, the stimulus serves both as an anchor to which one returns when thoughts drift somewhere else, and as a medium on which one concentrates to help keep thoughts from wandering.

The final meditative style we wish to discuss is Sufism. This type of meditation is probably the least known in the United States. The reasons for its relative obscurity are several. First, the exercises for inducing a meditative state in Sufism are quite different from the three types of meditation we have discussed so far. Second, the principles and styles of Sufi meditation are usually not made public. As a result, even if an individual did wish to develop a strong interest in Sufi meditation, he would not be able to do so merely by reading about it. He would have to join a Sufi meditation society and, as such, would be held responsible for keeping the "secrets" of the society from the general public.

However, on the basis of what is known from writings about Sufi meditation (Ornstein, 1977; Goleman, 1977; Shah, 1970), we do discover some reasons for the secretiveness of Sufi practices. Sufi meditators believe that public knowledge of their practices may lead to faulty applications of the exercises. They are most concerned about this because, to Sufi meditators, meditation exercises vary as a function of time and place. As a result, one Sufi exercise may be appropriate for one individual in a given place and time, while it is totally inappropriate for a different individual at the same place and time. Also, an exercise that is appropriate for a given individual at one time becomes inappropriate at another time. The reasons for these beliefs are neither known to Westerners nor discussed for lay consumption.

Despite the seemingly disparate methods of Sufi meditation and the unwillingness of Sufi meditators to make public their exercises, there are some commonalities among Sufi meditation exercises. One exercise calls for the meditator to move in circles. This whirling action is somewhat similar to an individual simply turning about in circles over and over again. On the surface it would appear that this exercise might make the practitioner nauseous at worst and dizzy at best. However, these sensations are eventually overcome and are replaced with a state of relaxation. This state or level of awareness appears to be different from what one experiences in the normal, waking state of consciousness.

The whirling action by some Sufi meditators, most notably the Maulavi or whirling dervishes of Turkey, is performed as a type of dance that is generally accompanied by the repetition of phrases or sounds called *zikr* (Goleman, 1977). These sounds begin as oral repetitions and later become silent ones. They are monotonous in tone and are believed to induce an altered state of awareness.

Because of the vast degree of individual differences in meditative styles used by Sufi meditators, it is only natural that not all such meditators perform the whirling exercise. In fact, many Sufi meditators use exercises that appear to be very similar to those used in the other types of meditation discussed previously (e.g., the lotus position, chanting a mantram). Other Sufi meditators simply sit in a comfortable position and chant a sound to produce a relaxed or concentrative state.

Since so many differences exist within the Sufi exercises, it seems obvious that Sufi meditation is a nonstandard form of meditation. However, regardless of the types of exercise performed, the goal of all Sufi meditators is the same: to achieve a state of awareness or consciousness that differs from the normal, waking state. This altered state enables meditators to concentrate on a given stimulus situation or environment while effectively blocking all other thoughts and feelings during meditation. Such concentration enables them to achieve a type of bliss or escape from the problems and troubles of the real world.

In fact, as a summary, one could state that regardless of the type of exercises or style of meditation, the goal of *all* meditators is the same: to temporarily alter the state of consciousness or awareness. Only during this altered state is an individual truly able to meditate or to block out the world as he or she experiences it during the normal, waking state of awareness.

CONTEMPORARY THEORIES OF MEDITATION

Three of the most recent theories concerning the process of meditation are those of Deikman (1966, 1971) and Ornstein (1972, 1977), Welwood (1977), and Washburn (1978). Although these theories have much in common in their explanations of the meditation process, they also differ from one another in their manner of explaining what happens during meditation and how a meditative state of consciousness can be achieved.

Deikman and Ornstein explain meditation in terms of a bimodal concept of consciousness. Briefly, the model distinguishes two modes of consciousness, an *active* mode and a *receptive* mode. The active mode is concerned with the focusing of awareness on an object in the environment and distinguishing or isolating the object from the context in which it is found. This is akin to the process of selective attention (Treisman and Geffen, 1967) mentioned briefly in Chapter 4. In addition, the active mode is analytic, sequential, and discursive in nature. The receptive mode permits the meditator to be open to experiences in the environment. In other words, rather than concentrating on an object, the meditator eventually (or, in some instances, immediately) comes in contact with experiences of the senses. Thus, the receptive mode is general, holistic, atemporal, and intuitive.

According to Deikman and Ornstein, we automatically shift from one mode of processing consciousness to another. However, the automatic process can be changed, and we accomplish this change through another process called *deautomatization*. Through this process we no longer automatically shift from one mode of processing to another. The principal mode for learning deautomatization is meditation. When we achieve this process successfully, our awareness opens up in a way that is similar to escaping the bounds that determine our behavior. Instead of being selective about what we attend to or attenuate, we permit ourselves, in a way, to start from the beginning in the processing of information. Rather than react to situations in a learned, automatic fashion, we allow learning to start anew. By doing so, we become more receptive to various stimuli or sensory-input information. This receptivity enables the active mode to take a brief vacation (Ornstein, 1972) from the old, learned, familiar environment of our everyday existence. Afterward, we can return or dishabituate to the normal environment and to the normal, waking state of awareness or consciousness, fully refreshed and ready to go again (an experience very similar to the relaxed feeling subjects report after hypnosis).

Another theory of meditation was proposed by Welwood (1977). This approach sees meditation as a means for making ourselves aware of experiences that we do not consciously notice. To explain how meditation helps us become cognizant of previously unnoticed behavior or experiences, Welwood proposes four levels of awareness: (1) the *situational ground*, which Washburn (1978) translates roughly as corresponding to the concept of the preconscious; (2) the *personal ground*, or the conceptualization of an individualized environment; (3) the *transpersonal ground*, in which an individual recognizes that an object of regard is merely an object within a larger and more complex environment; and (4) the *basic ground*, in which an object stands by itself in isolation (e.g., the object *is* the environment). These four levels form a system whereby meditation becomes an effective tool for helping an individual become aware of information, potentialities, and abilites that previously had existed at an unconscious level. In this sense, Welwood's theory is comparable to the Deikman-Ornstein theory; that is, meditation helps to diffuse information so that we become aware of previously unnoticed elements or objects in the environment. However, Welwood goes further in that he states that such diffusion is a continuous process; we diffuse to become aware of "new" information. This information is then diffused further, progressively and repeatedly, until the basic elements in the environment are uncovered for comprehension. Thus, in stepped fashion, meditation enables an individual to become more and more aware of his or her environment.

Washburn (1978) has pointed out several weaknesses in Welwood's theory. First, Welwood's theory artificially assumes a single, general unconscious when this may not be the case. Second, his theory postulates that diffusion is a sufficient rather than a necessary condition for bringing information and knowledge from the unconscious state to awareness. In light of these criticisms, Washburn has proposed a three-level theory of meditation. These levels include (1) *defocalization,* (2) *reduction of the intensity threshold of awareness,* and (3) *immobilization of psychic operations.*

Defocalization is quite similar to Welwood's concept of diffusion. However, Washburn stipulates that defocalization is a means of focusing on awareness but in a manner opposite to the process inherent in various forms of concentrative meditation (e.g., yoga, Zen). In concentrative meditation, attention is selective and is restricted to a single object, thought, or action. For a short period, selective attention functionally attenuates awareness to all other sources of stimulation in the environment. According to Washburn, such attenuation prevents the meditator from reaching the unconscious, further preventing a tapping of the receptive mode.

In Washburn's theory, meditation also reduces the intensity threshold of awareness. In the normal waking state, consciousness operates with a relatively high-intensity threshold. Meditation reduces this threshold by "calming the storm on the surface of consciousness" (Washburn, 1978, p. 54), thus permitting the contents of the unconscious to reach the level of awareness. When this occurs, a new threshold is established that is lower in intensity than its predecessor. Continued meditation thus becomes easier and easier, since it is no longer necessary to reach the previous high threshold. This process is comparable to Welwood's progressive process of diffusion.

The third factor in Washburn's theory, immobilization of psychic operations, is the state of complete, total, and motionless attention to the totality of experiences that arise during the meditative process. Through this operation, contact with the unconscious is secured and brought to conscious awareness by interfering with functions of the normal, waking state. This process is automatic and, as a result, meditators are unaware that it is happening.

In a comparison of the theories discussed, one commonality is evident. The goal in all three approaches is to tap the receptive mode of consciousness. Deikman and Ornstein specify that this comes about through initial concentration on a stimulus object, thus tapping the active mode. After continual practice with a concentrative meditation exercise, the active mode is replaced eventually by the receptive mode. On the other hand, Welwood and Washburn do not see the need for a concentrative exercise to stimulate the active mode before yielding to the receptive mode. Rather, they see meditation as a response of the receptive mode; concentrative exercises simply detract or interfere with reaching this mode.

Unfortunately, there is no experimental support for these three theories. To date, their predictions have not been tested. However, there does exist some support for the dishabituation concept of Deikman and Ornstein.

Before discussing dishabituation, we should briefly discuss habituation. This phenomenon occurs as a result of continual exposure to a stimulus situation. When we first come in contact with a novel stimulus, we attend to it readily. This produces what Sokolov (1963) referred to as an orienting response. As exposure to the stimulus continues, its novelty dissipates and the orienting response disappears. The result is an eventual "tuning out" of the stimulus event. For example, you may live in an environment where traffic noise is readily apparent. When you first moved to your habitat, the noise probably bothered you; it kept you from sleeping at night or from performing your daily activities in an undisturbed manner. However, after a while you became accustomed to the noise and you no longer noticed it, until a friend commented to you about how noisy it was in your house. Getting used to the noise in this situation is an example of habituation.

Dishabituation means not becoming accustomed to the noise, or becoming accustomed to it through some procedure like meditation. An experimental example of dishabituation through meditation is illustrated in a study by Anand, Chhina, and Singh (1961a, 1961b). A yoga meditator was shown a novel stimulus; his EEG, or brain-wave, activity was recorded at this time. During meditation, the subject produced alpha brain waves. There was no interruption of this wave production upon presentation of an external, novel stimulus. Such an interruption would normally occur for a nonmeditator. Also, when the subject was not meditating, the presentation of a novel stimulus did not produce the typical habituation effect. Thus, we can say that, in this study, the meditator had successfully dishabituated.

In a study by Kasamatsu and Hirai (1966), habituation to a stimulus was tested on a larger sample than that of Anand and associates. Zen masters and control (nonmeditating subjects) were exposed to a repeated clicking sound every fifteen seconds; their EEG activity was recorded during this time. The control subjects showed the typical habituation to the sound source, and their brain-wave activity indicated reception of the stimulus. After repeated presentations of the sound, brain-wave activity no longer responded to the sound source; that is, habituation had taken place. This was not the case with the meditators. Their brain-wave activity remained constant throughout a five-minute exposure period.

Thus it appears that, at least for advanced Zen meditators, dishabituation as defined by Deikman and Ornstein does take place. Whether this occurs via the route suggested by Deikman and Ornstein or by the route suggested by Welwood or Washburn is not known. Hopefully, future research will give us the answer to this question.

PHYSIOLOGICAL CORRELATES OF MEDITATION

As we mentioned at the beginning of this chapter, practitioners of meditation have long claimed that they are capable of inducing many changes in their physiological responses to events. For example, they claim they can voluntarily stop their heartbeat temporarily and that they can alter their normal breathing pattern. Are such feats possible? According to a growing body of scientific literature, some physiological changes can be induced with meditation.

As might be expected, most experiments on physiological controls of behavior during meditation have employed well-experienced meditators as subjects. One such study is by Sugi and Akutsu (1964), who used Zen monks from Japan. The researchers found that, during meditation, the monks were capable of decreasing their consumption of oxygen by 20 percent, which subsequently reduced their output of carbon dioxide. Anand, Chhina, and Singh (1961a, 1961b) reported a similar finding with their yoga meditator.

Changes of brain-wave activity have also been noted in well-practiced meditators. Kasamatsu and Hirai (1963) found that Zen monks were capable of producing a predominance of alpha activity with their eyes half open. This brain-wave pattern is usually present only when a subject is very relaxed and has his eyes closed. The Zen monks were also capable of controlling the amplitude and frequency of the alpha brain waves. For example, they demonstrated the ability to slow the frequency of the waves from the normal 8 to 13 Hz to 7 or 8 Hz. This seemingly voluntary control of alpha-wave production and activity also produced rhythmic theta waves of 6 to 7 Hz. (See Chapter 7 for a detailed description and explanation of various brain-wave patterns produced during relaxation and sleep.)

Perhaps one of the most comprehensive investigations of the effects of meditation on behavior was undertaken by Wallace and Benson (1972). Using practitioners of TM as subjects, they were able to support many of the long-standing claims made by meditators. They found that TM practitioners were capable of reducing oxygen consumption as well as carbon dioxide elimination during meditation (Fig. 6-4). The investigators also found a high correlate between TM and a marked reduction in blood lactate concentration (Fig. 6-5), a rapid rise in the electrical resistance of the skin (Fig. 6-6), an increase in the intensity of alpha brain waves, a slowing of the heartbeat, and an overall decrease in respiratory rate and in volume of air breathed. In other words, the results reported by Wallace and Benson substantiate and replicate some of the earlier experiments performed by other investigators with Zen monks and yoga meditators.

Also, as Wallace and Benson point out, there is little or no resemblance between the physiological changes noted in meditators and those found in hypnotized or sleeping subjects. For example, whereas after meditation there is a marked drop in oxygen consumption for about five to ten minutes, there is no such drop during hypnosis. Also, decreased oxygen consumption during sleep occurs over several hours.

WESTERN APPLICATIONS OF MEDITATION

The major reason that meditation has become so popular in the Western world is that certain benefits appear to be derived from practicing this art of the East. In addition, many forms of meditation are rather easy to learn and are relatively

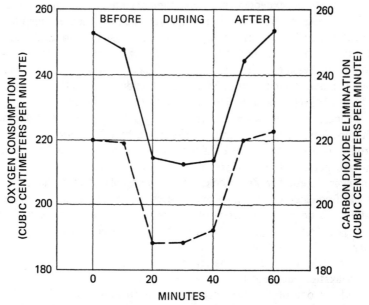

FIGURE 6-4.   *Oxygen consumption as a function of meditation (From: R. K. Wallace and H. Benson. The physiology of meditation.* Scientific American *226: 1972. 84–90. Copyright © 1972 by William Freeman and Co. Reprinted with permission.)*

undemanding. In addition, if the Western meditator perseveres in the practice of this newly acquired skill, he or she hopefully will achieve the desired benefits.

The primary benefit from practicing meditation is relaxation. For avid practitioners, relaxation will result ultimately in a reduced level of tension (Carrington, 1978). The decrease in tension level is manifested by a lessening of anxiety, disappearance of inappropriate startle responses, increased tolerance for frustration, improvement in psychosomatic conditions (e.g., headaches, asthma, hypertension), and a reduced need for psychotropic medication (Carrington, 1977). With the continued practice of meditative techniques, there also appears to be a heightening in energy level, an improvement in self-esteem, and an elevation and stabilization of mood state (Carrington, 1978). Furthermore, individuals who have meditated for, say, a few weeks at minimum report that they experience strong feelings of pleasure, sadness, anger, love, and other emotions that they suppressed previously (Glueck, 1973). As a result of the various benefits of practicing meditation, Carrington (1978) has advocated the incorporation of meditation in psychotherapy as an intervention to help individuals with some of the problems mentioned.

More recently, Walsh (1978) elaborated on some additional changes that occur during or as a consequence of meditation. One such change is in sleep habits. Intensive meditation over time effectively reduces the need for sleep.

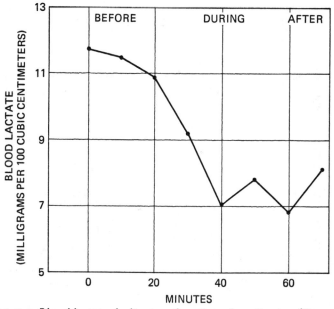

FIGURE 6-5. *Blood lactate decline as a function of meditation (From: R. K. Wallace and H. Benson. The physiology of meditation. Scientific American 226: 1972 84–90. Copyright © 1972 by William Freeman and Co. Reprinted with permission.)*

The sleep requirement decreases to about four hours per day, a dramatic reduction from the eight hours of sleep per day a nonmeditator usually needs. The decrease in the amount of sleep required by a meditator is not surprising. Since meditation is, in fact, a very relaxing experience, and relaxation of the body is one of the consequences of sleep, it makes sense that meditators would not require the usual eight hours of sleep per day.

In summary, it appears that many physiological and psychological changes can occur during and as a consequence of practicing meditation. Thus, meditation is another useful tool for helping us to understand our state of being and to identify various levels of consciousness and awareness. In the normal state of consciousness, we simply are not capable of changing or altering physiological responses of the autonomic nervous system. However, with extensive and intensive practice in meditation (especially yoga and TM), we can become adept at altering such responses. This is not to imply that meditation is the only procedure for achieving these results. Biofeedback (see Chapter 5) is also a beneficial tool for accomplishing this task. In fact, biofeedback does not require as much time to learn as meditation, nor does one need to become as adept at it as with meditation. However, conscientious meditators may practice their art or skill for a lifetime and therefore use it in their everyday experiences. This is not the case with biofeedback, which is generally employed to treat a specific

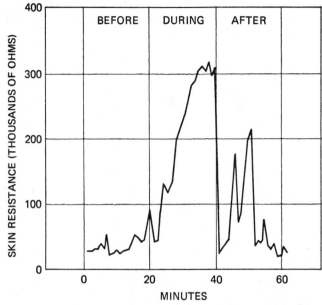

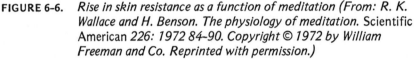

FIGURE 6-6.   *Rise in skin resistance as a function of meditation (From: R. K. Wallace and H. Benson. The physiology of meditation.* Scientific American *226: 1972 84–90. Copyright © 1972 by William Freeman and Co. Reprinted with permission.)*

problem at a specific time. Thus, meditation can be regarded as a slow, cumulative, long-term procedure for producing an altered state of consciousness.

As far as we know, meditation is a relatively safe procedure as compared with the use of drugs (see Chapter 3) for bringing about an altered state. Many life-long meditators claim that the high they achieve with meditation is as fulfilling as any they could achieve with drugs. In fact, they refer to meditation as a "natural high." If, as Weil (1972) has suggested, we have a drive to experience modes of awareness other than the normal, waking state, then meditation appears to be a safe outlet for satisfying that drive.

FOR FURTHER READING

Goleman, D. *The varieties of the meditative experience.* New York: E. P. Dutton, 1977.

Lerner, E. *Journey of insight meditation. A personal experience of the Buddha's way.* New York: Shocken, 1977.

Naranjo, C., and Ornstein, R. E. *On the psychology of meditation.* New York: Penguin, 1976.

chapter seven ══════════════════

Sleep and Dreams

If you are an average, healthy individual it is estimated that you will spend about one-third of your life in a state of sleep. Thus, when you reach the age of sixty, like Washington Irving's Rip van Winkle, you will have slept for about twenty years of your life. Moreover, during your twenty years of sleep it is estimated that you will have spent approximately four of these years dreaming. While sleep and dreams represent a dramatic departure from our normal state of awareness, they are at the same time a state of consciousness that each of us has experienced directly. Perhaps this familiarity with sleep and dreams has served as a breeding ground for questions about these phenomena.

Our current state of knowledge concerning sleep and dreams represents the combined research efforts of a variety of investigators working in such areas as clinical psychology, physiological psychology, and, more recently, psychophysiology. There are several reasons why psychologists and other behavioral scientists have studied sleep and dreams so extensively. Besides the fact that we spend a great portion of our life in the altered states of sleep and dreams, we also often drift into sleep, daydream, and enter states of consciousness in which we are not fully asleep and not fully awake. And we do all of these quite frequently. As a result, it is relatively easy to study these phenomena and to collect a wealth of data about them through introspective reports. Furthermore, in contrast to altered states with which not many of us are familiar, such as hypnosis, meditation, and drug experiences, we all have experienced sleep and dreams, and it is not considered odd to discuss these states with friends, professors, and other acquaintances. Before we survey the results of research efforts in sleep and dreams, let us examine the role of these phenomena in the psychology of consciousness.

SLEEP, DREAMS, AND CONSCIOUSNESS

Sleep and dreams are natural states of awareness and can be viewed most simply as parts of a single continuum that ranges from highly aroused excitement to death (Lindsley, 1952). Along this continuum, one can distinguish several different stages or levels of consciousness or arousal (see Fig. 7-1).

Strong, excited emotions, such as fear and rage, generally produce a restricted awareness and confusion in the individual. Attention during this state is at best narrowly focused and hazy and often leads to disorganized behavior. The level of alert attentiveness is accompanied by a selective attention that may vary or shift as the task demands. The individual is able to focus or concentrate well. This state of consciousness is correlated with a high degree of behavioral efficiency. Such behavior is characterized by selective, quick reactions with a high degree of organization. *Sleep* represents a state in which consciousness is interrupted temporarily; however, the level of consciousness may be fully restored by an appropriate stimulus, such as the sound of an alarm clock or your mother's voice calling you. Of course, dreams occur during this stage; some of them you can recall upon awakening, while some you forget. *Coma*

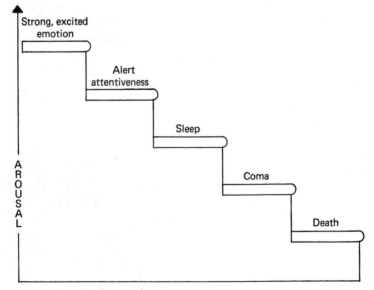

FIGURE 7-1. *Levels of arousal.*

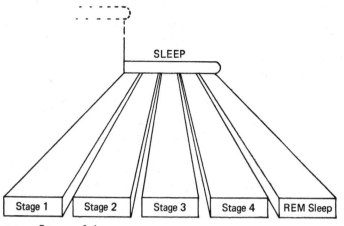

FIGURE 7-2. *Stages of sleep.*

is defined as a state in which there is complete loss of consciousness. After recovery (if recovery occurs), there is a complete amnesia about the entire coma period. While the individual is in a coma, he or she shows little or no response to external stimuli or internal needs. *Death,* the last stage, is thought to bring about a final and complete loss of awareness.

With the advent of modern electroencephalography, Loomis, Harvey, and Hobart (1937) noted that brain-wave recordings could be used to distinguish different stages of sleep. On the basis of electroencephalographic (EEG) records, the investigators were able to identify five distinct stages, ranging from awake to deep sleep. To represent that sleep occurs in stages, the step labeled "sleep" in Figure 7-1 has been expanded in Figure 7-2, and the stages of sleep have been identified with the more familiar Dement-Kleitman system (Dement and Kleitman, 1957).

We will give a detailed discussion of these stages of sleep later in this chapter. At this point it is important to identify some of the most significant scientific contributions that have led to our current understanding of the phenomena of sleep and dreams. What has history taught us about sleep and dreams? To help answer this question, let us examine the historical attempts to study these altered states of consciousness.

HISTORICAL DEVELOPMENT

Because sleep and dreams are such common human experiences of consciousness, it is probably safe to conclude that these phenomena have been of interest since the "dawn of humanity." It is evident that early humans imbued dreams with magical and mystical properties and viewed them as coming from outside themselves and containing omens of the future. Old Testament references to dreams provide clear examples of these beliefs. Joseph, through Pharaoh's dreams, was able to foretell a time of drought in Egypt, and Daniel was able to predict the coming of a period of "madness" in the life of King Nebuchadnezzar through the king's dreams.

The early Greeks and Romans were also extremely interested in sleep and dreams. In his collection of monographs on the biopsychological characteristics of animals, titled *Parva Naturalia,* Aristotle (384 B.C.-322 B.C.) devoted five chapters to dreams and predictions derived from dreams. On the basis of his own naturalistic observations, Aristotle concluded that dreams were not divine or supernatural but rather followed the laws of the mind. Lucretius (90 B.C.-15 B.C.), the Roman poet and philosopher, suggested that the little movements he had observed animals making while in a state of sleep were somehow related to dreaming.

Surprisingly, very little scientific inquiry into the nature of sleep and dreams was initiated until the late 1800s. Until that time, most of what was accepted concerning these phenomena [as described in Binn's (1846) *Anatomy of Sleep*], has been forged from natural observations, anecdotes, opinion, and a smattering of a growing body of scientifically based knowledge pertaining to human physiology. It is little wonder that Webb (1973), in describing this "dark age of sleep," refers to this time as an era during which "sleep and dreams were almost exclusively the property of poets and dream diviners" (p. 3).

Much of the early research in the quest for a brain sleep center took the form of clinical anatomical evidence. Gayet in France in 1875 and Mauthner in Austria in 1890 worked independently on finding the pathological cause of lethargy syndromes. Both noted the importance of a rostral midbrain lesion. On the basis of his observations, Mauthner proposed one of the earliest sleep-center hypotheses. He located this center in the gray matter of the brainstem that forms the walls and floor of the fourth ventricle.

The years 1916 through 1926 saw the development of a worldwide epidemic of encephalitis lethargica, more commonly called "sleeping sickness." Encephalitis lethargica is a degenerative inflammation of the brain and is thought to be virally produced. The disease is characterized by fever, lethargy or hypersomnia, and general motor symptoms (Marcus, 1972). The search for the pathological basis of this disease led von Economo, in 1929, to conclude that not one but two brain centers were involved in the control of sleep. There was a "waking center" that served to turn off sleep when properly stimulated and was located in the posterior hypothalamus and mesencephalic tegmentum (the floor of the midbrain). The brain center, which turned on sleep when properly activated, was thought to be located in the basal forebrain structures. This was labeled the "sleep center."

The late 1930s and the 1940s proved to be a most productive period in the search for brain centers that controlled the sleep/waking cycle. Partially responsible for this progress was the decision on the part of many investigators to turn to the use of nonhuman subjects so that more direct and controlled experimental manipulations could be employed. Two major research techniques were used. The first involved the lesioning or controlled destruction of specific neural structures and observation of the subject's subsequent behavioral changes (Bremer, 1937). Electrical stimulation was the second technique used (Sheer, 1961). It involved the excitation or activation of a specific neural site by the application of a series of short-duration, low-voltage electrical pulses and the noting of any subsequent change in the sleep/waking pattern.

Bremer believed that it was sensory input to the cerebrum that was responsible for keeping the brain "awake." His argument was based, at least in part, on the effects of lesions which interrupted sensory input via the sensory cranial nerves. He discovered that severing the brain stem at the midbrain level (*cerveau isolé*) would eliminate all cranial-nerve sensory input to the cerebrum except for vision and olfaction. On the other hand, the more caudal transection (*encephale isolé*) would leave all the cranial-nerve sensory input intact (see Fig. 7-3).

In studying the effects of various brain lesions on the sleep/waking cycle of the rat, Nauta (1946) found support not only for the presence of a waking center at the junction of the midbrain and hypothalamus, but also for the existence of a sleep center in the basal preoptic region. Nauta demonstrated that lesions in this area were followed by complete insomnia, motor hyperactivity, and, finally, within several days, death of the animals.

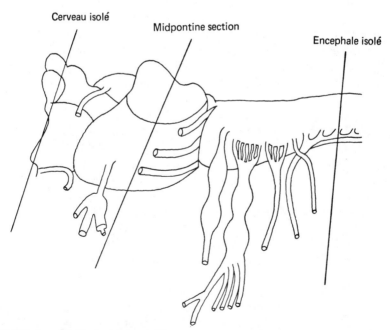

FIGURE 7-3. *Brain-stem transections.*

By the mid-1940s, then, scientists appeared to be on fairly sound footing in proposing the existence of a neural center located somewhere near the rostral midbrain, probably in the posterior hypothalamus, that served as a waking center for the intact organism. Of more questionable status, however, was the notion of a corresponding sleep center. The existence of a sleep center located in a thalamic nucleus, the *massa intermedia,* was suggested by the pioneering study with electrical stimulation reported by Hess (1944). Electrical stimulation of this center in cats induced a state of drowsiness or sleep with all the appropriate behavioral characteristics. The 1940s came to a close with the electrical stimulation studies of Moruzzi and Magoun (1949), who found that stimulation of the brain-stem reticular formation of cats produced an EEG pattern of desynchronization and other signs of wakefulness. In the same year, Lindsley, Bowden, and Magoun (1949) provided additional evidence implicating the reticular formation. They showed that midbrain lesions that interrupted the ascending fibers of this structure resulted in a constantly stuporous or sleeping animal. These findings provided an experimental basis for assuming the existence of both sleep centers and waking centers in the brain stem.

As the 1950s came to a close, it was generally accepted that regions necessary for both sleep and waking existed somewhere in the part of the brain stem referred to as the pons and the medulla. It was also evident at this point, in contradiction to Bremer (1937), that sensory input to the brain was not a necessary condition for an organism to demonstrate behavior signs of wakefulness.

The study of the electrophysiology of sleep and dreams actually had its origin with the discovery in 1875, by the English physiologist Richard Caton, that the brain continually produces low-voltage electrical fluctuations or waves. Using a galvanometer and recording from the exposed cerebral cortex of rabbits, Caton observed these brain-wave activities and noted that they ceased upon the death of the animal.

Caton's observations went virtually unnoticed by the scientific community until 1929, when the German psychiatrist Hans Berger, using human subjects, reported on a technique he had developed for recording the electrical activity of large populations of cortical neurons lying beneath the intact skull. Berger accomplished this by attaching surface electrodes to the scalp and forehead. This development signaled the advent of modern electroencephalography. The early 1930s saw the development of electroencephalography as a clinical tool (Gibbs, Davis, and Lennox, 1935; Walter, 1936), but it remained for Loomis, Harvey, and Hobart (1937) to demonstrate that Berger's technique could be used to measure the level(s) of consciousness. As we observed earlier, these investigators showed that cortical brain waves exhibited distinct changes in dominant frequency and amplitude with the onset of sleep and continued to change throughout the sleep period. Loomis and colleagues devised a system for classifying these EEG patterns into five distinct stages, ranging from wakefulness to deep sleep (Loomis, Harvey, and Hobart, 1937).

What little understanding scientists had before the 1950s concerning the nature of dreams was based almost exclusively on clinical observations. Two of the most influential psychoanalysts of the period, Sigmund Freud and Carl Jung, paid particular attention to the dreams and dreaming behavior of their clients. Freud referred to the dream as the "royal road to the unconscious." He believed that an understanding of a patient's dreams could provide the therapist with helpful clues as to what the client actually thought and felt. Freud's *The Interpretation of Dreams*, published in 1900, is still regarded as one of the most influential books on the topic. Jung, one of Freud's earliest disciples, eventually separated from Freud and set about the process of developing his own system, including his own theory of dream interpretation. Both theories will receive a more thorough treatment later in the chapter.

In 1892, Ladd speculated that the eyeballs of the sleeper moved during dreaming. Unfortunately, Ladd failed to pursue the observation and so it went unnoticed for more than fifty years. While carrying out some sleep studies, Kleitman and his graduate student Aserinsky noted that, periodically during the night, the eyes of the sleeping subject moved rapidly in a generally horizontal fashion. Kleitman and Aserinsky were able to demonstrate that during these periods of rapid eye movement (REM), dreaming occurs. (Aserinsky and Kleitman, 1953). However, before discussing REM activity further, let us look at the various brain-wave patterns, or EEGs, that commonly accompany sleep and dreams.

SLEEP, DREAMS, AND THE EEG

It has been estimated that the human brain consists of as many as 100 billion neurons (Hubel and Wiesel, 1979). These neurons are constantly involved in the reception of information about the environment (sensory input), the processing of such information, and the sending of neural messages to the muscles and glands of the body so that the individual can respond appropriately (motor output). In carrying out these functions, voltages of the nerve-cell membrane and electrical activity at the synapses are in a state of constant fluctuation. The combined electrical activity from large numbers of neurons and synapses, called brain waves, can be recorded by placing electrodes in contact with the scalp and with an instrument called an *electroencephalograph*. The resultant recording of the gross electrical activity of the brain (examples are illustrated in Fig. 7-4) is called an *electroencephalogram* (EEG).

Brain waves differ with respect to at least two major characteristics: amplitude (the height of the wave) and frequency or rate of occurrence. Much of the pattern of electrical activity in a typical EEG recording can best be described as irregular, low-amplitude activity with no particular pattern. Such activity is described as *desynchronized*. At other times, distinct, very regular

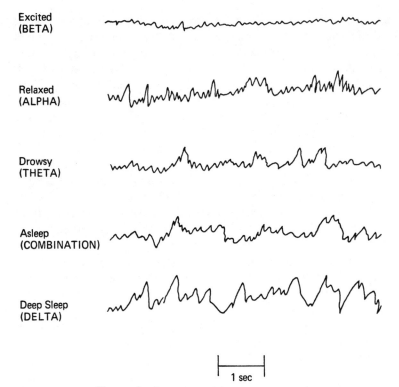

Excited
(BETA)

Relaxed
(ALPHA)

Drowsy
(THETA)

Asleep
(COMBINATION)

Deep Sleep
(DELTA)

|— 1 sec —|

FIGURE 7-4. *Human brain-wave activity.*

patterns of brain waves that are approximately the same amplitude and occur with a regular frequency can be detected on the EEG. This is called *synchronous* activity. On the basis of the number of waves per second (Hz), different patterns of synchronous activity have been assigned names corresponding to Greek letters.

One of the most common EEG rhythms is the *alpha* frequency, which varies from 8 to 13 Hz and has wave amplitudes ranging from 25 to 100 microvolts (μV). They are observed most frequently from electrodes situated over the occipital and parietal lobes of the cortex (see Chapter 2 for an illustration of the lobes of the human brain). Alpha activity occurs in the EEG patterns of healthy individuals when they are awake but in a quiet, resting state with their eyes shut. During sensory stimulation or attentive mental activity, alpha activity is reduced or is replaced by desynchronized activity.

Beta waves occur at frequencies of between 14 and 30 Hz and their amplitudes seldom exceed 20 μV. Such activity is often called "low-voltage, fast" beta activity. Beta activity is recorded most commonly from the parietal and frontal cortical regions. The beta wave is characteristic of wakefulness or arousal.

Among the less frequent patterns of synchronous brain-wave activity are *theta* and *delta* patterns. Theta rhythm was described initially by Walter and Dovey (1944) and includes waves in the range of 4-7 Hz and with moderately large amplitudes of less than 20 μV. Theta activity is a common pattern seen in EEG recordings of children under the age of ten when recorded from frontal and temporal cortical sites. Between the ages of eleven and twenty, theta waves decrease in both amplitude and frequency of occurrence. Delta activity is usually defined as large amplitude EEG waves of 0.5-4 Hz. The presence of delta waves in the EEG of waking adults is considered abnormal.

As we noted earlier, Loomis, Harvey, and Hobart (1935) observed that these cortical brain-wave patterns could be used to identify different stages of consciousness. On the basis of these findings and using EEG patterns as one criterion, these investigators were able to identify five stages that they believed represented increasing depths of sleep (or consciousness). A classification scheme used more frequently, and the one used in this chapter, was developed by Dement and Kleitman (1957). The Dement-Kleitman system identifies four stages of sleep depth and a fifth stage, Stage REM.

Imagine that you have agreed to participate as a research subject in a sleep and dream study and that this is the second night of your participation. The second night has been selected for purposes of this discussion because sleep researchers have observed that the data gathered during a subject's first night of participation in such a study is generally atypical. This is the so-called first-night effect (Antrobus, Fein, Jordan, Ellman, and Arkin, 1978). Once you have arrived at the sleep laboratory and completed your nightly ritual of preparing for bed, the researcher attaches surface electrodes to detect brain waves, eye movement, and muscle activity. The standard "hook-up" for studying sleep activity in the laboratory is shown in Figure 7-5.

Now you can get into bed, get comfortable, relax, and close your eyes. During this state of relaxed wakefulness there will be a change in cortical brain wave activity from the desynchronized beta activity commonly observed in the waking, alert individual to the synchronous, alpha activity of 8 to 13 Hz. Should you happen to open your eyes in response to a sudden stimulus or begin to think about some problem of the day at this point, the desynchronized activity will

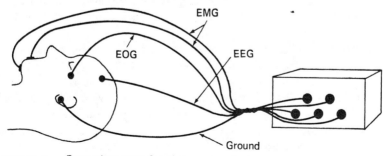

FIGURE 7-5.   *Recording sites for sleep research.*

return. On the other hand, should you happen to fall asleep at this time, you will enter the first stage of sleep, Stage 1.

"Drifting off to sleep" and other similar colloquial expressions imply that the process of going to sleep is a gradual one. While this is the popular or common view of the onset of sleep, it is far from the truth. Actually, the onset of sleep is instantaneous. One second you are aware, the next you are not. It is as though someone threw a switch that immediately put the portion of the brain that controls awareness on standby status. With the onset of Stage 1 sleep, your body begins to show signs of relaxation as muscle tonus diminishes, heart rate slows, and breathing becomes deeper and more regular. In this stage, cortical brain-wave activity is desynchronous, showing low-voltage mixed frequencies; 2 to 7 Hz is the most prominent frequency. This stage represents a transition in consciousness between wakefulness and the deeper stages of sleep to follow. During this relatively brief stage, it would be very easy to awaken you.

It is against this background of desynchronized EEG activity that brief bursts of sleep spindles and k-complexes begin to occur. This signals the onset of Stage 2 sleep. A sleep spindle is a sinusoidal wave that has a frequency of between 12 and 14 Hz. A k-complex is a biphasic wave form beginning with an initial sharp negative wave followed by positive components. Although you are soundly asleep by this stage, you could still be awakened easily.

By Stage 3 sleep your physiological signs, such as muscle tonus, heart rate, blood pressure, and body temperature, all show signs of decreasing. You are now soundly asleep and it would take a relatively strong stimulus to awaken you. The onset and termination of this stage is defined by the percentage of delta-wave activity on the EEG recording. Against the background of desynchronous cortical brain-wave activity punctuated by the k-complexes and sleep spindles of Stage 2, delta waves begin to appear. Stage 3 sleep begins when at least 20 percent of the EEG is composed of delta-wave activity.

During Stage 3, the frequency of delta-wave activity continues to increase until more than 50 percent of the EEG consists of these slow waves. When this occurs you have entered Stage 4 sleep. You are now in a very deep state of sleep and you would be extremely difficult to awaken. If you are aroused during this stage you would appear somewhat disoriented and it would take a little time for you to become conscious of your surroundings. If you are allowed to sleep uninterrupted, you would begin to drift from Stage 4 into Stage 3 and then into Stage 2.

At Stage 4, which occurs sometime during the second hour of sleep, EEG and physiological changes indicate the presence of REM sleep. The EEG during this stage consist of relatively low-voltage mixed frequencies punctuated by occasional bursts of alpha activity. If you think that this description of EEG activity sounds familiar, you are correct. In fact, because the EEG of REM sleep resembles that of Stage 1 so closely, this stage of sleep is often called *paradoxical* sleep. Although the EEG pattern is similar to that of Stage 1 sleep, it would be much more difficult to arouse you from Stage REM than it would be from Stage 1.

The term *REM sleep* was coined first by Dement and refers to the fact that the eyes of the sleeper can be seen darting back and forth beneath closed eyelids at a rate of approximately fifty to sixty times per minute (Dement and Kleitman, 1957). In addition to changes in the EEG and the electrooculogram (EOG), a record of eye movement, other bodily changes also occur during REM sleep. Respiration and pulse rates increase and become irregular during this stage. Blood pressure also increases. The sleeper shows a profound loss of muscle tonus, although twitches or spasms in the limbs are often observed. Finally, male subjects often experience penile erections during Stage REM sleep.

Earlier we mentioned what has come to be one of the most fascinating characteristics of REM sleep: dreaming. Having observed that, during the course of a night's sleep, the eyes of the subject periodically move back and forth rapidly, Aserinsky and Kleitman (1953) began to awaken and question subjects during both REM and non-REM (NREM) sleep. The investigators observed that 74 percent of the subjects reported detailed accounts of their dreams when awakened during REM sleep, while only 7 percent were able to report dreams when awakened during any other sleep stage. While these findings forced the conclusion that dreaming does occur during REM periods, they did not negate the possibility that dreaming could occur during NREM periods as well. Foulkes (1962) and Rechtschaffen, Verdone, and Wheaton (1963) have provided results indicating that dreaming does in fact occur during NREM states, but that these dreams are more difficult to recall on awakening than those that occur during REM periods. Electroencephalographic records obtained during each of the sleep stages are shown in Figure 7-6.

There are wide individual variations in patterns of sleep, but most adults complete a full cycle of sleep stages every 90 to120 minutes. If your night's sleep in the laboratory was a typical one, most of the deep sleep (Stages 3 and 4) you experienced occurred during the first third of the sleep period, while the bulk of the REM sleep occurred during the final third of the night (Hartmann, 1973). As the night progresses, the length of each REM period increases, while Stages 3 and 4 diminish and all but disappear (see Fig. 7-7).

Sleep patterns have also been noted to vary with age. Webb and Agnew (1971) found that the percentage of total time spent in Stage 4 sleep decreases as a function of age. Other investigators (Korner, 1968; Roffwarg, Muzio, and Dement, 1966) have observed similar decreases in percentage of total time spent in Stage REM sleep as the individual grows older. What happens, however, if we are totally deprived of the altered state of consciousness we call sleep? Let us discuss this state of affairs briefly.

SLEEP DEPRIVATION

Most of us try to allow ourselves between six and ten hours of sleep per night; and if we miss a night's sleep or greatly reduce the amount of sleep for any

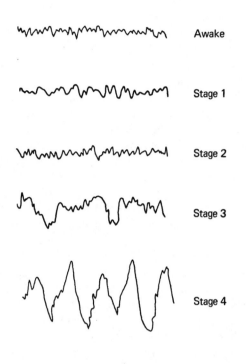

Awake

Stage 1

Stage 2

Stage 3

Stage 4

Stage REM

FIGURE 7-6.   *Electroencephalographic recordings from the frontal lobe of stages of wakefulness and sleep.*

reason, we feel ill-used and tend to express such feelings the next day in the form of irritability, inattentiveness, and general lackluster performance. If we can agree that this is a common experience when we have been deprived of a single night's repose (which means we have gone without sleep for twenty-four hours or so), then the next question might well be, "What are the consequences of more prolonged periods of sleep deprivation?"

Sleep-deprivation studies with both human and animal subjects were performed as early as the 1890s. However, it really was not until the 1950s that sleep researchers began to focus some of their attention and efforts on this problem. Certainly one major impetus to this sudden surge of research had to be the newly acquired knowledge that, in certain countries, prolonged periods of sleep deprivation combined with emotional and physical abuse were being used to induce personality disorders in noncooperative prisoners of the state.

Can prolonged periods of "sleep starvation" actually alter our normal state of consciousness? If such effects do occur, what is their nature? Are they relatively transitory or are they permanent? These are the sorts of questions that the sleep researchers tried to answer in a variety of ways. A frequently cited study of sleep deprivation is Peter Tripp's bid to stay awake for 200 consecutive

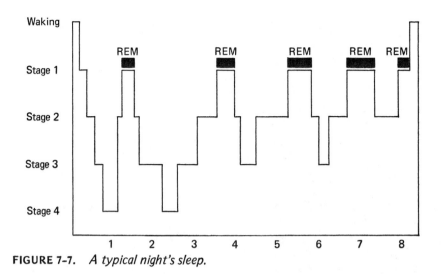

FIGURE 7-7. *A typical night's sleep.*

hours to raise money for the March of Dimes. Tripp, a New York disk jockey, made daily broadcasts from his booth at Times Square, where crowds gathered to watch him. During the course of this self-imposed sleep starvation, Tripp was given medical and neurological examinations, performance tests, and psychological tests. He was watched closely by a number of sleep researchers, including Dement, Lubin, and Wolff. Almost from the beginning, Tripp had to fight off a strong tendency to go to sleep. As he neared the halfway mark (100 hours) it became evident that Tripp was experiencing great difficulty in terms of memory, attention, and even simple mental tasks that required only minimal thought. He also had visual hallucinations. Luce (1965) described the last day of the 200-hour sleepless period:

> By 170 hours the agony had become almost unbearable to watch. At times Tripp was no longer sure he was himself, and frequently tried to gain proof of his identity. Although he behaved as if he were awake, his brain patterns resembled those of sleep. In his psychotic delusions he was convinced that the doctors were in a conspiracy against him to send him to jail. On the last morning of his wakathon, Tripp was examined by Dr. Wolff of Cornell. The late Dr. Wolff had a somewhat archaic manner of dress, and to Tripp he must have appeared funereal. Tripp undressed, as requested, and lay down on the table for medical examination, but as he gazed up at the doctor he came to the gruesome decision that the man was actually an undertaker, about to bury him alive. With this grim insight, Tripp leapt for the door, and tore into the Astor hall with several doctors in pursuit. At the end of the 200 sleepless hours, nightmare hallucination and reality had merged, and he felt he was the victim of a sadistic conspiracy among the doctors.

With some persuasion, Tripp managed to make a final appearance in the glass-windowed booth in Times Square, and after
his broadcast he went to sleep for 13 hours (pp. 19–20).

When Tripp awoke from his recovery sleep, the terrors, hallucinations, and
mental deterioration had vanished. A three-month mild depression was the only
residual effect he experienced.

Five years later, an effort to break the record for consecutive hours of
wakefulness was made by a seventeen-year-old high school student named Randy
Gardner. He was highly motivated and in excellent health. The attempt was
made in the familiar confines of his own home, and he had the aid of two
schoolmates and Dr. William Dement. Under these conditions he was able to
better the *Guinness Book of World Records* listing of 260 hours by four hours.
Although Randy experienced some memory lapses, irritability, and difficulty
in concentrating, he demonstrated no psychotic behavior or serious emotional
change during the entire period. Dement and his colleagues did note that Randy
experienced some neurological difficulties, including blurred vision, involuntary
eye movements, and an EEG pattern which resembled that of a sleeping person, regardless of whether his eyes were opened or closed (Johnson, Slye, and
Dement, 1965). Having set his record, Randy held a press conference and then
went to bed, where he spent the next fourteen and a half hours in a sleep domi-
nated by Stages 4 and REM. On awakening, he appeared to have suffered no ill
effects from his ordeal.

Why the differences in the effects of sleep deprivation between Peter Tripp
and Randy Gardner? The lack of experimental controls in these observations
makes it extremely difficult to pinpoint any single factor. However, a list of
possible explanations would include age, physical health, and prestudy psychological makeup of the subjects; setting of the studies; and the kinds of
demands placed on the subjects during their ordeals.

Laboratory research suggests that, during total sleep deprivation, subjects
may evidence decrements in performance. To account for such performance
deficits, Williams and Lubin (1959) proposed a *lapse hypothesis.* They suggested
that a subject under total sleep deprivation demonstrated an uneven slowing of
performance that led to an eventual absence of the appropriate task-related
response. Edwards (1941) observed that highly motivated, sleep-deprived subjects were able to maintain an acceptable level of task performance, but only
with tremendous difficulty. While the underlying mechanisms are still not
fully understood, it is clear from laboratory findings that sleep starvation is
accompanied by impairment of memory. While it generally has been accepted
that sleep deprivation affects short-term memory (Lubin, Moses, Johnson, and
Naitoh, 1974), Vojtěchovský, Šarfatová, Votava, and Feit (1971) have presented
evidence that suggests that long-term memory also may be impaired. Finally,
laboratory research (Hartmann, Baekeland, Zwilling, and Hoy, 1971; Webb and
Agnew, 1974) shows that, when total sleep time is reduced, the amount of time

actually spent in Stage 4 sleep does not decrease. In fact, if the reduction is severe, Stage 4 time may actually increase (Dement and Greenberg, 1966; Johnson and MacLeod, 1973).

Until now we have dealt with the effects of total sleep loss. One might also question what the effects of a more selective deprivation, say, deprivation of a single stage of sleep, might be. Dement (1960) was one of the first researchers to deprive subjects selectively of Stage REM sleep. In his research, adults were allowed to sleep normally in the laboratory, except that whenever a subject entered Stage REM he or she was awakened by the investigator and then allowed to return to sleep. Dement continued this procedure for five successive nights. He observed that, with the passage of time, subjects had to be awakened more frequently, indicating that progressive deprivation of REM sleep increases the tendency to enter REM sleep. During their first "normal" night's sleep, the REM-deprived subjects spent approximately 60 percent more time in REM sleep than they had during a comparable prestudy baseline period. This phenomenon was called the *REM-rebound* effect, since it appeared as though subjects were trying to make up for the lost Stage REM sleep. The REM-rebound effect has since been replicated many times (Clemes and Dement, 1967; Dement, Greenberg, and Klein, 1966; Sampson, 1966).

Fisher (1966) noted that penile erections, which normally occur during Stage REM sleep, begin to occur during NREM sleep in REM-sleep-deprived male subjects. Tilley and Empson (1978) found that human memory may be affected subtly by Stage REM deprivation. Nevertheless, Webb (1974) suggests that, contrary to early studies (Dement and Greenberg, 1966), REM-sleep-deprivation studies have failed to demonstrate any harmful psychological effects.

SLEEP LEARNING

Most of the memory traces of my undergraduate experiences have long since been tucked away neatly into a corner of my preconscious. However, the memory of at least one experience—a certain midterm examination in Latin 101—stands out very clearly. For me, Latin was one of those courses that fulfilled a college requirement and was not one of my favorite or most interesting classes. For some reason, probably pure procrastination, my preparation for this exam was delayed until the evening before the exam was scheduled. Now it may have been the lateness of the hour, the "exciting" nature of the material, or the quiet of the room, but at 3:00 A.M. I closed my book, about a chapter short of completion, lay down, and slept until one-half hour before my Latin class. That semester I missed an "A" in Latin by three points. I remember reviewing my midterm exam and rationalizing my C+ exam grade in terms of everyone having to sleep sometime.

Perhaps you have had a similar experience and felt that sleep could be best described and classified as one of those inevitable wastes of time. However, passing from a conscious state of wakefulness to one of sleep does not mean a sudden cessation of brain activity. Further, it has been demonstrated that the sleeper is not completely unaware of his or her environment during sleep (Goodenough, Witkin, Koulack, and Cohen, 1975; Arkin and Antrobus, 1978).

It is quite possible that an experience like the one I described, combined with this sort of thinking, led to the examination of *hypnopedia*, or sleep learning. While a great many claims have been made for the effectiveness of sleep learning, laboratory findings have failed to offer much support for such claims (Emmons and Simon, 1956). Reviewing this literature, Rubin (1968) and Aarons (1976) observed that many of these studies were poorly controlled. Adequately controlled studies indicate that, while the subject does not actually learn material presented during sleep (with accompanying sleep brain-wave patterns), the learning of such material when he or she is awake (beta waves) appears to be facilitated slightly as compared with the rate at which he or she learns similiar but new material. In short, there appears to be a positive savings score on learning similar material.

ON DREAMS AND DREAMING

When we dream, what do we dream about? Research has demonstrated that dream content is infinitely varied. Obviously, dream content is also a very private experience. Through EEG and EOG recordings it may be possible for the experimenter to determine whether a sleeping subject is dreaming. However, the only way the researcher can discover what the subject is dreaming about is to ask the subject. Daytime dream recall, although it presents certain methodological problems (Schwartz, Weinstein, and Arkin, 1978), is one way of studying dream content. As its name suggests, the subject, on awakening, is requested to give an account of the dream or dreams he or she had during the previous night's sleep. The procedure is a bit like keeping a dream diary. Another approach to the study of dream content involves using EEG and EOG recordings to determine when the subject is dreaming, awakening him or her immediately after the dream period, and asking for a verbal report of the dream. One advantage of this research technique over daytime dream recall is that it eliminates dependency on the subject's memory.

Some researchers (Hall, 1951; Hall and Van de Castle, 1966; Snyder, 1970) have used the dream logs of a large number of college students as their data base and tabulated the themes of these dreams to provide information concerning dream content. Most dreams involve two or three persons, usually strangers, and one or two familiar objects. Men dream about other men almost twice as often as they dream about women, while women dream about men and other women with equal frequency. Despite what your friends may have told you about their dreams, the probability is very low that your dreams will be populated by famous figures, such as Robert Redford, Suzanne Somers, or Hank Aaron. Animals appear in dreams; however, the ever-popular "dream monster" is almost never encountered. Generally some kind of activity, most frequently some form of movement, is found in dreams. The second most common activity is talking, followed in frequency by sitting, watching, socializing, and playing, in that order. Dream themes more often portray bad news, misfortune, and failure than success; aggressive themes are slightly more frequent than friendly encounters. Although sex-related dream themes are certainly not uncommon, their observed frequency of approximately 10 percent is far less than what one might predict in view of the importance attached to sex by Freudian psychoanalysts.

Some 30 percent of all dreams reported had color, while the remainder were colorless. One investigation (Kahn, Dement, Fisher, and Barmack, 1962) obtained results that suggest that all dreams are in color. The researchers explain that such a small number of dreams are reported as having color because color is forgotten during the time between the dream experience and the time of recall. The data base for this study was obtained by awakening the subject immediately after the dream and carefully questioning him or her concerning the color content of the dream.

In discussing the topic of dreams and dreaming in my psychology classes, I often ask students to estimate the frequency with which they dream. In almost every class I have found one or two students who swear that they never dream. Such a claim must fly in the face of the REM evidence: It is clear that everyone dreams every night (Faraday, 1972). However, as is the case with almost all human behavior, there are individual differences in the clarity with which we recall our dreams. Dreams may be difficult to recall because of some characteristic of the dream's content. Thus, exciting dreams are easier to recall than dull ones, and bizarre dreams are easier to recall than ordinary ones. It is also possible that some property of sleep that distinguishes it from other levels of consciousness can explain why dream recall is so difficult (Goodenough, 1978).

SLEEP DISORDERS

Before closing this discussion of sleep and dreams, we need to sample from what perhaps is the most dramatic aspect of this phenomenon: sleep disorders, that is, disorders of consciousness.

One of the most common sleep disorders is *insomnia*. Estimates suggest that as much as 25 percent of the population experiences some form of this syndrome on a fairly regular basis. Dement (1972) refers to insomnia as "an illness that is caused by the treatment." The very sleeping pill prescribed by the doctor to regulate the patient's sleep may well produce the sleep disturbance. Initially, the sleep medication may cause a suppression of REM sleep; but if the dosage of the medication is not increased, this effect will eventually habituate. As you might predict, once medication is discontinued, the individual experiences a tremendous REM-rebound effect. The sudden increase in REM-sleep leads to sleeplessness that is often accompanied by vivid nightmares (Oswald, 1968). Now the patient is convinced he or she has a bad case of insomnia and so returns to the sleeping pill, and the cycle begins once more.

While insomnia may take several forms, each form results in the same thing, a loss of sleep. The individual may experience great difficulty in initially falling asleep. This is sometimes referred to as a sleep-onset disorder. Other forms of insomnia include a tendency to wake up repeatedly during the night, and a tendency to wake up very early in the morning coupled with an inability to go back to sleep.

Another sleep disorder, *sleep apnea*, was identified first by Gastaut and Broughton (1965) in patients who complained of hypersomnia, and later by Guilleminault, Eldridge, and Dement (1973) in association with insomnia. As the name suggests, sleep apnea is characterized by brief periods during which the sleeping person stops breathing. These periods generally last for between 15 and 60 seconds. For the person who suffers from sleep apnea, the change from the waking to the sleeping state has the effect of "turning off" the respiratory centers of the brain. This causes the muscles necessary for breathing—the diaphragm and the intercostal muscles—to stop working. Under such conditions there can be no exchange of oxygen and carbon dioxide, so the amount of oxygen carried by the red blood cells decreases to extremely low levels while the carbon dioxide in the blood continues to increase. In response to these changes in blood gas levels, the respiratory centers of the central nervous system and the respiratory muscles begin to function once more. However, there is yet another problem. Because the loss of muscle tonus that normally accompanies sleep is exaggerated in sleep apnea, the throat collapses, effectively cutting off the flow of air to the lungs. Thus, oxygen levels continue to decrease and carbon dioxide levels increase until they reach dangerous levels and the individual is briefly aroused. After a series of gasping breaths, during which time the blood gases return to normal levels, the patient goes back to sleep and the cycle begins again (Dement, 1972). The specific cause of sleep apnea is as yet unknown.

Narcolepsy is another common sleep disorder. Individuals suffering from narcolepsy experience sudden and recurrent attacks of sleep and a desire to sleep during the waking hours. Most narcoleptics also experience other periodic disorders that occur frequently enough to be included as a part of the narcolepsy syndrome. These symptoms include cataplexy, sleep paralysis, and hypnogogic hallucinations. Cataplexy refers to a sudden loss of muscle tone and postural reflexes. During these seizures the patient is fully awake and aware of what is happening in the environment. Sleep paralysis is an inability to move that occurs in relation to falling asleep or awakening. Hypnogogic hallucinations are very vivid, often frightening, dreams that occur at the onset of sleep.

Earlier in the chapter we noted that the normal onset of sleep is characterized by NREM brain-wave activity. Laboratory studies of narcoleptic patients, however, have demonstrated that these individuals begin their night's sleep with a REM phase (Rechtschaffen, Wolpert, Dement, Mitchell, and Fisher, 1963). These results led Rechtschaffen and colleagues to predict that the daytime sleep attacks of the narcoleptic may well be attacks of REM sleep. This prediction was later confirmed in the laboratory (Rechtschaffen and Dement, 1969). The exact cause of this condition is unknown. Findings such as those cited above, however, have led Dement, Holman, and Guilleminault (1976) to suggest that narcolepsy may be due to a physiological defect in the REM-sleep control mechanism.

Several sleep disorders have in common the fact that they predominantly affect the sleep of children. These disorders include sleepwalking, bedwetting, and night terrors.

Children who suffer from sleepwalking, or *somnambulism*, usually go to sleep normally, but sometime during the night they arise and walk in their sleep. If unchecked they may go from room to room, leave the house, and even perform rather complex tasks. During sleepwalking the child's eyes are partially or fully open, and the child is able to avoid obstacles, listen when spoken to, and obey commands. After fifteen minutes to a half hour of such behavior, the sleepwalker generally will return to bed on his or her own. In the morning the child usually remembers none of these nocturnal events.

Nocturnal enuresis, or bedwetting, is often associated with dreams in which the child is urinating into a toilet. The child awakens only to discover that he or she has wet the bed. Turner and Taylor (1974) estimate that as many as four million to five million children and adolescents in the United States suffer from this embarassing condition.

Parvor nocturnus, or night terrors, are events that normally occur during the early part of the night and leave a child in an apparent state of terror, thrashing and screaming, unable to communicate what is wrong, and completely inconsolable. Concomitant with the night terror attack is a severe physiological upheaval. Kahn, Fisher, and Edwards (1978) suggest that, during severe attacks, the heart rate may almost triple. Increases in both rate and magnitude of respiration and in skin conductance are also observed. Such episodes are generally of short duration, and characteristically the child returns to sleep once the attack passes. Despite the apparent intensity of the experience, the child often forgets it by morning.

Since it would appear that at least some dream content is associated with these sleep disorders, it may come as a surprise that they normally occur near the end of one of the first Stage 4 (deep sleep) periods. Although the exact causes of these disorders remain unknown, a review of the literature suggests at least two hypotheses. Some investigators say that the behaviors observed in such disorders may be an expression of emotional conflicts that the child represses during the waking hours. Other researchers contend that such disorders develop as a result of an immature central nervous system (Broughton, 1968).

Now that we have considered the mechanisms of sleep and dreams and the research in this area of consciousness, we will consider the theoretical interpretations of some of the findings.

THEORIES OF SLEEP AND DREAMS

In discussing the sleep and dreams as states of consciousness, we need to ask several questions: Why do we sleep? What are the functions of dreams? Questions such as these have long puzzled both the layperson and the researcher. From time to time, investigators in the field have offered their "best guesses" (hypotheses) on the basis of the clinical and laboratory evidence available. Let us examine some of the "guesses" as to what sleep and dreams are all about in the realm of consciousness.

Sleep Theory

Theoretical responses to the question, "Why do we sleep?" have been many and varied. Rather than attempt to identify each of the theoretical explanations that has been offered—a task well beyond the scope of this chapter—we have attempted to classify these explanations into five representational categories.

With the advent of new data about and increased interest in hematology (the study of blood) came the first categories of sleep theory, the **humoral theories.** Such theories suggest that some substance residing in the blood brings about a dysfunction of the central nervous system that results in sleep. One theory representative of this category, the *circulatory theory*, suggests that sleep occurs as a result of the brain being deprived of its normal amount of oxygen.

Several investigators, such as Bartley and Chute (1947), have proposed a *reparative theory* of sleep. These researchers argue that cortical activity that occurs during the waking period brings about cortical cellular changes. Since such cortical functions as the processing of sensory information, processing of memory, and thinking diminish or cease during sleep, the investigators conclude that it is during the sleep period that the necessary cellular repairs are made.

A number of years ago sleep was seen as a passive process. In short, sleep was described simply as a cessation of the active condition of wakefulness, not unlike the state of unconsciousness. This view of sleep has been incorporated into some modern theories of sleep. Of the modern **passive theories** of sleep, perhaps one of the best known is Lindsley's (1960) *reticular hypothesis*. According to this explanation, sleep is the result of the cessation of ascending impulses in the ascending reticular activating system.

In sharp contrast to the passive theories stand the **active theories** of sleep. Rather than view sleep as a process resulting from the deactivation of a system, active theories suggest that sleep is an active process produced by the activation of a sleep-producing system. All active theories of sleep contend that different neural mechanisms are involved in the control of wakefulness and sleeping.

Finally, some theories suggest that sleep is an evolved mechanism which has a particular survival function. One such evolutionary theory of sleep, proposed by Zepelin and Rechtschaffen (1974), contends that the sleep process evolved as a system for conserving energy.

From the foregoing discussion, it should be obvious that there is no dearth of "best guesses" as to why we sleep. However, none of the theories offered to date has been clearly substantiated when subjected to the rigors of laboratory research. Thus, the question of "Why do we sleep?" remains unanswered.

Dream Theory

As we noted earlier, Sigmund Freud and Carl Jung, through their clinical observations, did a great deal to enhance the clinical respectability of dreams. Freud suggested that the function of dreams was twofold. First, dreams prevent the sleeping individual from being awakened by minor environmental disturbances. In this regard, Freud wrote, "The dream is the guardian of sleep" (Freud, 1913). Freud's theory seems to be supported by the fact that many such disturbances during the night often find their way into the dreams of the sleeper. For example, once I dreamed of being chased through the desert by bandits who were shooting at me. In my dream I was hot and thirsty. When I awoke the next morning, I was indeed hot and thirsty. I had forgotten to turn down the thermostat before retiring, and the indoor thermometer read almost eighty degrees. I have not yet determined the source of the gunshots. Perhaps they were the product of the sounds made by the window blinds slapping against the wall. Possibly you can recall having a similar dream experience.

Wish fulfillment is the second function of dreams proposed by Freud. Simply stated, Freud believed that unconscious impulses were responsible for dreams, and the goal of dreams was the gratification of some drive. Thus, the hungry person dreams of food; the student, of graduating; and the failure, of success.

Jung (as discussed by Hall and Lindzey, 1978) suggested that dreams were more than unconscious wishes. Jung saw two functions or purposes of dreams. First, he felt that dreams were prospective. This means that dreams help the dreamer to prepare for events anticipated for the immediate future. The test you must take tomorrow or the next day may be the main feature of your dream tonight. Second, Jung's proposed function of dreams is closely tied to his theory of personality. According to this theory, personality is composed of a number of subsystems, and the goal of personality development is to unify these parts into an integrated whole. For this to be accomplished, Jung believed that all the parts of the personality had to develop fully. If the development of any one subsystem is neglected, then it will find expression in the form of dreams.

We all encounter various problems during the course of the day. These problems range from "Which date do I accept for Friday night?" to "Should I invest the money, time, and energy necessary to get a college education, or should I enter the work force now?" Some of these problems lend themselves to an immediate solution, while others require considerably more thought. French and Fromm (1964) have suggested that dreams are simply attempts by the individual to solve such problems. The function of dreams is to help the dreamer define the problem more clearly.

More recently, Cartwright (1977) proposed a cognitive theory of dreaming. Cartwright suggests that dreams may have two major functions. First, they provide the individual with an opportunity to attend to fantasy and to his or her own impulses. Cartwright argues that this opportunity enables the subject to focus more clearly on the world of reality during the waking hours. Second, dreams have a coping function. By affording the dreamer an opportunity to regulate inner feelings, dreams help the individual adapt better to stressful situations of the real world.

As with sleep theories, dream theories differ widely. The more classical dream theories, such as those of Freud and Jung, suffer from a vagueness that makes it extremely difficult to subject them to the rigors of experimental scrutiny. Attempts to take more recently developed theories into the research laboratory have generally produced results that can best be described as contradictory and are often confounded by uncontrolled variables. In summary, then, the questions "Why do we sleep?" and "What are the functions of dreams?" must, for now, remain unanswered.

In conclusion, many questions concerning the study of sleep and dreams within the psychology of consciousness have not been answered, either by theory or by research. This situation reflects only the present state of science. However, we have discovered much information concerning sleep and dreams as states of consciousness. For example, as an altered state, we know that sleep is not one state of consciousness, but rather several states, or, at least, that sleep consists of several levels. These levels are defined by differences in recorded brain-wave activity (EEG) that correspond to each stage of sleep. We know that each stage is different, not only in terms of EEG activity, but also in terms of consciousness experiences. For example, one stage may correspond to light sleep, while another may correspond to deep sleep. While in these stages, the sleeper has distinctly different experiences of consciousness or awareness. During another stage of sleep, dreams generally occur. Therefore, at least when we discuss sleep and dreams as altered states of consciousness, it is not difficult to see (and experience) that we do not simply have just a wakeful state of consciousness and a sleep state of consciousness. The process is much more complex. We hope that, with time, science will help to reduce some of the complexity and help us to understand better the role of sleep and dreams, not only as physiological events, but also as unique experiences that comprise altered states of consciousness.

FOR FURTHER READING

Dement, W. C. *Some must watch while some must sleep: exploring the world of sleep.* New York: Norton, 1976.

Diamond, E. *The science of dreams.* Garden City, NY: Doubleday, 1962.

Kramer, M. *Dream psychology and the new biology of dreaming.* Springfield, IL: C C Thomas, 1969.

Webb, W. B. *Sleep: the gentle tyrant.* Englewood Cliffs, NJ: Prentice-Hall, 1975.

chapter eight ════════════════

Sensory Deprivation

Sitting here looking out the window of my study, I can see my seven-year-old daughter providing two of her playmates with an explanation, complete with elaborate gestures and gory details, of her most recent loss—her two upper front teeth. This backyard drama is being played out against a background of "acid rock" which emanates from the bedroom of my teenage son. I have yet to discover a way of preventing these soundwaves from terrorizing my auditory receptors. The day has been clear and sunny, and the sunshine pouring through the study window feels warm and pleasant on my back. Since noon, I have been nursing along, with great care, the main course for this evening's dinner—stuffed cabbage rolls. Only now has the aroma begun to escape the confines of the kitchen to stimulate my olfactory receptors. Being the chef in our home carries with it certain advantages. The one I exercise most frequently is that of being the official taster. Thus, on my last trip to the kitchen to coax my creation, I paused long enough to satisfy the curiosity of my taste buds with a sip of the cream sauce. The movement of my arm as I write, the noise of the cars driving past the house, the light touch of my shirt against my skin, and the hunger pangs I feel are among the many other environmental stimuli, both internal and external, of which currently I am aware.

In large part, this stimulation will govern my behavior. The stimuli serve to initiate, maintain, or sustain certain physiological processes and bring about certain behavioral consequences. Thus, if the "noise" of my son's latest rock album becomes too loud, I will cease my writing, open the doors of my study, and, in my stern, fatherly voice, explain to him the imminent danger his record and stereo system will face if the sound level is not diminished immediately.

The environment I have described fairly teems with stimulation, but the important point to remember is that it is a brief and incomplete description of a *typical* environment. This will become evident if you put down your book for a minute and make a partial list of stimuli in your present environment of which you are cognizant. Now imagine that you are transported to another kind of environment, one that does not contain any of the kinds of stimulation that you encounter normally in your daily life. Consider the small life raft of a lone crash survivor, adrift under a cloudless sky with nothing but endless ocean in sight; the small, dark, quiet cell of a prisoner in isolation; or the tank of water in the subject room of a sensory deprivation laboratory into which the subject, blindfolded and nude, is immersed. These environments all have at least one thing in common: the normal daily exposure to stimulation is absent. After several days in this strange, new environment, how might you function? Can an environment so devoid of stimulation actually affect one's level of consciousness and thus one's perceptual judgments, learning, and problem-solving behaviors? These questions, as well as others you may have thought of, will be addressed in this chapter.

Before we plunge headlong into a discussion of sensory deprivation, it is necessary to have a clear understanding of what is meant by this term. Actually, it is impossible to create a situation of complete sensory deprivation for a human subject. Even by using a well-ventilated, soundproof, and lightproof room we would not be able to eliminate all possible sensory stimulation. Our nude subject would still hear the pounding of the heart, the sounds generated by breathing, and perhaps an occasional growl of the stomach. Additional sensory stimulation may come from muscle activity involved in movement, body odors, and skin contact with another surface. In a sense, then, the term *sensory deprivation* is a misnomer in that it implies that the level of all sensory stimulation is subthreshold for all the sensory modalities. For purposes of our discussion we will adopt the definition of sensory deprivation proposed by Corso (1967): that sensory deprivation indicates that the level of stimulation has been reduced or altered in such a way as to no longer conform to an individual's normal variety or range of exposure.

SENSORY DEPRIVATION AND CONSCIOUSNESS

In Chapter 6 (meditation), we observed that certain meditative techniques involve the use of some external stimulus upon which the meditator learns to focus attention and to exclude from consciousness all other external forms of stimulation. In the case of sensory deprivation, it would appear that an altered state of consciousness is achieved also through a reduction in perceived external stimulation. However, unlike meditation, this reduction is not achieved by some mental process; rather it is accomplished by the direct experimental manipulation of the environment. That manipulation in sensory deprivation does lead to an altered state of awareness seems clear from the research data obtained to date. For example, sensory deprivation may produce hallucinations or a change in a state of consciousness similar to that observed in subjects under the influence of an hallucinogenic drug (see Chapter 3). Many of these changes will be described in greater detail in this chapter.

We have noted that, generally, individuals enter into situations that typically produce an altered state of consciousness in order to achieve a desired goal. Thus, a person may elect to enter a program of biofeedback training to heighten his or her awareness of specific bodily responses in order to develop conscious control over those responses. For the person who is able to master a technique, meditation affords an opportunity to enter into an altered state of consciousness and, in doing so, bring about a "mystical" experience. Finally, a person who experiences chronic pain may choose to undergo hypnosis in hopes of reducing the felt pain.

What can sensory deprivation offer the individual? Why would a person decide to enter a sensory-deprived situation? At first glance you might be inclined to respond negatively to both of these questions. Certainly, any review of the literature on sensory deprivation, both natural observations and experimental research data, suggests very little in the way of positive outcomes for individuals who undergo such an experience. In the final section of this chapter, however, we will focus on at least one possible positive outgrowth of research on sensory deprivation and the altered state of awareness it establishes. Before discussing the ways in which sensory deprivation changes states or levels of consciousness, let us trace the development of this manipulation.

HISTORICAL BACKGROUND

The topic of sensory deprivation certainly is not new to those interested in human behavior. Since earliest times such deprivation has existed in the form of solitude and social isolation. The Bible provides a number of references to such isolation experiences. Moses, withdrawing from the multitudes, ascended Mount Sinai, where he spent forty days and nights alone; there he received the commandments from God. John the Baptist spent much of his early life in the isolation of the desert, where he developed the mystical qualities he would need to fulfill his ministry. Finally, Jesus, after being baptized by John, went out into the wilderness alone, where he overcame the temptations of the devil.

More detailed descriptions of the experiences of prisoners, writers, explorers, mystics, and others under conditions of extreme isolation have been made public. For example, Admiral Richard Byrd (1938) chronicled his experiences of being isolated for six months in a small hut buried beneath the snows of the Antarctic. The small, unchanging surroundings of his hut combined with the quiet of the seemingly unending polar nights that served as Byrd's environment for this period can best be described as monotonous, confining, and unchanging. Although he undertook the ordeal voluntarily, Byrd soon discovered that life under such conditions was anything but peaceful and serene. His early reactions centered around a fear that his rescuers would not reach him in time; these fears gave way to an overwhelming apathy. It took an almost herculean effort for Byrd to attend to the life-sustaining necessities of eating, drinking, and keeping warm. He also experienced hallucinations. By the fourth month Byrd had entered a severe depression. He reported an extremely strong need for the kinds of stimulation we normally take for granted—sounds, odors, human touch, and so on. During this time, Byrd also reported feelings of loss of identity and of floating freely through space. Obviously, Byrd's descriptions suffered from the limitations inherent in any anecdotal report, but they undoubtedly served to attract the interest of psychological researchers as well as the general public.

Shurley (1961) has suggested that the experimental approach to sensory deprivation came about as a result of the convergence of three major lines of influence. First, the developments in neurophysiological techniques and electrophysiological methods provided an avalanche of new findings and led to a revision of the physiological model of the central nervous system. Instead of viewing the brain as a switchboard mechanism for connecting an appropriate response to a stimulus, the new model took into account such phenomena as reverberating circuits, neural feedback systems, and arousal centers (Hebb, 1949).

The second major influence was based on numerous investigations by psychological researchers into the effects of sensory deprivation on the developmental processes and learning of nonhuman subjects. It would seem logical that the impetus for this research came, at least in part, from the many case reports of feral humans. Carl von Linnaeus (1707-1778) first introduced the term *feral man* in his 1758 edition of the *Systema Naturae*. He used it to describe cases in which a human child has been cared for, in complete social isolation from other human beings, either by animals or by only indirect contact with human caretakers. One of the best known of these cases is that of the Wild Boy of Aveyron (Itard, 1932).

By the early 1950s it became apparent that, for the sake of national security, it was important that United States researchers investigate and attempt to understand the factors involved in thought-reform movements, indoctrination programs, and brainwashing techniques. Disturbing newspaper accounts of captured American soldiers defecting to the enemy and confessing to all sorts of war atrocities began to appear. The publication of General William F. Dean's (1954) account of his own experiences at the hands of his Communist captors, combined with the newspaper reports, served to heighten public as well as government interest and speculation that the enemy had developed a new, secret method of breaking the mind.

It was at Canada's McGill University in 1953 that these three major influences—development of neurophysiological techniques and electrophysio-logical methods, subhuman research in sensory deprivation effects, and a possible threat to national security—finally converged to bring about the development of an initial research program that focused on stimulus reduction and decreased sensory variability. Besides formalizing the question of sensory deprivation, the McGill University studies opened a whole new track for psychological research, theory, and speculation (Brownfield, 1965).

SENSORY DEPRIVATION THEORY

The preceding sections of this chapter have made reference to both naturalistic and experimental observations of the effects of sensory deprivation on human behavior. At some point in such a discussion it is reasonable to expect that the curious student will question how these effects can best be explained within the framework of psychology. To account for these findings, a number of interesting theoretical statements have been posited by investigators of this phenomenon.

Concentrating on the hallucinatory experiences reported by some sensory deprivation subjects, Rosenzweig (1959) suggested that the condition of sensory deprivation is somewhat analogous to that of schizophrenia. Rosenzweig contends that the symptoms of the schizophrenic are brought about by disruptions in internal processes that in turn destroy the orderly associations of sensory and perceptual material. Thus, even though the schizophrenic may be experiencing considerable stimulation, he or she simply is unable to establish the relevance of such input to ongoing cognitive processes. Likewise, subjects of sensory depriva-tion studies also find it extremely difficult to attach meaning to the sensory input. In this case, however, the problem does not stem from any disruption of internal processes, but rather from the manipulation of external environmental conditions such that sensory stimuli are restricted, depatterned, or redundant. To Rosenzweig, then, it is not the deprivation of external stimuli, but rather the deprivation of relevance or meaning that leads to the effects (especially hallucinations) observed under conditions of sensory deprivation.

Robertson (1961) assumes that under normal conditions an individual's response is a result of the interaction of external and internal stimuli. As we use the term here, internal stimuli refer to feelings, memories, images, and thoughts that predispose the individual to attend to and perceive certain stimuli in the environment while ignoring others. It follows that under conditions of sensory deprivation the hypothesized interaction between external and internal stimuli is substantially reduced, and behavior is determined almost completely by various internal stimuli. This condition leads to a state of preoccupation during which the subject's perceptual and cognitive activities are considerably restricted and internally directed. The subject gives excessive attention to what remains of the external stimulation, and with this suggestibility develops. Robertson suggests that the subject, faced with diminished external stimulation and with internal stimuli for which there is no normal background of external stimulation, experiences a heightened suggestibility, and the behavioral effects of sensory deprivation are manifested.

To provide a somewhat different explanation for the effects of sensory deprivation, Lindsley (1961) looked to the neurophysiology of the organism and, more specifically, to the functioning of the ascending reticular activating system (ARAS). Under normal conditions, two major functions are subserved by the neurons of the lower brain stem that make up the ARAS. First, the ARAS acts as a kind of relay station. The ARAS receives information in the form of neural impulses from each of the sensory receptors and in turn transmits messages centrally to other structures of the brain, especially the cortex. The ARAS neural impulses alert or arouse the cortex, which plays an essential role in the occurrence of normal perception. If for any reason the ARAS is not functioning, sensory information from the receptors will still reach the appropriate cortical projection centers. However, the cortex will not be activated sufficiently so that the processes of sensory discrimination and perception can occur. The second major function of the ARAS under normal conditions can best be described as a self-regulating or adjustive function. On the basis of its own neural activity and that of the cortex, which it monitors, the ARAS regulates the amount of its own sensory input. Put another way, the ARAS is functionally capable of monitoring its own inout-output levels of neural excitation. This regulatory function led Lindsley to posit the concept of an adaptation level. According to this concept, the ARAS, on the basis of the amount of input from various sensory receptors, adjusts its neural output to the cortex so as to establish a correspondingly high, neutral, or low level of arousal. As you might expect, under conditions of sensory deprivation this level of arousal decreases markedly, with attendant boredom, inactivity, and finally sleep. A characteristic of the compensatory adjustment process is that it is limited. It is suggested that if these limits are exceeded, as they most certainly are in the case of sensory deprivation, behavior deteriorates and becomes disorganized.

Finally, Ziskind (1965) suggests that the psychological symptoms that come about during sensory deprivation are not the result of reduced sensory input per se, but rather of the reduced level of arousal that is also present during such an experience. Ziskind sees this reduction in awareness level as the condition necessary for the development of sensory-deprived mental symptoms. The reduction in awareness occurs in conjunction with internal and external stimuli and goal-directed actions, which Ziskind calls the sufficient condition. The sufficient condition apparently is related, in part at least, to the instructions and psychological set or demand characteristics of the experiment (Orne, 1959, 1979).

As you might have surmised, there certainly is no lack of theoretical speculation and explanation for the behavioral phenomena associated with the sensory deprivation experience. The major problem is one of accumulating critical evidence in support of one or more of these theoretical positions.

EXPERIMENTAL PROCEDURES

Although the specific conditions of sensory deprivation vary from experiment to experiment, it is possible to identify at least three distinct, basic procedures employed by researchers to reduce sensory input from the environment to the subject. The first of these approaches attempts to achieve an absolute reduction of sensory stimulation. To accomplish this, researchers such as Lilly (1956) and Shurley (1960) have used a large tank filled with continuously flowing water maintained at a temperature of 93.5° F (34.5° C). The subject, nude except for a blacked-out face mask attached to breathing tubes, was immersed in the tank. (Fig. 8-1). This technique substantially diminishes gravity, light, and temperature stimuli to the subject. The tank itself usually is located in a room constructed so that light, sound, vibration, odor, and taste sensations are markedly reduced. A schematic of a laboratory designed for this kind of sensory deprivation is shown in Figure 8-2. The overall system provides a constant environment with maximal reduction of ambient physical stimuli. Once the subject is immersed in the tank, he or she is requested to get comfortable and to remain motionless for several hours. Either during or after the study, a subject may be requested to report on his or her experiences. Subjects were allowed to terminate their participation in the study at any time and for any reason.

The second major approach employed by researchers in stimulus deprivation (e.g., Bexton, Heron, and Scott [1954]) is to reduce or alter the patterns and relationships in sensory input from the environment. Their subjects were required to lie on a comfortable bed located in a lighted, semisoundproof

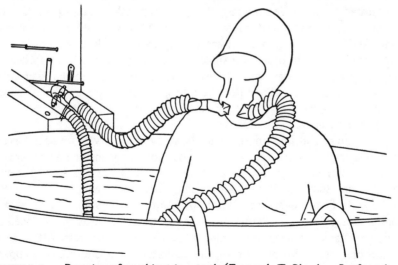

FIGURE 8-1. *Drawing of a subject in a tank (From: J. T. Shurley. Profound experimental sensory isolation.* American Journal of Psychiatry *117: 1960 539-545. Copyright © 1960, the American Psychiatric Association. Reprinted with permission.)*

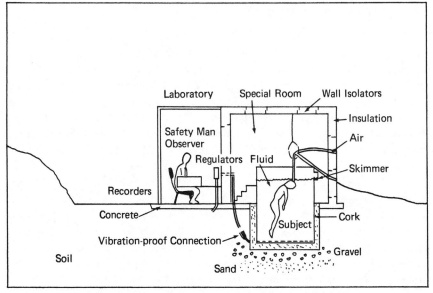

FIGURE 8-2. *Drawing of a sensory-deprivation flotation tank (From: J. T. Shurley. Profound experimental sensory isolation. American Journal of Psychiatry 117: 1960 539–545. Copyright © 1960, the American Psychiatric Association. Reprinted with permission.)*

cubicle. Subjects wore translucent goggles that allowed the passage only of a diffuse light. Auditory stimulation was held constant by placing the subject's head in a U-shaped pillow of foam rubber and by using the sound of an exhaust fan located in the ceiling directly above the subject's head to provide a continuous masking noise. Each subject was required to wear gloves, and his or her hands and arms were encased in cardboard tubes to reduce the possibility of tactile stimulation. In order that subjects could communicate their needs to the experimenter, a two-way speaker system was embedded into the foam rubber pillow. Subjects were fed and permitted to go to the restroom when necessary. Again, subjects were able to terminate their participation in the experiment whenever they desired.

The third and final approach to the study of sensory deprivation has been to impose highly structured or monotonous conditions in the sensory environment rather than reduce the levels of stimulation. The apparatus employed by investigators such as Wexler, Mendelson, Leiderman, and Solomon (1958) is shown in Figure 8-3. The subject, with arms and legs encased in rigid but comfortable cylinders to limit movement and tactile stimulation, is placed in a polio-type tank respirator containing a specially built mattress. Although the subject breathes on his or her own, the respirator motor is turned on to provide a dull, monotonous masking noise. Room lighting is kept at a minimum. A large hood placed around the respirator prevents the subject from seeing anything but the front of the tank and the blank white walls and ceiling. Food in the form of

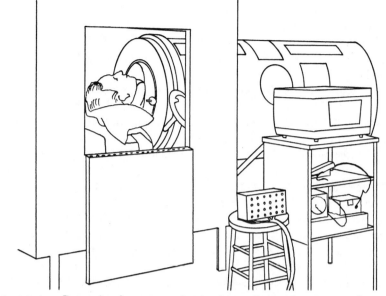

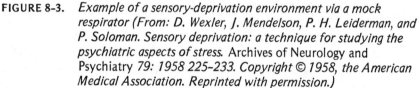

FIGURE 8-3. *Example of a sensory-deprivation environment via a mock respirator (From: D. Wexler, J. Mendelson, P. H. Leiderman, and P. Soloman. Sensory deprivation: a technique for studying the psychiatric aspects of stress.* Archives of Neurology and Psychiatry *79: 1958 225-233. Copyright © 1958, the American Medical Association. Reprinted with permission.)*

an eggnog mixture is available through a feeding tube placed near the subject's mouth, and bedpans or urinals are provided upon request.

In summary, the investigator is faced with the selection of one of the following major methodological approaches: (1) absolute reduction of sensory stimulation; (2) reduction or change in the patterns and relationships in the sensory input; and (3) imposition of highly structured or monotonous conditions in the sensory environment. Whichever approach is selected, an extremely complex experimental environment is required. Having reviewed the common experimental methodologies employed in the study of sensory deprivation we are now ready to determine what effects, if any, this phenomenon may have upon consciousness or arousal.

THE McGILL STUDIES

Historically there have been any number of recorded natural observations of sensory deprivation experiences. However, the initial experimentally controlled attack on this problem was carried out at McGill University (Bexton,

Heron, and Scott, 1954; Doane, Mahatoo, Heron, and Scott, 1959; Heron, Bexton, and Hebb, 1953; Heron, Doane, and Scott, 1956; Scott, Bexton, Heron, and Doane, 1959). Because this series of studies defined the problem and set the tone for future research in this area, it is important that we review some of the details here.

In these studies, the goal of the researchers was to reduce or alter the patterns and relationships in the sensory input from the environment by providing an experimental setting much like the one illustrated in Figure 8-3. Brief time-out periods were allowed for meals and bathroom needs, but subjects otherwise remained in this very restricted environment until they requested to terminate the experience. As an incentive, each subject was offered twenty dollars for each day they remained in this strange environment. (While this may not seem like much money, you should keep two facts in mind: First, this series of studies was carried out in the 1950s, when twenty dollars had much greater buying power than it does today. Second, the subjects were all male college undergraduates, and as I remember those days, male college students are generally in a continuous state of financial embarrassment.) Despite the potential financial gains, the experimental conditions were sufficiently intolerable so that most subjects terminated their participation within four days.

As you might have predicted, most subjects spent the early part of their participation catching up on their sleep. Later they slept less, became bored, and seemed to need some stimulation. To this end they began singing and talking to themselves, tapping the cylinders together, or using the cylinders to explore the cubicle. They became restless and engaged in a great deal of random movement. Postexperimentally, subjects described their experience as extremely unpleasant. Upon leaving the experimental situation, individuals reported a number of aftereffects, including disturbances in visual perception, confusion, headaches, mild nausea, and fatigue.

Subjects reported some cognitive and perceptual disturbances during the time they spent in the cubicle. Many experienced an inability to concentrate on a single topic for any length of time. Some of these subjects, so desperate for some form of stimulation, attempted to review their studies or to solve self-initiated intellectual problems; however, they found such activity extremely difficult and soon gave it up, lapsing instead into a period of daydreaming and simply allowing their minds to wander. Several subjects reported experiencing "blank periods," during which they were unable to think of anything at all.

Reports such as these prompted some members of the McGill group to try to measure the cognitive and perceptual effects of sensory deprivation. Some twenty-eight perceptual and cognitive tasks were administered to subjects before, during, and after their deprivation experience. While the group results suggested that certain of the tested functions were impaired after sensory deprivation, some subjects appeared to be completely unaffected. Certainly one interpretation of these findings is that the sensory deprivation experience brings about the deterioration of certain perceptual and cognitive skills. However, these same results can also be accounted for, at least in part, by a decrease in the subject's motivation.

During the experimental sessions, the researchers observed an unusual degree of emotional lability on the part of most subjects. In the early phase of the session subjects reported being elated; however, with the passage of time subjects became more irritable. Perhaps the most interesting of all the findings of the McGill studies was the occurrence of hallucinations reported by the subjects. Visual hallucinations varied considerably in their degree of complexity, ranging from simple light flashes and geometric forms to much more complex, dreamlike scenes, such as "a procession of squirrels with sacks over their shoulders marching purposefully across a snow field and out of the field of vision" (Bexton, Heron, and Scott, 1954). The hallucinatory experiences reported were not confined to this single sensory modality. Subjects also reported auditory, kinesthetic, and somesthetic hallucinations. For example, one subject described a "miniature rocketship" shooting pellets at his arm, while another reported hearing a music box. Finally, feelings of "otherness" and bodily "strangeness" were also reported. One subject indicated that his mind seemed to be a ball of cotton wool floating above his body.

EFFECTS OF SENSORY DEPRIVATION

It was the McGill University studies that asked the right questions and provided some of the initial answers concerning the effects of prolonged exposure to a sensory-deprived environment on consciousness and, ultimately, behavior. It remained for the researchers who followed to both replicate and refine the results of these early studies.

You will recall that subjects in the McGill studies reported some qualitative disturbances in perceptual functioning and sensitivity. Some of these subjective reports were confirmed later by the use of preexposure and postexposure measures. The post-McGill literature on sensory deprivation also suggests that sensory deprivation may lead to some disruption of visual perception. Attempts to identify precisely which perceptual tasks are affected and to determine to what degree such tasks are affected indicate that increased time distortion, diminished color perception, apparent movement, loss of spatial, temporal, and tactual orientation, and perhaps distortions in size and shape constancy can be expected in sensory-deprived subjects (Batten, 1961; Freedman and Greenblatt, 1959; Freedman and Held, 1960; MacNeill and Zubek, 1967; Walters and Quinn, 1961; Zubek, 1969; Zubek, Pushkar, Sansom, and Gowing, 1961; Zubek and MacNeill, 1966).

Many subjects in the McGill investigations reported some difficulty in thinking coherently and in concentrating for any length of time. You will remember that some of these subjects reported trying to review their studies or to solve self-initiated problems, only to become frustrated and give up. Are cognitive and intellectual functions subject to interruption as a result of prolonged exposure to a sensory-deprived environment? If so, which specific functions are typically affected? These were the questions for which the post-McGill investigators sought answers. Their findings indicate that sensory deprivation does not appear to result in a general loss of cognitive functioning. It does, however, appear to bring about a deterioration of certain specific functions. Thus, Robertson and Wolter (1963) found that performance of tasks that involved reasoning and problem solving may be impaired, while Zubek, Sansom, and Prysiazniuk (1960) found that only recent memory was significantly affected.

Subjective reports such as ". . .like having a dream while awake" led McGill investigators Bexton, Heron, and Scott (1954) to suspect that one effect of sensory deprivation might be hallucinations. To test this hypothesis, the investigators requested from the remaining subjects more detailed accounts of any "visual imagery" they experienced. The results and those of more recent studies (Kubzansky, 1961; Suedfeld, 1980) suggest strongly that hallucinations are definitely a part of the sensory deprivation experience.

Before you are lulled into the (false) belief that total agreement exists among researchers on the effects of sensory-deprived environments, we should note that a review of the literature on sensory deprivation reveals a substantial number of discrepancies. Certainly some of these discrepancies can be accounted for, at least in part, by the use of different deprivation manipulations and testing techniques. However, there do appear to be a number of other variables that may influence the response of the subjects to this type of environment. These include subject variables such as preexposure personality traits (Arnhoff and Leon, 1963; Hull and Zubek, 1962) and sociocultural factors; experimental variables (Orne, 1962, 1979); and situational variables such as restriction of mobility (Zubek and Wilgosh, 1963), time uncertainty (Vernon and McGill, 1963), and duration. The goal of future research in sensory deprivation must be clarification of the role of such factors in the production of sensory deprivation effects.

CLINICAL POTENTIAL OF SENSORY DEPRIVATION

Earlier in this chapter we posed the question, "Are there any positive aspects of the sensory deprivation experience?" Now that we have reviewed the effects of a sensory-deprived environment as observed under controlled experimental conditions you may find it difficult to view this phenomenon in a positive vein. Keep in mind, however, that what these studies have demonstrated is that by limiting or modifying the environmental stimuli, it is possible to produce marked changes in consciousness levels and subsequently in behavior, without the use of drugs or other medical techniques.

The work of Rosenzweig (1959) and later of Suedfeld (1980) suggests that the presence of the factors mentioned earlier underlies the production of hallucinatory activity in the schizophrenic. Rosenzweig proposed the possible existence of a similarity between these two hallucinatory systems. Suedfeld observed that under conditions of sensory deprivation the subject's attention focuses on his or her feelings, memories, thoughts, and other internal stimuli; such a focus increases the probability of hallucinations. While it is true that there is no experimental manipulation of the sensory environment of schizophrenics, such persons nevertheless withdraw from the environment for prolonged periods. It is possible that schizophrenic hallucinations may be a consequence of such prolonged withdrawal.

In addition to providing the clinical researcher with a possible model of the schizophrenic hallucination, sensory deprivation has been viewed recently as a possible psychotherapeutic procedure (Suedfeld, 1980). Thus, sensory deprivation has been used for producing a state of relaxation and for control of cigarette smoking. One might well ask how such a potentially negative experience could be employed to bring about such desirable results. Again, any precise answer to such questions must await the execution of more definitive research. We do know, however, that sensory deprivation induces an altered state of consciousness that helps the subject to become aware of information in an altered environment. Perhaps this state enables the subject to learn to relax in certain anxiety-inducing situations or to come to grips with a habit, such as smoking. Obviously, more preferred methods exist for dealing with habit control and relaxation (see Chapters 4, 5, and 6). However, sensory deprivation perhaps does enable the individual to understand his or her potentialities and thus can be a successful tool in dealing with certain situations requiring behavioral change.

As a manipulation for helping us understand the psychology of consciousness, it is very clear, except for the recent research of Suedfeld, that sensory deprivation is no longer as popular a technique as it was in the 1950s (e.g., Bexton, Heron, and Scott, 1954). However, it definitely does produce a change in states or levels of consciousness. We saw earlier that sleep and hallucinations are produced when persons are deprived of changes in sensory input. Therefore, although sensory deprivation is dated as a technique for studying levels of consciousness, it is still useful. In addition, it still has much to offer in helping us understand consciousness and its altered states more fully.

FOR FURTHER READING

Brownfield, C. A. *Isolation: clinical and experimental approaches.* New York: Random House, 1965.

Byrd, R. E. *Alone.* New York: Putnam, 1938.

Dean, W. F. *General Dean's Story.* New York: Viking Press, 1954.

Suedfeld, P. *Restricted environmental stimulation: research and clinical applications.* New York: Wiley-Interscience, 1980.

Zubek, J. P. (ed.) *Sensory deprivation: fifteen years of research.* New York: Appleton-Century-Crofts, 1969.

chapter nine ═══════════════════════════

Mysticism

Most of us have observed or heard of instances where individuals who supposedly were paralyzed were empowered to walk again through a process called faith healing. They are led to a stage where a religious leader asks them questions concerning their beliefs. The leader then is observed to lay his hands on the head of the afflicted party or on the part of the body that requires attention. After a few seconds or minutes, a spiritual shout emanates from the leader as he orders the afflicted to walk or stand up or the like. The audience then shouts "Hallelujah!" or other words of praise as the once afflicted person is now observed to perform an act he or she previously was not able to do. Is it really possible that such a phenomenon is taking place? Can belief in faith healing really bring about a cure for paralysis or for a disease that physicians are incapable of treating or have given up on finding a cure or treatment? Can related phenomena, such as witchcraft or voodoo, also be employed to treat problems as severe as paralysis or other afflictions? Can voodoo and witchcraft be used to put a curse on someone and bring them bad luck? These are some of the issues that will be discussed in this chapter as we consider mysticism as an area of study in the psychology of consciousness.

MYSTICISM AND CONSCIOUSNESS

After having read the first eight chapters of this book, you might say to yourself, "But weren't many of the topics already discussed concerned in some respects with mysticism?" In a general sense, the answer to this question is yes. Certainly the topics of hypnosis and drug-altered states of behavior have a mystical element to them. However, mysticism as defined here refers to belief in a power (supernatural or other) that plays a key role in helping to produce what appears to be an altered state of consciousness or a change in behavior. This behavior usually exhibits itself, for example, in cure of a disease without the use of medicine or in the ability to stand or walk after being considered paralyzed and unable to perform these physical feats. As defined here, then, mysticism refers to three phenomena: (1) witchcraft, (2) voodoo, and (3) faith healing.

Although each of these phenomena has purportedly been used to "cure" people of a problem, many would consider them to be very different from one another. It is true that each has its own separate history and set of perpetuated myths. However, they are similar in that the end result of each is to bring about a change in consciousness that can then bring about a change in behavior. Each is practiced by a different group in a different culture, and those who believe in one phenomenon tend not to believe in the others and chastise those who do. Because of this, witchcraft, voodoo, and faith healing will be discussed separately as we examine their scientific validity as a means for altering consciousness and treating afflictions.

WITCHCRAFT

The topic of witchcraft immediately brings to mind an image of an old woman dresssed in black wearing a funny pointed hat and riding a broom. When she is off her broom, she may be at work near a large iron kettle stirring up a strange brew for some purpose. This, in fact, is the image most of us have of a witch from associations with Halloween or *The Wizard of Oz*. Witchcraft also brings to mind the history of the witch trials of Salem, Massachusetts, in 1692 (Burr, 1914), during which people were tortured or executed for presumably possessing strange powers.

Are there now or have there ever been witches who possess mystical or strange powers capable of altering another individual's state or level of consciousness? In other words, can one individual induce an altered state of consciousness in another individual? The history of witchcraft (Spanos, 1978) suggests that many individuals throughout the centuries have been accused of possessing witchlike abilities or behaviors. These included the ability to cause disease and death, to destroy crops, and to produce natural disasters such as storms and earthquakes. Accused individuals also purportedly belonged to "an international satanic conspiracy dedicated to the defamation of God. . ." (Spanos, 1978, p. 420). Supposedly they also could fly to *sabbats*, or nocturnal orgies, where they had sexual intercourse with a variety of demons, animals, and each other; they also killed and ate children and performed a parody of Christian rituals.

These "powers" or strange behaviors, however, were really nonexistent. Rather, their existence often was imagined or created by individuals who exhibited symptoms similar to those found in schizophrenia (e.g., hallucinations) or neurotic hysteria (e.g., psychosomatic ailments; Bromberg, 1954). These individuals then accused someone in the community (usually an older woman) of being a witch. The accusation generally came about after some symptom(s) arose while the accuser was in proximity of the accused.

It is important to clarify a common misconception. People who exhibited strange behaviors were themselves never accused of being witches (Oesterreich, 1966). The accused, more often than not, were ordinary individuals whom, for one reason or another, the afflicted party disliked. The more prominent or well liked was the accuser, the greater the likelihood of an innocent person being accused, tried, and convicted of being a witch. As this climate prevailed and spread, so did the myth of the existence of agents of the devil, or witches.

Those believed to be victims of witchcraft were considered to be demonically possessed. This was considered an involuntary occurrence and was usually treated by means of exorcism and/or prayer and fasting (Kelly, 1974). Such treatment would seem to help some of the afflicted.

It should be pointed out that many individuals who exhibited symptoms believed to be induced by witchcraft were not faking the symptoms. They were simply suffering from one or more behavioral and/or physical disorders and strongly believed that witchcraft was to blame for their state of affairs (Spanos, 1978). Some of the disorders scientists now believe were to blame for a person's feeling bewitched included ergot poisoning. This was especially the case for the Salem witch incidences (Caporael, 1976). Ergot is a fungus (*Claviceps purpurea*) that can infest rye and other cereal grains. When ingested it can produce several neurological disorders including convulsions, a symptom often exhibited by people in Salem, Massachusetts, who believed they were bewitched.

However, Spanos and Gottlieb (1976) dispute the assertion that ergot had anything to do with supposed witchcraft symptoms. After a careful analysis of the available data of exhibited symptoms of reported sufferers, they concluded that ergot poisoning produced many symptoms besides the usual convulsions. These include vomiting, diarrhea, a livid skin color, sensations of heat and cold in the extremities, spastic muscle contractions in the extremeties, and severe itching. Besides the convulsions, the other symptoms were absent from sufferers. As a result, they concluded that the ergot poisoning hypothesis as an explanation for the symptoms of sufferers of so-called witchcraft should be dismissed as being highly unlikely.

Instead, they hypothesized that the witchcraft symptoms were the result of a belief in demonic possession. This was common during the time of the Salem trials, and such a belief would account for the exhibited symptoms which closely corresponded to popular stereotyped views of possession. These symptoms included creeping under chairs, demonstrating odd postures and gestures, and uttering foolish speech (Calef, 1914).

Of course, as was mentioned earlier, mental illness also produced "symptoms" of being bewitched. Schizophrenics, individual who generally lose contact with reality and may experience hallucinations, could have been considered to have been bewitched in an era when little was known of mental disorders. Hysterical neurotics may have thought themselves bewitched since a doctor could find nothing physically wrong with them. Witchcraft was simply an easy explanation for a disorder that was not understood. Such individuals were simply considered possessed by demonic influences, and the manner of treatment involved the exorcising of such influences.

During the exorcism, afflicted individuals would often faint or exhibit behavior that differed from their normal state of consciousness. Some, for example, had a strange look in their eyes. This behavior generally came about as a result of a belief in a supernatural healing power. Since they "believed," they could be "cured." And in many instances, exorcism appeared to work. Psychosomatic symptoms (ones not physiologically produced) disappeared, and the afflicted believed they had been exorcised of demonic possession, originally brought about through witchcraft.

As is obvious, witchcraft was a creation of ignorance in an era when a majority of the populus believed in such a phenomenon (Trevor-Roper, 1969; Midelfort, 1972; Spanos, 1978). There never were real witches who could do the strange things of which they were accused. There really were no altered states of consciousness existing in the "bewitched." Accusers believed that this was the case only because they had no other explanation. They believed the devil afflicted them through a witch intermediary, and that exorcism or prayer was the best procedure for dealing with this situation.

Even today some people believe in witchcraft and in the powers of witches. In fact, there is a religion known as Wicca whose "witch" parishioners believe in Mother Nature as a source of guidance, especially to help in a healing situation. This belief is not as widespread now as it was in the fifteenth, sixteenth, or seventeenth centuries, but it does indeed exist. It also is possible for psychosomatic symptoms to develop in these individuals and for them to attribute the symptom to witchcraft. In such a circumstance, a nontraditional treatment, such as exorcism, may help alleviate the problem, just as it helped the afflicted centuries ago. In addition, the afflicted people also exhibit strange behaviors during the treatment, as if they were in an altered state of consciousness, leading observers to believe that the treatment is alleviating the symptoms. For the true believers in witchcraft and exorcism, such treatment does work. However, remember that since a belief in witchcraft may have produced the problem, belief in the treatment for witchcraft may solve the problem. In any case, an altered state of consciousness did not occur. In all likelihood, the person developed a symptom in a normal, waking state of consciousness; he or she may not have been aware that the symptom was taking place, nor did he or she necessarily volunteer the production of the symptom. As a result, the afflicted person can be "cured" in a normal, waking state of consciousness, even though the person truly believes that he or she was in an altered state when the "cure" was effected.

VOODOO

Voodoo is a phenomenon related to witchcraft. As with witchcraft, we have stereotypes of voodoo. These include the insertion of needles or pins in dolls that represent people to bring evil upon them. We also associate voodoo with dancing in strange ways, often under the influence of a drug, to cast a spell on another person. Is voodoo, like witchcraft, a phenomenon of the imagination? How does it differ from witchcraft?

Unlike witchcraft, voodoo is alien to the Western world. Many people in Western countries have been accused of witchcraft and subsequently punished or executed. However, we have not heard of people in Western countries being accused of practicing voodoo. The major reason for this is that, except for some examples of voodoo practice in Louisiana (Hurston, 1978), voodoo is practiced primarily in places such as Haiti, Trinidad, Brazil, and some African countries such as Kenya and Zambia (Sargant, 1975).

Voodoo practices differ in each of these areas. One of the most stereotypic versions is that which is practiced in Haiti (Mars and Devereux, 1951). After a period of dancing and drumming, gods and goddesses are called upon to possess the bodies of attending worshipers and believers. The possession is referred to as *loa*. Once a person has been possessed or mounted (as believers refer to the process), strange behaviors begin to occur. For example, parts of the body may become immobile. Sargant (1975) describes one person who, when he believed he was possessed by loa, suddenly found his foot stuck to the ground. When he tried to move his other foot, he found it also stuck to the ground.

When the so-called mounting by loa is complete, for all intents and purposes, the believer *is* loa. The worshipper's free will and "soul" are temporarily expelled. This behavior persists until the worshiper collapses or comes close to doing so. Afterwards, the worshiper feels psychologically and physically renewed, as if all ills had left his or her body. If the worshiper was ill prior to possession, the mounting may play a role in bringing about a cure or, at least, in helping to alleviate some of the symptoms.

Because those who believe in voodoo obviously feel that is practice can help rid them of their ills (Fosshage and Olsen, 1978), it often serves just that purpose. Those who are strong believers in voodoo will exhibit a "possession," or trance state, because they have been brought up in the belief that such altered states of consciousness exist. Furthermore, they are taught from early childhood that many illnesses are curable via voodoo possession. Thus, demand characteristics (Orne, 1959, 1979) have been induced from an early age concerning how to behave when possession takes place. The individual attends a voodoo ceremony and hears drums and sees dancing. These are cues to join in the festivities. He or she sees others becoming exhausted while appearing to enter an altered state of awareness or consciousness. This shows the individual the appropriate mode of behavior during the ceremony. He or she complies, exhibiting the exhaustion and the appearance of an altered state, followed by collapse or near collapse. After being revived, the individual feels much better and credits voodoo with his or her present state of health. So the belief in voodoo continues and is perpetuated.

Does an altered state of awareness take place during the voodoo ceremony? This is very difficult to answer, for, as in Sufi meditation (see Chapter 6), voodoo practitioners are not at liberty to divulge any secrets concerning the production of the altered state. However, whether or not there is an altered state, believers do change their behavior during the voodoo ceremony. Thus, the belief in voodoo seems to be the major variable in producing the so-called altered state. If a person believes sufficiently that voodoo can cure a particular ill, and that ill has a psychological basis, it is possible that voodoo can help.

Unfortunately, scientific investigations of voodoo are virtually nonexistent. This is probably the result of two factors: (1) voodoo is not practiced to any significant degree in the Western world, and (2) scientists simply are not interested in voodoo. Since both factors are rather pervasive, it is not likely that we shall see an upsurge in the study of voodoo. However, the informed student of the psychology of consciousness should be made aware of the existence of this practice and its possible value in helping its believers enter what may be an altered state of consciousness. In this state, behavior does appear to differ from that of the normal, waking state of awareness and often changes, especially if voodoo is being applied to some existing psychosomatic illness.

At the beginning of this section we referred to the practice of sticking pins in dolls to bring about evil. This voodoo practice is confined mostly to television and movie portrayals. No reference could be found to its wide use anywhere in the literature. Again, however, if such a practice is employed, it would be effective only for believers in voodoo. Only an adherent to voodoo beliefs could possibly experience pain in sympathy with a pin inserted in a doll. Furthermore, the believer could experience such pain only if they witnessed or knew that someone was sticking the doll. This stereotype of voodoo should really be dismissed, for it does not represent voodoo as it is really practiced. As we mentioned previously, one of the major functions of voodoo is to treat afflictions.

FAITH HEALING

Basically, voodoo is a form of faith healing. However, when we speak of faith healing, we generally envision a type of religious ceremony in which someone is helping an afflicted person to overcome a disease or medical problem. Today, faith healing in the Western world is as popular as it has always been. Many often seek a faith cure when a medical cure has failed, while others resort to a faith cure as their only means of treating a problem. Does faith healing work? Does an altered state of consciousness take place before, during, or after faith healing? These are some of the questions we will address here.

Although faith healing is generally associated with some sects of Protestant Christianity, it is also found in various forms in Catholicism and Judaism. For example, exorcism was and still is practiced to some extent by some Catholics. This form of faith healing requires the presence of a priest to rid the person's body of a supposed evil spirit that possesses it. In Judaism, faith healing has been employed in what has been referred to as Jewish Science (Meyer, 1965), a counterpart to Christian Science. In both Jewish and Christian Science, believers feel that a variety of maladies can be treated through prayer to a deity who has power to cure them of their affliction. Strong prayer may induce the person to experience a change in the normal, waking state of consciousness. Those who seek cures primarily with prayer often report that, during such prayer, they felt removed from their normal, waking state. This distance helped them come closer to their deity, who helped cure their illness. In all likelihood, major physical illnesses could not be treated successfully with prayer alone, although many religious adherents would disagree with us (Ricalla, 1975). However, a variety of psychosomatic problems can be alleviated, and many individuals find relief from their troubles through the power of prayer and a strong religious belief in prayer as a way to deal with illness.

The most popularized form of faith healing is the type we often see on Sunday morning television or at revival meetings where a religious leader "lays hands" on an afflicted believer and tries to cure him or her of a malady. Related to this is a form of faith healing in which the afflicted person is asked to handle a poisonous snake (Sargant, 1975). If the person survives the encounter with the snake, he or she may experience a cure. In both forms of faith healing, it is common to see the believer undergo a psychological transformation that appears to involve a change in his or her state of consciousness.

Laying On Of Hands

This form of faith healing is the one with which most of us are familiar. The stereotypic version involves an afflicted person who comes to a religious revival meeting in search of a cure. At some point in the religious service, the preacher asks all who wish to be healed of an affliction to come forward. The scene then resembles that of the crippled being led to the preacher in a wheelchair or hobbling toward him on crutches. These individuals are then paraded by as the preacher asks each if they believe in Jesus and if they believe Jesus can cure them of their afflictions. After they respond in the affirmative, the preacher lays his hands on the head or on another part of the believer. This is a symbolic gesture of a transference of healing power from Jesus through the hands of the faith healer. A prayer may or may not be said at this point. The believer then is observed to experience either a sense of euphoria or, in many instances, a loss of waking consciousness. If the believer does not faint, he or she appears to at least have experienced some transformation in consciousness from the normal, waking state. The audience then observes as some of the afflicted begin to walk after being "crippled" for so many years. Of course, this produces a definite religious high for the previously afflicted believer as well as for those observing.

Did healing really occur? Was there a change in consciousness by which healing was achieved? As with voodoo, believers in faith healing may experience relief from an affliction or, in some instances, a bona fide cure (Whitlock, 1978). Most people who have experienced a faith cure probably were afflicted with a psychosomatic illness. Therefore, if they truly believed that Jesus, through the aid of the faith healer, could help them, it is very possible that they indeed were helped.

What about those who truly believed that Jesus could help them and yet were not cured? Often they are simply accused of not being true believers. Since Jesus could detect lack of true faith, the cure did not come about. A more realistic suggestion is that their illness was not psychosomatic. Therefore, a faith cure would not be as effective for them as it would be for a person afflicted with a psychosomatic illness.

Snake Handling

A similar circumstance exists for the form of faith healing that calls for the handling of poisonous snakes (Sargant, 1975). In this procedure, a poisonous snake is handed to an afflicted individual. He is told that if he truly believes in Jesus, he will be protected from the snake and will be cured of any illness he has. If he survives, all who are observing are assured of his faith. If he is bitten and dies, this is only an indication that he was not a true believer. Of course, what is often not told to the parishioners who attend such revivals is that some people have an immunity to the poison of certain snakes. Therefore, whether or not they are believers, they will not die from the snake venom. Some are hypersensitive to the venom and, whether or not they are true believers, they stand an excellent chance of dying if they are bitten by a snake.

As in the laying on of hands, those who attend a snake-handling revival meeting and eventually handle a snake will exhibit what appears to be a change in their normal, waking state of consciousness. This is likely the result of induced fear or simply a reaction to the venom of the snake. Of course, a survivor of a snake bite will credit his survival to his religious beliefs. This information is passed on to other members of the religious community, and the snake-handling practice of faith healing continues.

It should be obvious that witchcraft, voodoo, and faith healing have a common denominator: they all involve a belief that illness can be cured through nonmedical means. While we will not dispute this assertion, it should be stressed that the treatment of afflictions through nonmedical resources is restricted generally to those who believe strongly enough that witchcraft, voodoo, and faith healing can help them. If they so believe, they have a chance to experience a faith cure.

Mysticism may or may not involve an altered state of consciousness. It does, however, provide us with knowledge of how it can be possible to control an affliction with thought and belief rather than with conventional medicine or psychotherapy. Perhaps if there were greater stress in our complex world upon individuals trying to help themselves, we would see more emphasis put on faith cures. If this happens, we also will see more scientists becoming interested in mysticism. Such increased interest hopefully will be an impetus for expanding our knowledge of these areas of the psychology of consciousness.

FOR FURTHER READING

Harrell, D. E. *All things are possible.* Bloomington, IN: Indiana University Press, 1975.
Meyer, D. *The positive thinkers.* New York: Doubleday, 1965.
Sargant, W. *The mind possessed.* New York: Penguin, 1975.

chapter ten ══════════════

Parapsychology

Historically, parapsychology or psychic research (psi) has probably been one of the most interesting and controversial areas of study in the realm of consciousness. There are few nonpsychologists who will not admit to an interest in this area. The topic is often written about in popular magazines and is discussed on television and radio programs. Many would like nothing better than to be able to "read minds" or to make objects move in space with mental control. Can you imagine how nice it might be to read someone's mind, like the brightest student's during an exam? Or your boyfriend's or girlfriend's thoughts? However, few will admit to being able to perform these feats, although many believe that some people possess such abilities. Among scientists, especially psychologists and other behavioral scientists, a very small minority admit to the possibility of extrasensory perception (ESP) or psychokinetic (PK) abilities. In fact, to express a belief in such possibilities is often akin to being a scientific heretic, a believer in the occult.

Why is the study of parapsychology so controversial? Is there any scientific evidence to support the claims of some that they can read minds or other such feats? If so, do such claims indicate a special ability of some people to control consciously mind over matter? These issues as well as others will be discussed here.

PARAPSYCHOLOGY AND CONSCIOUSNESS

Parapsychology literally means "along side" psychology. This root definition implies that this area of interest is not within the mainstream of psychological study. In fact, this indeed is the status of this subject matter. However, those who conduct scientific investigations in psi claim that some people on some occasions are capable of processing information without relying on the five senses (vision, audition, taste, smell, and touch). Such people supposedly can relate information to an investigator that is beyond the normal limits of consciousness or awareness. As a result, although you and I may not be able to sense or detect consciously a phenomenon or event, people with this ability theoretically can experience it. If it does exist and if it can be isolated and controlled for scientific study, such ability may help us to understand yet another piece of information within the workings of the human system. As we have already seen, this system is capable of consciously controlling or altering behavior that we once believed could not be so controlled. If some behavior can be manipulated or controlled outside the normal limits of our senses, this would be a remarkable discovery indeed. Such a discovery perhaps would enable us to have a tighter grasp on the limits of our abilities and potentialities. As we discuss psi as an area of investigation within the psychology of consciousness, we shall discover whether this is possible.

HISTORICAL DEVELOPMENT

Although stories about the ability to read minds or move objects by thought have circulated for centuries, it was not until 1822 that scientists organized to study parapsychology. In that year, the Society for Psychical Research was founded in London by F.W.H. Myers (1843-1901), Edmund Gurney (1847-1888), and Henry Sidgwick (1838-1900). Sidgwick became the first president of the organization. One of the most notable members of the society was Sir Arthur Conan Doyle (1859-1930), author of the many Sherlock Holmes detective stories. An American version of this society was organized in Boston in 1885 with the purpose of investigating claims of telepathy, clairvoyance, precognition, and other forms of paranormal cognition.

The most prevalent investigation in the early scientific years of parapsychology centered around *mediumship*, or communication with the dead. In fact, several very prominent psychologists were attracted to parapsychology because of their interest in communicating with a discarnate personality. These individuals included William James (Murphy and Ballou, 1969), who played a major role in the early development of the psychology of consciousness (see Chapter 1), and William McDougall (1871-1938).

James believed that psychic research was an important and little understood area of the human mind and its powers. He felt it necessary that this area be investigated by "any means at our disposal if progress in understanding was to be achieved" (Murphy and Ballou, 1969, p. 12). He further believed that a phenomenon was not necessarily untrue simply because it conflicted with known principles of science, as many believe to be the case with parapsychology.

McDougall probably played the most important role in the development of the scientific investigation of parapsychology in the United States. In 1927, while at Duke University, McDougall set up the first laboratory devoted to the investigation of psi, specifically to the study of telepathy, clairvoyance, precognition, and psychokinesis. McDougall was also at the time a very influential force in the council of the Society for Psychical Research.

McDougall brought to Duke two biologists, J. B. Rhine (1895–1980), who is often credited with coining the term *parapsychology* (Wallechinsky and Wallace, 1975), and his wife, Louisa E. Rhine (1891–   ), who had been experimenting with psi at Harvard University. The Rhines's major area of interest did not fall within the categories of study for which McDougall had organized his laboratory. Rather, they were interested in the area that was the impetus for the development of psi research, the question of survival after death. Although their research involved having a medium in one room try to read the thoughts of a subject in another room, they could not deduce how such thought transference could take place. They hypothesized that it was either the result of a dead person communicating with the medium by acting as an intermediary to relay information, or that telepathy was taking place between the medium and the subject. The latter hypothesis seemed more reasonable to them (and far easier to test experimentally) than the former. As a result, they commenced their investigation of mental telepathy with the aid of research support from the Rockefeller Foundation and the U.S. Navy. They published the first formal report of their findings in a book entitled *Extrasensory Perception* (1934). This important publication described the Rhines's many experiments with subjects' abilities to deduce symbols on a deck of cards. These cards were called Zener cards after the originator of the deck, Karl Zener (1903–1964).

This deck consisted of twenty-five cards with five identical cards in five different suits (see Fig. 10–1). The suits consisted of crosses, circles, stars, wavy lines, or squares. The probability odds of guessing the correct card were one in five. Thus, a typical subject would guess five cards correctly out of twenty-five presented. To guess all twenty-five correctly produced odds of 298, 023, 223, 876, 953, 125 to one. According to the Rhine report, one subject by the name of Hubert Pearce, a divinity student at Duke, remarkably beat those odds and guessed all twenty-five cards correctly. However, he was unable to repeat this phenomenal performance.

Ever since scientists began to investigate parapsychological phenomena, card-guessing ability has been one of the most researched areas. The technical

FIGURE 10-1.   *The five suits depicted on Zener ESP cards.*

term for this ability is *telepathy* when the experimenter can see the cards while the subject tries to guess their identity. *Precognition* is used when the subject tries to guess the cards or card order as they will be arranged before the experimenter arranges them. When the experimenter does not know the identity or order of the cards and the subject guesses their identity, the ability is known as *clairvoyance*. Each of these powers will be discussed later under the general rubric of extrasensory perception. In turn, extrasensory perception is distinguished from psychokinesis which involves the possibility of being able to move objects through thought. Both ESP and PK have been scientifically investigated by many researchers (Moss and Butler, 1978; Rao, 1966, 1979; Rhine, 1964; Rhine and Pratt, 1957; Rhine, 1961, 1970) with many positive and negative findings being reported.

EXTRASENSORY PERCEPTION

Extrasensory perception generally refers to the phenomena of clairvoyance, precognition, and telepathy. *Clairvoyance,* broadly defined, is the ability to experience the occurrence of an event without physically perceiving it. In other words, the event is experienced in an extrasensory manner. Pratt (1973a, 1973b) reports an example of an individual who claimed to have such an ability. His name was Pavel Stepanek and he lived in Prague, Czechoslovakia. In an experiment designed to test clairvoyant abilities, Stepanek was requested to guess on many trials whether a given card, placed in a covered container, was white or colored. Before the testing session, all of the cards and covers were ordered randomly so that not even the experimenter knew what type of card was in a given container. Thus the experimenter could not convey any information to the subject regarding the card's identity. This is the procedure necessary for conducting a scientific experiment in clairvoyance. After examining Stepanek's guesses over a series of trials, researchers discovered that this individual significantly exceeded chance in correctly identifying the color of cards hidden from both the subject and the experimenter. Pratt mentions that this ability was not a random or spurious one, for Stepanek was able to demonstrate this feat over and over again, not only for Pratt but for other investigators as well (Beloff, 1968).

The case of Pavel Stepanek is an interesting one indeed. Here is a demonstration of the ability of an individual to experience an event accurately (above chance) without reliance on his five senses. Does this finding scientifically establish the existence of the ESP component of clairvoyance? Although the evidence seems to be convincing in the case of Stepanek, it is still unclear how he performed his feat. In addition to the possibility of ESP, learning as a function of trials cannot be totally discounted as an alternative. For example, if one guesses (correctly or incorrectly) the same color of a card for a series of responses, one probably will switch to another color after a while. Could it be that Stepanek became very skilled in developing a strategy for producing accurate guesses? It is not possible to answer this question because investigations in clairvoyance generally tend to ignore alternatives to psi as an explanation for results. Perhaps future investigators will make a greater effort to consider such explanations.

Another area of ESP is *precognition*. Precognition is the ability to predict a future event. Do you ever remember being able to predict a future occurrence? Do you remember how shocked or surprised you were when the event really happened? Did it occur by coincidence, or is precognition possible? Such a possibility formed the basis of an experiment by Friedman, Schmeidler, and Dean (1976). Subjects were asked to predict which of five possible targets (put in random order of rank) would be selected by an experimenter on each of twenty calls or trials. This paradigm differs from the one employed in clair-voyance experiments because the experimenter knows the identity of the targets to be guessed. Also, the subject makes a prediction concerning what an experimenter *will do* rather than what he or she *did*. If the subject's response matched the first item of the target set, the score was five; if it matched the second, the score was four, and so on. With this system, the mean chance expec-tation is three. Subjects scored significantly above chance, but only if they were in a nonaggressive mood and lacked the need for social affection. Mood states were determined before the experiment by having subjects complete the Nowlis (1965) Mood Adjective Checklist.

It is not clear why these mood states were necessary for subjects to score above chance. There seems to be no logical reason why precognition would require these states. There also is no definitive evidence that the data of Fried-man and associates support the existence of precognitive abilities. Perhaps, as we discussed in the case of clairvoyance, subjects became skillful at developing a strategy for guessing on the basis of a learning experience over twenty trials. Obviously there is no way to resolve the controversy over whether Friedman and associates really demonstrated precognition. However, they did make a scientific attempt to determine the possible existence of the phenomenon. Hopefully, with many more such attempts, science will be able to give us some clues as to whether precognition is a bona fide phenomenon.

The third major area of ESP, *telepathy*, is the ability to read someone's mind and to relate to others the thoughts that are perceived in this fashion. As with precognition and clairvoyance, the possible existence of telepathic skills has been scientifically investigated. To repeat briefly what we mentioned earlier, telepathy differs from both clairvoyance and precognition because it requires that the experimenter look at a target while the subject tries to guess the target's identity. Therefore, telepathy is akin to mind reading.

In addition to Rhine's experiments with Zener cards (1934), Tart (1966, 1977b) continued telepathy research in a similar vein. He hypothesized that giving a subject immediate feedback in a repeated card-guessing task would stabilize psi performance by permitting talented individuals to develop a strategy for learning which cards had a greater chance of appearing on subsequent guesses. According to Tart, Palmer, and Redington (1979a, 1979b), such learning could take place because of internal processes that enable the subject to gain conscious control of ESP functioning. In essence, the subject made "mental snapshots" in reaching a response decision, stored such snapshots in memory along with the feedback knowledge of the success or failure of each response, and then examined the stored data to determine which internal events constituted a guide for a useful ESP guessing strategy.

The experiments conducted by Tart and colleagues have produced some evidence that many subject are capable of card-guessing above chance probability. Although the results are not as impressive as those produced by Hubert Pearce in the Rhine report (1934), they do present evidence that card-guessing above chance definitely is possible. The question is whether this skill requires ESP. It seems that Tart's data can easily be explained in nonparapsychological terms, namely, that good subjects have the ability to memorize card sequences, much as good poker players can remember which cards have been played previously in an expended deck. Because of the feedback manipulation, the assertion that ESP was necessary for above-chance performance is at best a tenuous argument. As Irwin (1937a, 1937b) has demonstrated in his card-guessing experiments, the ability to be an above-chance card-guesser may relate more to the subject's ability to process available information, as in a perception or cognition task (see Lindsey and Norman, 1977; Kahneman, 1973), than to possession of ESP abilities.

In ESP experiments, subjects are classified as one of two types. They are either "sheep" (believers in ESP) or "goats" (disbelievers or doubters of the existence of ESP). Research has tended to show that "sheep" generally score better than chance on ESP tasks, while "goats" tend to score at or below random chance (Schmeidler and McConnell, 1958; Palmer, 1971). Besides being a "sheep" or a "goat," are other factors important in being able to demonstrate ESP abilities? This is not an easy question to answer. However, Rhine (1934, 1961) has reported that subjects who demonstrated ESP in his experiments did not fall into one particular age group. His subjects have ranged in age from four to sixty years. For college students who have served as subjects, grades have not been a predictive factor in determining who can demonstrate ESP. In addition, there exists no evidence to demonstrate that ESP ability is related to gender.

Factors that appear to improve ESP abilities include one's level of confidence (persons who are more confident demonstrate greater abilities) and concentration. Krippner, Hickman, Auerhahn, and Harris (1972) have also discovered that, for some subjects, ESP abilities are improved when there is a full moon. We can only speculate why any of these factors influence ESP abilities. Does one's level of consciousness change when one is more confident about performing a certain task and when one concentrates on the task? In Chapter 4, we learned that both of these factors appeared to be important in determining who was hypnotizable. Therefore, it is also possible that these factors may play a role in determining who can demonstrate certain ESP abilities. However, this is only a matter of conjecture.

As for the influence of moon phase on ESP abilities, a physical force may be working on behavior and consciousness in a manner similar to that which controls tide levels. Since this suggestion is highly speculative with no supporting evidence, a scientific conclusion is not possible. However, would it not be interesting if such a phenomenon were taking place?

PSYCHOKINESIS

Some scientists have studied the role of physical events in parapsychology in terms of their possible influence in PK. The study of PK generally involves an individual who is able to move an object(s) by mind control—that is, without being in physical contact with it.

There are several examples of PK in the parapsychology literature. One classic case was reported by Aylesworth (1975), in which an Englishman, Harry Price, observed a young girl who appeared to be able to depress a telegraph key without touching it. Doubting the PK abilities of the girl, Price had her repeat the performance under some very stringent controls. He blew a soap and glycerin bubble over the telegraph key and also placed the setup in a glass enclosure. After this, he further enclosed the apparatus in a wire cage. All of these precautions hopefully would guarantee that the girl could not have physical contact with the telegraph key. Price was astonished to see that she again depressed the telegraph key.

Other examples of PK have been reported in the Duke University laboratories of the Rhines (1970). Basically, the Rhines studied PK because of their concern for methodological control during investigations of parapsychological phenomena. They wondered, for example, whether a subject could accurately report a number of Zener cards and, if this number exceeded chance guessing, whether this was because the subject possessed clairvoyant or telepathic abilities. Or could it be that the subject would control via PK the order in which the cards were presented to him or her? In an attempt to answer these questions, the Rhines used a subject in a PK experiment who had previously demonstrated clairvoyant abilities with the Zener cards. This time, instead of having the subject report the symbol on each card, he was to report the exact order of the cards before and after they were shuffled. The researchers observed no difference between these two sessions, although in both instances the subject exceeded chance guessing. As a result, it appeared that the ability to name Zener card symbols could be multidetermined. That is, it could be attributed to clairvoyance, telepathy, PK, or perhaps just good guessing!

It was obvious to the Rhines that it would not be possible to isolate the various ESP and PK phenomena in the card-guessing task. Although several subjects in the Duke experiments demonstrated the ability to guess Zener cards accurately above the chance guessing level, it was not possible to draw a conclusion concerning the reasons for their ability to demonstrate this feat.

Thus, the Rhines began to experiment with another task to determine whether PK could exist. This was a dice-throwing task. In one such experiment (Rhine and Brier, 1968), subjects were asked to throw two dice in an attempt to have their sum total greater than seven. Of a possible thirty-six combinations of two dice, fifteen are greater than seven. Subjects threw the dice for a total of 6,744 times. They managed to accumulate 3,110 throws in which the total of the dice exceeded seven. The odds against doing so are about a billion to one when 2,810 throws of dice totaling greater than seven are expected by chance. Again, however, a question arose regarding whether subjects were controlling the dice by PK or whether they knew how the dice would land via precognition. Obviously, this question frequently arises in experiments such as this and must be dealt with if such experiments are to be conducted in a controlled fashion.

Although Rhine and colleagues have studied PK in the laboratory for many years, there are also examples of PK phenomena in the natural environment. Pratt and Roll (1958) report the case of the James H. Herrmann family of Seaford, New York. For several weeks, this family complained of rather strange occurrences in their home. They reported objects moving for no apparent reason. For example, a figurine flew through the air and a bottle of shampoo moved across the bathroom shelf. There were a total of sixty-seven such events before the Herrmanns sought assistance.

These so-called *poltergeist* happenings were believed to be the result of PK. Poltergeist is a German word meaning "noisy spirit" and generally refers to strange happenings such as those that occurred in the Herrmann home. Pratt and Roll discovered that objects never moved in the home when it was unoccupied. However, when the Herrmann son, James Jr., was present, objects began to move. Pratt and Roll observed five of these so-called PK movements, and they did not believe that trickery or deception was involved. In fact, Pratt (1973a) reports several additional instances of poltergeist events that are similar in nature to the Herrmann example. In one case, a court reporter from Oakland, California, named James Hazlewood reported some strange happenings in his office. A dictaphone foot pedal moved from a cabinet; light bulbs in a fixture became unscrewed, fell, and broke; and a metal top of a typewriter went through an open window and fell to the street below.

Are these poltergeist phenomena examples of PK in the real world? This is not an easy question to answer, for many of the PK or poltergeist events are reported after the fact and therefore cannot be verified scientifically. However, similar examples continue to be reported and therefore cannot be dismissed lightly. Until more examples can be demonstrated under controlled laboratory settings, the scientific community will not accept the poltergeist phenomenon.

Some of the most interesting demonstrations of PK were exhibited by an Israeli named Uri Geller. Geller claimed to be able to break metal rings simply through concentration. He also claimed to be able to start broken clocks by concentrating on them. As reported by Aylesworth (1975), Geller demonstrated bending a ring that belonged to Friedbert Karger of the Max Planck Institute in Berlin. While Geller visited the space scientist Werner von Braun, the scientist's calculator ceased to function. This also happened at the Stanford Research Institute in California when Geller appeared as a subject for an experiment by two physicists, Russell Targ and Harold Puthoff.

Targ and Puthoff (1974) conducted several experiments on Geller. All of the experiments were filmed or videotaped to be certain that the scientists would not miss anything, such as a sleight-of-hand trick or other deception. In one experiment, Geller unbalanced a precision scientific scale. He also bent a steel band to an angle that would have required about 100 pounds of pressure. Geller accomplished this without coming in physical contact with the objects.

Needless to say, the PK demonstrations by Geller and others are highly controversial. Can some of the feats performed by Geller be magic? In other words, could a magician replicate the so-called PK demonstrations? Many investigators say yes. However, if all of Geller's feats are trickery, then he is indeed an excellent magician.

Another PK phenomenon is called *Kirlian photography*. This process was discovered by two Russian scientists, Semyon and Valentina Kirlian (Moss and Johnson, 1974; Krippner and Rubin, 1974). The basis behind this phenomenon is the notion that a form of energy flows from acupuncture points on the human body (although such photography has also been demonstrated with plants). The Kirlians believe they have discovered a process that can photograph this bioplasmic energy.

The actual Kirlian process involves the use of an electric Telsa coil (a type of transformer) that is connected to two metal plates. An object (usually a finger) is then placed between the plates, where a piece of film touches the object. Electricity is then turned on and a high-energy frequency is generated that causes the film to record an "aura" or "halo." Variations in the color and form of the halo are considered descriptors of mood states. For example, a red, blotchy halo is indicative of anxiety. A glowing halo indicates a relaxed state (the greater the glow, the more relaxed the person is). Since the energy flow does not appear to be controlled by the five senses, parapsychologists believe it is controlled by PK.

Whether this is really the case cannot be stated at this time. Montandon (1977), however, believes that Kirlian photography and the resultant auras are related to palmar sweating; therefore, such photography has a physical basis that is autonomically controlled. That is, it is controlled involuntarily by the autonomic nervous system (ANS) (see Chapter 5). If this is the case, and if Kirlian photography is an accurate recording of ANS activity, the potential uses of Kirlian photography are limitless. For example, the technique might someday serve as a lie detector in recording levels of anxiety or nervousness. Or it might be useful in helping individuals understand their level of anxiety and subsequently decrease or control this level, much as in biofeedback training. Of course, these suggestions are speculative and are based on the assumption that Kirlian photography is not an illustration of PK. Only time will help us understand this process more fully.

THEORIES OF PARAPSYCHOLOGY

In order for science to progress in a particular area of concern, it is essential that theories either exist or can be established to explain the various phenomena considered under the general rubric of the topic. In an area such as psi, which has many critics and doubters, this requisite is especially crucial. Some researchers (Moss and Butler, 1978; Scriven, 1976) have argued that there exist no bona fide theories of parapsychology. It is true that there is an absence of a general, comprehensive theory that is considered scientifically adequate to integrate and explain some psi phenomena; this matter is elaborated upon at length by Rao (1977). The most recent theoretical accounts of psi include those by Walker (1975), Stanford (1974, 1977a, 1977b), and Schmidt (1975).

Walker's theory is based on the notion that ESP and PK are products of hidden variables in quantum mechanics. He states that this is possible because the mathematical formalism of quantum mechanics does not specify exactly what constitutes an observation or measurement of an event. Because of this deficiency, hidden variables are conceived that are essentially inaccessible to physical measurement. These variables function independently of space/time constraints.

Walker believes that hidden variables exist in consciousness as a part of one's "will" and, as a result, may not be directly observable or measurable. The hidden variables can then produce physical changes in the environment that cannot be accounted for by any physical variable. This permits phenomena such as ESP and PK to take place without science being able to determine their physical or biological loci.

The attempt to explain psi as a function of physics, specifically a measurement problem of quantum mechanics, is an interesting avenue in parapsychology. Unfortunately, Walker's theory is not scientifically testable, since it is impossible to locate these hidden variables for potential manipulation. Also, Walker's assumption that ESP and PK are the result of physical events remains unproved. Furthermore, to argue that something occurs as a result of something "hidden" is like trying to catch a ghost with an invisible net. To look for psi by proposing "hidden variables" is a very poor approach to explaining a supposed scientific relationship.

Stanford (1974, 1977a, 1977b) proposed a theory of psi that appears to incorporate and elaborate on the idea of mind projection (Rhine, 1945, 1953). Specifically, in addition to using other sense modalities, the individual also employs psi to scan the environment. In this way, psi may be considered a "sixth sense." In a particular need situation, an individual uses ESP as well as other senses to gather necessary information about the world. When the individual obtains extrasensory information, he or she may use it to satisfy a need or what Stanford calls the psi-mediated instrumental response (PMIR). Stanford explains PK as "a response mode for PMIR." Thus, PMIR may be a kind of goal-relevant response that comes about as a result of extrasensory means via PK.

Basically, Stanford proposes that all psi responses are mediated, instrumental, and serve to satisfy a need. Unfortunately, as with Walker's theory, there is no scientific basis or evidence for his conclusions. If psi functions as Stanford predicts, it should be possible to test his assumptions with use of basic instrumental learning techniques, such as shaping, extinction, and so on. This is not possible, however, because we do not know what behavior to shape or extinguish. Until Stanford can define this "sixth sense" more operationally and explain how it functions, his theory will not help advance our knowledge of parapsychology.

Probably the most sophisticated attempt to develop a theory of psi was made by Schmidt (1975). He proposed a mathematical explanation of psi that postulated the existence of "psi sources." These mathematically derived sources, according to Schmidt, act similarly to the behavior exhibited by successful PK subjects. His theory proposes a psi axiom that leads mathematically to spatial and temporal independence of psi. Also, the different forms of psi, such as PK, precognition, and clairvoyance, appear as logical consequences of one psi axiom.

Although Schmidt's theory sounds very impressive, Schmidt is applying mathematics to unobservables. There is nothing intrinsically wrong with doing so, except that mathematical models of behavior often do not have a basis in the real world. To date, Schmidt has not shown such a basis; until he does, his model will remain interesting but not scientifically predictive.

Although researchers have attempted to explain psi in theoretical terms, all theories to date have received little or no experimental support. This is an unfortunate state of the science of parapsychology and is undoubtedly one of the major reasons why a large number of scientists, especially psychologists, do not take research in parapsychology very seriously.

The major problems that haunt parapsychology as an area of study in the psychology of consciousness were enumerated recently by Moss and Butler (1978). These include:

1. inadequate reporting of test procedures and experimental designs;
2. failure to replicate most parapsychology experiments;

3. an absence of psychological, predictive laws and theories of psi;
4. lack of harmony between psi and established physical and biological laws and theories;
5. an absence of generally observable (i.e., by most of us) psi phenomena in the real world and, therefore, an absence of practical applications of psi; and
6. a general absence of scientific evidence in the laboratory to establish the existence of psi phenomena.

In a response to these criticisms, Rao (1979) accused Moss and Butler of being biased in reaching their conclusions. He believes that an accumulation of evidence reported in two scientific publications for psi research, the *Journal of Parapsychology* and the *Journal of the American Society for Psychical Research*, basically contradicts each of the six points made by Moss and Butler. Rao goes on to say that although the points made by Moss and Butler may be true for a small number of psi experiments, their suggestions are no less true for psychology experiments in general. For example, Rao stressed that most experimental psychologists do not attempt to replicate their studies, and, as a result, it is often not known whether they are replicable. Psi experiments, however, are often replicated successfully (Honorton, 1978).

Despite Rao's arguments to defend psi and psi research, there are problems with his defense. For instance, it is simply not true that experimental psychologists do not attempt to replicate their findings. Also, there are other problems that face investigators in the field of parapsychology in addition to those enumerated by Moss and Butler (and many of theirs are still valid despite Rao's defense). There is the problem of good ESP and PK subjects being unable to replicate their own performance. On one day or trial, they exhibit an above-chance performance, while on another day or trial, the performance is at or below chance level. This has been dubbed the "decline effect" (Pratt and Woodruff, 1939; Pratt, 1973b; Woodruff and Rhine, 1942; Anderson, 1959). Does this observation indicate that ESP or PK performances are spurious or occur by coincidence? Many believe so. Those who defend psi findings (e.g., Rao, 1979), however, believe that psi performances are not controllable and therefore are not predictable. Thus, it is not unusual to discover strong psi abilities in an individual on some occasions and reduced or nonexistent abilities on others. As Stanford (1974) has theorized, psi is a sixth sense; sometimes we use it and sometimes we do not.

In the final analysis, the study of parapsychology may simply reveal that strange happenings have been observed or reported in the laboratory and in the real world that cannot be explained by traditional laws and theories of science. Investigators such as Stanford, Schmidt, Walker, Rhine, and others have proposed explanations for these happenings. Some believe that these explanations may help us ultimately to understand these occurrences. Others believe that such happenings are spurious events that are probably attributable to physical, biological, or psychological laws, although we have not as yet been able to discover such laws. And some believe there simply are no real strange happenings that cannot be explained by a magician.

As you can see, a conclusion concerning the validity of psi is not possible at this time. As with many areas of consciousness we have discussed (e.g., hypnosis, meditation, biofeedback), there will always be critics and disbelievers. With regard to parapsychology, most researchers today maintain a fairly healthy skepticism toward this topic. While they keep an open mind, they have many doubts about the likelihood of this area becoming an important part of psychological study. Also, the other areas of consciousness have provided us with practical applications, regardless of whether scientists believe the manipulations are totally valid. This has not been the case with parapsychology, and until this happens, the study of psi will always remain as controversial as it is now.

FOR FURTHER READING

Aylesworth, T. G. *ESP.* New York: Watts, 1975.

Cohen, D. *ESP: the search beyond the senses.* New York: Harcourt, Brace, Jovanovich, 1973.

Koestler, A. *The roots of coincidence.* New York: Random House, 1972.

Rhine, J. B., and Brier, R. (eds.) *Parapsychology today.* New York: Citadel Press, 1968.

Tart, C. T.; Puthoff, H. E.; and Targ, R. (eds.) *Mind at large.* New York: Praeger, 1979.

chapter eleven ═══════════════

The Future

After having discussed the psychology of consciousness, we wish to spend a few pages speculating on what we see as the future of this area of study. Although much of what we discuss here will be our own opinions, remember that this area of psychology is now in a *zeitgeist;* its popularity undoubtedly will spread to many other areas of psychology and related behavioral sciences. With this thought in mind, we will try to put the future of consciousness in its proper perspective.

As we mentioned in Chapter 1, our approach in this book has been to show that consciousness is a multilevel or multistate phenomenon. One of these levels, obviously is our normal or unaltered state of awareness. This level is our baseline for comparison with other levels of consciousness that may arise (e.g., levels of sleep) or that may be produced (e.g., drug-altered states). We can all relate easily to the baseline level or state. It is easy to compare our wakeful level of consciousness with that of someone else's, such as a friend's. Likewise, that friend can relate to your experiences of wakefulness.

However, when consciousness shifts to a different level, communication may break down. For example, even though we have all experienced the different levels of sleep as discussed in Chapter 7, can one individual communicate his or her stage 3 sleep with another person's? In terms of brain-wave activity, stage 3 sleep is fairly similar from one individual to another. Unfortunately, this level of consciousness cannot be compared verbally or in a psychological sense because generally we cannot recall our stage 3 experiences. Hence, this level of consciousness is not capable of being compared in the same sense that our experiences of wakefulness can be compared.

This example may not be as easy to identify with as, perhaps, that of stage REM. Recall that the stage REM level of consciousness is associated with dream production. Yet how easy is it to compare your stage REM experiences to those of your friends? Try it. You will find that such comparisons are not easy. First, individuals vary in their ability to recall dreams. Second, all dreams are qualitatively different. Finally, dreams vary within the same individual. What one dreams in one evening may differ considerably from what one dreams on another occasion.

Even induced levels of consciousness create interesting dilemmas. After a group of individuals has meditated, they all may share a common experience, such as relaxation. Yet each person may have experienced this level of consciousness in a different way. One may have had a tension-relieving experience, while another may have had a so-called religious experience.

The point we are trying to make is that, although consciousness is a phenomenon that can be studied in an empirical fashion, it is necessary for science to come to grips with problems facing this area of psychology. These include the development of methods for summarizing the vast individual differences in experiencing levels or states of consciousness. The development of adequate procedures for assessing and describing levels of consciousness is also necessary. Finally, it is mandatory that scientifically testable theories be developed for the areas of investigation under the rubric of consciousness so that experiments can be derived. This has been accomplished to some extent, but many of the theories discussed throughout this book are not strong. Either they are not based on generalizable data collected in a scientific manner, or they fail to define terms and concepts operationally so as to make the theory scientifically testable. Without strong and empirically testable theories of consciousness, this area of study cannot progress to become and remain an important area within psychology and related behavioral sciences. At the end of this chapter we shall elaborate on some of our ideas for a theory of consciousness.

We are well familiar with the fact that all the topics in this book represent controversial areas of study. Yet these areas are what many people believe psychology is all about. This observation can be verified by reading certain popular magazines and weekly newspapers. If most people believe such notions, which are known to be distortions of the total picture, investigators must put to rest these misconceptions through empirical experimentation. A strong bias still exists in the scientific community that prevents researchers from engaging in such investigations. However, the psychology of consciousness has much to offer, and perhaps the development of strong theories and experiments will break down this bias.

FUTURE APPLICATIONS OF CONSCIOUSNESS

The future of each of the areas we have discussed will depend on many factors, as we have already said. We would like to give some indication of what we see happening in these areas.

As we tried to make clear in Chapter 3, consciousness-altering drugs have been used for a variety of beneficial purposes. This was the reason they were originally produced. However, many of these drugs are abused. One would not think that good might come of abused drugs, but, in fact, this has happened in several instances. The misuse of marijuana has led to two important applications that might not have come about as soon if not for information obtained from the misusers. One of these applications has been in the treatment of excessive eye pressure, or glaucoma. An individual who suffered from this condition discovered that, after smoking marijuana, his eye condition improved, as verified by ophthalmologic examination. Reporting this to his ophthalmologist led to several laboratory experiments, which verified that marijuana can be beneficial in the treatment of glaucoma (Hepler and Frank, 1971; Green, 1979; Cohen, 1980).

Similarly, several patients receiving chemotherapy for the treatment of cancer reported that use of marijuana reduced their experiences of nausea following such treatment. This discovery has been verified in the laboratory (Borison, McCarthy, and London, 1978; McCarthy and Borison, 1977). Marijuana has also had beneficial effects on symptoms of asthma, epilepsy, depression, and alcoholism (Cohen, 1980). These discoveries may not have been made as quickly as they were had it not been for the misuse of the drug by patients suffering from these conditions. Although we by no means advocate the use of marijuana, it is not too speculative to predict that several more discoveries of the beneficial effects of using the substance will be made in the 1980s and 1990s. Such discoveries may also be forthcoming for other drugs of abuse that were discussed in Chapter 3.

With respect to future applications of hypnosis (Chapter 4), Wallace (1979) has speculated that this manipulation could be employed to help individuals with the problem of poor concentration. For example, students from elementary grades through college who have difficulty studying may find some assistance through hypnosis. They could be taught to focus their attention on the material they must study and to attenuate distractions that interfere with their task. Similarly, hypnosis could be employed to help athletes concentrate better during sports activities and thereby improve their game. Such applications have received little attention from investigators in the field of the psychology of consciousness.

Other applications of hypnosis will include its continued and expanded use in habit control, especially for controlling smoking, weight, and stress. We would not be surprised to see a proliferation of professional clinics where individuals could be helped to control a specific habit with the aid of hypnosis.

Law enforcement has also begun to use hynosis to help with the solution of crimes. Specifically, it has been used to assist witnesses to a crime to recall information that is not easily retrievable otherwise. Although use of this application appears to be in the future, it has already come under considerable scrutiny. Loftus (1979, 1980) believes that hypnosis helps people to relax, to concentrate, and to cooperate with the questions of a hypnotist. Unfortunately, for this reason, she believes that the suggestibility of a witness is so heightened that the person "recalls" events that may have never occurred. This suggestion has been true in some situations, but it has helped to solve some crimes. We should see expanded use of it in the 1980s and 1990s.

We envision hypnosis being used increasingly as an analgesic manipulation for helping people overcome experienced pain. This application was discussed in Chapter 4, and we believe it will be used more commonly in future years, especially to control the pain of arthritis, rheumatism, and various forms of cancer (Hilgard and Hilgard, 1975).

With respect to biofeedback (Chapter 5), we see the use of this manipulation expanding greatly in the future. As with hypnosis, we believe the 1980s and 1990s will see the development and proliferation of biofeedback clinics. Here people can be helped to control tension and migraine headaches, anxiety, hypertension, and other problems that have been shown to be alleviated with the intervention of biofeedback training (this claim is by no means universal; e.g., Kewman and Roberts, 1979; Blanchard and Epstein, 1978). We also believe that biofeedback will be used more widely for the treatment of such problems as stuttering (Lanyon, Barrington, and Newman, 1976), epilepsy, teeth grinding, muscle spasms, and backaches (Coleman, Butcher, and Carson, 1980). One note of caution: in order for the potential of biofeedback to be assessed thoroughly as a clinical intervention, more carefully controlled experiments must be undertaken in the next few decades.

As with hypnosis and biofeedback, we see the continuing development of meditation clinics—or "societies," as they often refer to themselves—in the 1980s and 1990s. Perhaps we will even see the development of centers, under the auspices of physicians or psychologists, devoted to the use of consciousness-altering techniques as a whole. In such places, hypnosis, biofeedback, meditation, and other interventions will be offered to assist people who have problems that can be alleviated with consciousness-changing techniques.

We also envision the continued use of meditation techniques (Chapter 6) to help people control stress and anxiety through relaxation. As with hypnosis, meditation will also be employed to help with problems of concentration.

Future years will also produce much research that will help us to understand sleep and dreams better (Chapter 7). We would not be surprised to see great strides in finding nonchemical methods for treating sleep disorders, such as those described in Chapter 7. Several consciousness-altering techniques (e.g., hypnosis and meditation) have already been shown to be helpful in dealing with insomnia. We still do not fully understand the physiological processes underlying sleep and dreams. Perhaps the coming decades will help shed light on these areas of study as they relate to consciousness.

Future applications of sensory deprivation (Chapter 8) include its use in a technique called *tank therapy* (Daniel, 1981). In tank therapy, a person lies down in a tank of water and Epsom salts (similar to that used by Lilly, 1956), that is heated to 93° F (33.9° C). After a few minutes, the person begins to feel weightless from the buoyancy and relaxation that ensues. Some patients of such therapy (which may include traditional talk therapy while in the tank) report that it has had a beneficial effect in helping them with a variety of psychological problems. However, as you will recall from Chapter 8, many other effects also occur, including hallucinations. Therefore, although sensory deprivation may be therapeutic for some, it can be equally detrimental for others. As a result, the wisdom and beneficial applications of tank therapy are uncertain.

The future of mysticism (Chapter 9) is not as clear as for other consciousness-related topics. At the time of this writing, there appears to be an increase in the role and popularity of religion and spiritualism in the United States—at least the public display of such, especially on television. This increased visibility will probably lead to an increase in the number of individuals who try faith healing as a means of treating problems and ailments. This is because faith healing is so widely publicized on many televised religious programs. The increased use of faith healing is not necessarily bad, for many have found this technique to be of benefit. This is especially true for the treatment of many psychosomatic illnesses (although "healed" patients did not and do not know that their problem was of a psychological origin). Beyond a potential increase in the use of faith healing, we do not feel that the study of mysticism will advance in a significant scientific manner in the 1980s and 1990s.

Parapsychology (Chapter 10) is an area of consciousness that will continue to interest laypeople. However, we do not see that this area will advance beyond its present state. For advancement to occur, reliable and valid tests of so-called psi phenomena must be established and empirical theories must be produced. In the many years of investigating these phenomena, such tests and theories seem not to be forthcoming, and we do not think that this situation will change. Therefore, most scientists will continue to hold this topic in low esteem, and the area will remain at the bottom of the ladder of science.

The psychology of consciousness has much to accomplish in the years to come. Many of the areas under the rubric of consciousness also have much to offer science, and we expect research in these areas to progress and flourish as this aspect of psychology regains prestige among scientists. Other areas will remain low in scientific prestige. Hopefully, the psychology of consciousness, a facet neglected since the advent and growth of behaviorism in the early 1900s, will become a major area of concern and study by psychologists and other behavioral scientists.

TOWARD A THEORY OF CONSCIOUSNESS

Now that you have read about the psychology of consciousness, it is time to try to make some theoretical sense of it, if possible. In Chapter 1 you read about several proposed theories of consciousness. There appeared to be some good thoughts in those theories, but they need to be tied together with theories that do not claim necessarily to be general theories of consciousness. We shall now attempt to tie some of the loose ends together.

First, a theory of consciousness must contain an element of variability. That is, regardless of any prediction(s) in a theory, individual differences will always exist. This is one reason why consciousness is so difficult to study. Individual differences are abundant for all the areas we have discussed in this book. Therefore, an hypothesis or a law within a theory will never hold true for all individuals. We only hope it will be predictive for most of the population.

Second—and we have stressed this, as have other researchers (e.g., Hilgard, 1977b)—that consciousness is not a single state or level. It is a process consisting of many levels or states. One of these states is quite obvious—the normal, waking state. The other states are all departures from this state, and we often refer to them as altered states. Altered states can be elicited either naturally, as during sleep (which itself has several different levels of consciousness), or artificially, as with drugs, sensory deprivation, hypnosis, and meditation.

Consciousness is also something we have all experienced. This is true not only for the waking state but also for altered states. For some, the experience of consciousness was a natural altered state; for others, it was an artificial altered state. Because of this difference, although many responses cannot be measured directly, as behaviorists would prefer, such responses can at least be communicated, often with some degree of reliability and validity. This permits scientists to study consciousness and to test hypotheses and laws of behavior relating to areas of consciousness.

Altered states of consciousness must contain an element of pleasure. We believe this to be the case because so many individuals (all of us, perhaps) are seeking to attain an altered state, often on a regular basis. This altered state must also be more pleasurable than the waking state, for many individuals often prefer the altered state to the waking state. Perhaps Weil (1972) was correct: we have an innate drive to experience modes of awareness. Although the drive may be innate, we must learn to utilize the drive, perhaps in a manner similar to deautomatization (Ornstein, 1972), as described in Chapter 6. Perhaps this effect can be accomplished through experimentation, such as with drugs, meditation, hypnosis, biofeedback, and so on. On the other hand, a good night's sleep with a few fantastic dreams can accomplish this.

Finally, as Tart (1975, 1977) has proposed, consciousness is a very complex process, one we are just beginning to understand. Because of the present state of knowledge with respect to the process of consciousness, it will take many years (perhaps decades or centuries) before we understand as much as is possible about how humans are capable of doing what we have described in this book. The task will be immensely difficult, if not nearly impossible, but many scientists will have much pleasure and anguish in trying to unravel the mysteries of the human psyche, especially one of the greatest mysteries of all: how our brain works at various levels of consciousness—the psychology of consciousness.

References

Aarons, L. Sleep-assisted instruction. *Psychological Bulletin* 83: 1–40, 1976.

Abelson, H. I., and Fishburne, P. M. *Nonmedical Use of Psychoactive Substances.* Princeton, NJ: Response Analysis Corporation, 1976.

Aghajanian, G. K., Haigler, H. J., and Bloom, F. E. Lysergic acid diethylamide and serotonin: direct actions on serotonin-containing neurons. *Life Science* 11: 615–622, 1972.

Akil, H., Watson, S., Sullivan, S., and Barchas, J. D. Enkephalin-like material in normal human cerebrospinal fluid: measurement and levels. *Life Science* 23: 121–126, 1978.

American Medical Association, Department of Mental Health. The crutch that cripples: drug dependence. Part 1. *Today's Health* 46: 11–12, 70–72, 1968.

Anand, B. K., Chhina, G. S., and Singh. B. Some aspects of electroencephalographic studies in Yogis. *Electroencephalography and Clinical Neurophysiology* 13: 452–456, 1961a.

Anand, B. K., Chhina, G. S., and Singh, B. Studies on Shri Ramanand Yogi during his stay in an air-tight box. *Indian Journal of Medical Research* 49: 82–89, 1961b.

Anderson, M. A precognition experiment comparing time intervals of a few days and one year. *Journal of Parapsychology* 23: 81–89, 1959.

Andreychuck, T., and Skriver, C. Hypnosis and biofeedback in the treatment of migraine headaches. *International Journal of Clinical and Experimental Hypnosis* 23: 172–183, 1975.

Antrobus, J. S., Fein, G., Jordan, L., Ellman, S. J., and Arkin, A. M. Measurement and design in research on sleep reports. In *The Mind in Sleep: Psychology and Psychophysiology*, A. M. Arkin, J. S. Antrobus, and S. J. Ellman (eds.). Hillsdale, NJ: Lawrence Erlbaum Associates, 1978.

Arkin, A. M., and Antrobus, J. S. The effects of external stimuli applied to and during sleep on sleep experience. In *The Mind in Sleep: Psychology and Psychophysiology.* A. M. Arkin, J. S. Antrobus, and S. J. Ellman (eds.). Hillsdale, NJ: Lawrence Erlbaum Associates, 1978.

Arnhoff, G. N., and Leon, H. V. Sex differences in response to short-term sensory deprivation and isolation. *Perceptual and Motor Skills* 17: 81-82, 1963.

Aserinsky, E., and Kleitman, N. Regularly occurring periods of eye motility and concomitant phenomena during sleep. *Science* 118: 273-274, 1953.

Ashley, R. *Cocaine: Its History, Uses, and Effects.* New York: Warner Books, 1976.

Aylesworth, T. G. *ESP.* New York: Watts, 1975.

Bakal, D. A. A biopsychological perspective. *Psychological Bulletin* 82: 376-382, 1975.

Barber, T. X. Experimental evidence for a theory of hypnotic behavior. II. Experimental controls in hypnotic age regression. *International Journal of Clinical and Experimental Hypnosis* 9: 181-193, 1961.

Barber, T. X. *Hypnosis: A Scientific Approach.* Princeton, NJ: Van Nostrand, 1969.

Barber, T. X. *LSD, Marihuana, Yoga, and Hypnosis.* Chicago: Aldine, 1970.

Barber, T. X., and Glass, L. B. Significant factors in hypnotic behavior. *Journal of Abnormal and Social Psychology* 64: 222-228, 1962.

Barber, T. X., Spanos, N. P., and Chaves, J. F. *Hypnotism, Imagination, and Human Potentialities.* New York: Pergamon Press, 1974.

Barkley, R. A., Hastings, J. E., and Jackson, T. L., Jr. The effects of rapid smoking and hypnosis in the treatment of smoking behavior. *International Journal of Clinical and Experimental Hypnosis* 25: 7-17, 1977.

Barron, F., Jarvik, M. E., and Bunnell, S. The hallucinogenic drugs. *Scientific American* 210: 29-37, 1964.

Bartley, S. H., and Chute. E. *Fatigue and Impairment in Man.* New York: McGraw-Hill, 1947.

Batten, D. E. The effects of sensory deprivation on auditory and visual sensitivity. Ph.D. diss., Washington State University, 1961.

Bell, J. S. The use of EEG theta biofeedback in the treatment of a patient with sleep-onset insomnia. *Biofeedback and Self-Regulation* 4: 229-237, 1979.

Beloff, J. ESP: Proof from Prague? *New Scientist* 40: 76-77, 1968.

Benjamins, J. Alpha feedback relaxation procedures with high and low mental image clarity: an analogue desensitization study. Paper presented at the annual meeting of the Biofeedback Society of America, Albuquerque, March 1978.

Benson, H., Shapiro, D., Tursky, B., and Schwartz, G. E. Decreased systolic blood pressure through operant conditioning techniques in patients with essential hypertension. *Science* 173: 740–742, 1971.

Berman, A. L. *The Brain Stem of the Cat.* Madison: University of Wisconsin Press, 1968.

Besner, H. Biofeedback: possible placebo in treating chronic onset insomnia. Paper presented at the annual meeting of the Biofeedback Society of America, Albuquerque, March 1978.

Bexton, W. H., Heron, W., and Scott, T. H. Effects of decreased variation in the sensory environment. *Canadian Journal of Psychology* 8: 70–76, 1954.

Birk, L., Crider, A., Shapiro, D., and Tursky, B. Operant electrodermal conditioning under partial curarization. *Journal of Comparative and Physiological Psychology* 62: 165–166, 1966.

Blacker, K. H., Jones, R. T., Stone, G. C., and Pfefferbaum, D. Chronic users of LSD: the acidheads. *American Journal of Psychiatry* 125: 97–107, 1968.

Blanchard, E. B., and Epstein, L. H. *A Biofeedback Primer.* Reading, MA: Addison-Wesley, 1978.

Bonvallet, M., and Allen, M. B., Jr. Prolonged spontaneous and evoked reticular activation following discrete bulbar lesions. *Electroencephalography and Clinical Neurophysiology* 15: 969–988, 1963.

Boring, E. G. *A History of Experimental Psychology.* New York: Appleton-Century-Crofts, 1929.

Borison, H. L., McCarthy, L. E., and London, S. W. Cannabinoids and emesis. *New England Journal of Medicine* 298: 1480–1481, 1978.

Bowers, K. S. *Hypnosis for the Seriously Curious.* Monterey, CA: Brooks/Cole, 1976.

Bradshaw, J. L., and Nettleton, N. C. The nature of hemispheric specialization in man. *Behavioral and Brain Sciences* 4: 51–91, 1981.

Brecher, E. M., and The Editors of Consumer Reports. *Licit and Illicit Drugs.* Mount Vernon, NY: Consumers Union, 1972.

Bremer, F. L'activité cérébrale au cours du sommeil et de la narcose. Contribution à l'étude du mécanisme du sommeil. *Bulletin de l'Academie Royale de Belgique* 4: 68–86, 1937.

Bremer, F. Preoptic hypnogenic focus and mesencephalic reticular formation. *Brain Research* 21: 132–134, 1970.

Bromberg, W. *The Mind of Man: A History of Psychotherapy and Psychoanalysis.* New York: J.B. Lippincott, 1954.

Broughton, R. Sleep disorders: disorders of arousal? *Science* 159: 1070–1079, 1968.

Brown, B. B. Recognition of aspects of consciousness through association with EEG alpha activity represented by a light signal. *Psychophysiology* 6: 442–452, 1970.

Brown, H. Some anticholinergic-like behavioral effects of trans(-)-Δ^8 tetra-hydrocannabinol. *Psychopharmacologia* 21: 294–301, 1971.

Brown, H. Possible anticholinesterase-like effects of trans(-)-Δ^8 and -Δ^9 tetra-hydrocannabinol as observed in the general motor activity of mice. *Psychopharmacologia* 27: 111–116, 1972.

Brown, T. S., and Wallace, P. M. *Physiological Psychology.* New York: Academic Press, 1980.

Brownfield, C. A. *Isolation: Clinical and Experimental Approaches.* New York: Random House, 1965.

Bruner, J. *On Knowing: Essays for the Left Hand.* New York: Atheneum, 1965.

Budzynski, T. H., Stoyva, J. M., and Adler, C. Feedback-induced muscle relaxation: application to tension headache. *Journal of Behavior Therapy and Experimental Psychiatry* 1: 205–211, 1970.

Budzynski, T. H., Stoyva, J. M., Adler, C. S., and Mullaney, D. J. EMG biofeedback and tension headache: a controlled outcome study. *Psychosomatic Medicine* 35: 484–496, 1973.

Burr, G. L. (ed.) *Narratives of the Witchcraft Cases 1648–1706.* New York: Scribner's, 1914.

Byrd, R. E. *Alone.* New York: G. P. Putnam's Sons, 1938.

Calef, R. More wonders from the invisible world. In *Narratives of the Witchcraft Cases 1648–1706,* G. L. Burr (ed.). New York: Scribner's, 1914.

Caporael, L. R. Ergotism: the Satan loosed in Salem? *Science* 192: 21–26, 1976.

Carrington, P. *Freedom in Meditation.* New York: Doubleday, 1977.

Carrington, P. The uses of meditation in psychotherapy. In *Expanding Dimensions of Consciousness.* A. A. Sugarman and R. E. Tarter (eds.). New York: Springer, 1978.

Cartwright, R. D. *Nightlife: Explorations in Dreaming.* Englewood Cliffs, NJ: Prentice-Hall, 1977.

Chagas, C. Studies on the mechanisms of curarization. *Annals of New York Academy of Sciences* 81: 345–357, 1959.

Chesney, M. A., and Shelton, J. L. A comparison of muscle relaxation and electromyogram biofeedback treatments for muscle contraction headache. *Journal of Behavior Therapy and Experimental Psychiatry* 7: 221–225, 1976.

Christie, M. J., and Todd, J. L. Experimenter-subject-situational interactions. In *Research in Psychophysiology.* P. H. Venables and M. J. Christie (eds.). London: Wiley, 1975.

Clemes, S. R., and Dement, W. C. Effects of REM sleep deprivation on psychological functioning. *Journal of Nervous and Mental Disease* 144: 488–491, 1967.

Cohen, S. Statement before the Subcommittee to Investigate Juvenile Delinquency of the U.S. Senate Committee on the Judiciary on Drug Abuse, December 15, 1971.

Cohen, S. Therapeutic aspects. In *Marijuana Research Findings: 1980.* NIDA Research Monograph no. 31. R. C. Peterson (ed.). Rockville, MD: Department of Health and Human Services, 1980.

Coleman, J. C. Butcher, J. N., and Carson, R. C. *Abnormal Psychology and Modern Life* (6th ed.). Glenview, IL: Scott, Foresman, 1980.

Conn, J. H., and Conn, R. N. Discussion of T. X. Barber's 'Hypnosis as a causal variable in present-day psychology': a critical analysis. *International Journal of Clinical and Experimental Hypnosis* 16: 106-110, 1967.

Corso, J. F. *The Experimental Psychology of Sensory Behavior.* New York: Holt, Rinehart, and Winston, 1967.

Crider, A., Schwartz, G. E., and Shnidman, S. R. On the criteria for instrumental autonomic conditioning: a reply to Katkin and Murray. *Psychological Bulletin* 71: 455-461, 1969.

Cunningham, M. D., and Murphy, P. J. The effects of bilateral EEG biofeedback on verbal, visual-spatial, and creative skills in learning disabled male aolescents. Paper presented at the annual meeting of the Biofeedback Society of America, Albuquerque, March 1978.

Dahlström, A., and Fuxe, K. Evidence for the existence of monoamine-containing neurons in the central nervous system. I. Demonstration of monoamines in the cell bodies of the brainstem neurons. *Acta Physiological Scandinavica* 62: 1-55, 1964.

Dalessio, D. J. *Wolff's Headache and Other Head Pain* (3rd ed.). New York: Oxford University Press, 1972.

Daniel, A. Off the couch and into the tub. *Time* January 12, 1981, p. 45.

Davenport-Slack, B. A comparative evaluation of obstetrical hypnosis and antenatal childbirth training. *International Journal of Clinical and Experimental Hypnosis* 23: 266-281, 1975.

Dean, W. F. *General Dean's Story.* New York: Viking Press, 1954.

Deikman, A. J. Deautomatization and the mystic experience. *Psychiatry* 29: 324-338, 1966.

Deikman, A. J. Bimodal consciousness. *Archives of General Psychiatry* 45: 481-489, 1971.

Dement, W. C. The effect of dream deprivation. *Science* 131: 1705-1707, 1960.

Dement, W. C. *Some Must Watch While Some Must Sleep.* San Francisco: W. H. Freeman, 1972.

Dement, W. C., and Greenberg, S. Changes in total amount of stage four sleep as a function of partial sleep deprivation. *Electroencephalography and Clinical Neurophysiology* 20: 523-526, 1966.

Dement, W. C., Greenberg, S., and Klein, R. The effect of partial REM sleep deprivation and delayed recovery. *Journal of Psychiatric Research* 4: 141-152, 1966.

Dement, W. C., Holman, R. B., and Guilleminault, C. Neurochemical and neuropharmacological foundations of the sleep disorders. *Psychopharmacology Communications* 2: 77-90, 1976.

Dement, W. C., and Kleitman, N. Cyclic variations in EEG during sleep and their relation to eye movement, body motility, and dreaming. *Electroencephalography and Clinical Neurophysiology* 9: 673-690, 1957.

Dengrove, E. *Hypnosis and Behavior Therapy.* Springfield, IL: Charles C Thomas, 1976.

Deutsch, M., Canavan, D., and Rubin, J. Effects of size of conflict and sex of experimenter upon interpersonal bargaining. *Journal of Experimental Social Psychology* 7: 258-267, 1971.

Dewan, E. D. Occipital alpha rhythm, eye position and lens accommodation. *Nature* 214: 975-977, 1967.

Diamond, M. J. Modification of hypnotizability: a review. *Psychological Bulletin* 81: 180-198, 1974.

Doane, B. K., Mahatoo, W., Heron, W., and Scott, T. H. Changes in perceptual function after isolation. *Canadian Journal of Psychology* 13: 210-219, 1959

Domhoff, C W. But why did they sit on the king's right in the first place? *Psychcanalytic Review* 56: 586-596, 1969-1970.

Doyle, A C. *The Sign of the Four.* In *The Complete Sherlock Holmes.* New York: Garden City Publishing, 1938.

Ebin, D. (ed.) *The Drug Experience: First Person Accounts of Addicts, Writers, Scientists and Others.* New York: O'Ryan Press, 1961.

Edwards, A. S. Effects of the loss of one hundred hours of sleep. *American Journal of Psychology* 54: 80-91, 1941.

Ellinwood, E. H. Amphetamine psychosis: a multi-dimensional process. *Seminars in Psychiatry* 6: 208-226, 1969.

Emmons, W. H., and Simon, C. W. The non-recall of material presented during sleep. *American Journal of Psychology* 69: 79-81, 1956.

Evans, F. J. Hypnosis and sleep: techniques for exploring cognitive activity during sleep. In *Hypnosis: Developments in Research and New Perspectives.* E. Fromm and R. E. Shor (eds.). New York: Aldine, 1979.

Faraday, A. *Dream Power.* New York: Coward, McCann, and Geoghegan, 1972.

Feinstein, B., and Sterman, M. B. Effects on sensorimotor rhythm biofeedback training on insomnia. Paper presented at the annual meeting of the Biofeedback Research Society, Colorado Springs, February 1974.

Fishburne, P. M., Abelson, H. I., and Cisin, I. (eds.). *National Survey of Drug Abuse: Main Findings, 1979.* Rockville, MD: National Institute of Drug Abuse, 1979.

Fisher, C. Dreaming and sexuality. In *Psychoanalysis: A General Psychology.* L. Lowenstein, M. Newman, M. M. Schur, and A. Solnit (eds.). New York: International University Press, 1966.

Fisher, L. E., and Kotses, H. Race differences and experimenter race effect in galvanic skin response. *Psychophysiology* 10: 578-582, 1973.

Fisher, L. E., and Kotses, H. Experimenter and subject sex effects in the skin conductance response. *Psychophysiology* 11: 191-196, 1974.

Fisher, S. Problems of interpretation and controls in hypnotic research. In *Hypnosis: Current Problems.* G. H. Estabrooks (ed.). New York: Harper & Row, 1962.

Fosshage, J. L., and Olsen, P. (eds.). *Healing: Implications for Psychotherapy.* New York: Human Sciences, 1978.

Foulkes, D. Dream reports from different stages of sleep. *Journal of Abnormal and Social Psychology* 65: 14-25, 1962.

Fowler, R. L., and Kimmel, H. D. Operant conditioning of the GSR. *Journal of Experimental Psychology* 63: 563-567, 1962.

Fredericks, L. E. The value of teaching hypnosis in the practice of anesthesiology. *International Journal of Clinical and Experimental Hypnosis* 28: 6-15, 1980.

Freedman, S. J., and Greenblatt, M. Studies in human isolation. WADC Technical Report no. 59-266. Wright-Patterson AFB, OH: Aero-Medical Laboratory, Wright Air Development Center, 1959.

Freedman, S. J., and Held, R. Sensory deprivation and perceptual lag. *Perceptual and Motor Skills* 11: 277-280, 1960.

French, T., and Fromm, E. *Dream Interpretation: A New Approach.* New York: Basic Books, 1964.

Freud, S. On the general effect of cocaine. Lecture given at Psychiatric Union, March 5, 1885. Reprinted in *Drug Dependence* 5: 17, 1970.

Freud, S. *Totem and Taboo.* London: Penguin, 1913.

Fridlund, A. J., Fowler, S. C., and Pritchard, D. A. Striate muscle tension patterning in frontalis EMG biofeedback. *Psychophysiology* 17: 47-55, 1980.

Friedman, R. M., Schmeidler, G. R., and Dean, E. D. Ranked-target scoring for mood and intragroup effects in precognitive ESP. *Journal of the American Society for Psychical Research* 70: 195-206, 1976.

Frohlich, E. D. Hypertension and hypertensive heart disease. In *Quick Reference to Cardiovascular Diseases.* E. K. Chung (ed.). Philadelphia: J. B. Lippincott, 1977.

Fromm, E. and Shor, R. E. (eds.). *Hypnosis: Developments in Research and New erspectives.* New York: Aldine, 1979.

Fuchs, K., Hoch, Z., and Kleinhauz, M. Hypno-desentization therapy of vaginismus. Paper presented at the International Congress of Hypnosis and Psychosomatic Medicine, Philadelphia, 1976.

Fuchs, K., Hoch, Z., Paldi, E., Abromovici, H., Brandes, J. M., Timor-Tritsch, I., and Kleinhauz, M. Hypno-desentization therapy of vaginismus: Part I. In vitro method. Part II. In vivo method. *International Journal of Clinical and Experimental Hypnosis* 21: 144-156, 1973.

Fujimori, M., and Himwich, H. E. Electrographic analysis of amphetamine and its methoxy derivatives with reference to their sites of EEG alerting in the rabbit brain. *International Journal of Neuropharmacology* 8: 601–615, 1969.

Fuller, G. D. Current status of biofeedback in clinical practice. *American Psychologist* 33: 39–48, 1978.

Fuxe, K., and Jonsson, G. Further mapping of central 5-hydroxytryptamine neurons: studies with the neurotoxic dihydroxytryptamines. *Advancements in Biochemical Psychopharmacology* 10: 1–12, 1974.

Gaarder, K. R., and Montgomery, P. S. *Clinical Biofeedback: A Procedural Manual.* Baltimore: Williams and Wilkins, 1977.

Galaburda, A. M., LeMay, M., Kemper, T. L., and Geschwind, N. Right–left asymmetries in the brain. *Science* 199: 852–856, 1978.

Galin, D., and Ornstein, R. E. Lateral specialization of cognitive mode: An EEG study. *Psychophysiology* 9: 412–418, 1972.

Gannon, L., and Sternbach, R. A. Alpha enhancement as a treatment for pain: a case study. *Behavior Therapy and Experimental Psychiatry* 2: 209–213, 1971.

Gastaut, H., and Broughton, R. A clinical polygraphic study of episodic phenomena during sleep. (academic address). In *Recent Advances in Biological Psychiatry*, vol. 7. J. Wortis (ed.). New York: Plenum Press, 1965.

Gatchel, R. J., and Price, K. P. *Clinical Applications of Biofeedback: Appraisal and Status.* New York: Pergamon Press, 1979.

Gazzaniga, M. S., Bogen, J. E., and Sperry, R. W. Observations on visual perception after disconnection of the cerebral hemispheres in man. *Brain* 8: 221–236, 1965.

Gazzaniga, M. S., and Sperry, R. W. Language after section of the cerebral commissures. *Brain* 90: 131–148, 1967.

Geschwind, N., and Levitsky, W. Human brain: left-right asymmetries in temporal speech regions. *Science* 161: 186–187, 1968.

Gibbs, F. A., Davis. H., and Lennox, W. G. The electroencephalogram in epilepsy and in conditions of impaired consciousness. *Archives of Neurology and Psychiatry* 34: 1133–1148, 1935.

Glueck, B. Quoted in the *Hartford Courant*, May 27, 1973, p. 6.

Glueck, B. C., and Stroebel, C. F. Biofeedback and meditation in the treatment of psychiatric illnesses. *Comprehensive Psychiatry* 16: 303–321, 1975.

Goleman, D. *The Varieties of the Meditative Experience.* New York: Dutton, 1977.

Goleman, D., and Davidson, R. J. *Consciousness: Brain, States of Awareness, and Mysticism.* New York: Harper & Row, 1979.

Goodenough, D. R. Dream recall: history and current status of the field. In *The Mind in Sleep: Psychology and Psychophysiology.* A. M. Arkin, J. S. Atrobus, and S. J. Ellman (eds.). Hillsdale, NJ: Lawrence Erlbaum Associates, 1978.

Goodenough, D. R., Witkin, H. A., Koulack, D., and Cohen, H. The effects of stress films on dream affect and on respiration and eye movement during rapid-eye movement sleep. *Psychophysiology* 15: 313-320, 1975.

Gordon, H. W., and Sperry, R. W. Olfaction following surgical disconnection of the hemisphere in man. Paper presented at the annual meetings of the Psychonomic Society, Austin, TX, 1968.

Graham, G. W. Hypnotic treatment for migraine headaches. *International Journal of Clinical and Experimental Hypnosis* 23: 165-171, 1975.

Green, K. *The Ocular Effects of Cannabinoids.* Vol. 1. *Current Topics in Eye Research.* New York: Academic Press, 1979.

Grilly, D. M. A Reply to Miller's 'The habit of Sherlock Holmes.' *Transactions and Studies of the College of Physicians of Philadelphia* (third series) 45: 252-257, 1978.

Grinspoon, L. Marihuana. *Scientific American* 221: 17-25, 1969.

Guerra, F. *The Pre-Columbian Mind.* New York: Seminar Press, 1971.

Guilleminault, C., Eldridge, F. L., and Dement, W. C. Insomnia with sleep apnea: a new syndrome. *Science* 181: 856-858, 1973.

Gutmann, M. C., and Benson, H. Interaction of environmental factors and systemic arterial blood pressure: a review. *Medicine* 50: 543-553, 1971.

Haber, R. N., and Haber, R. B. Eidetic imagery. I. Frequency. *Perceptual and Motor Skills* 19: 131-138, 1964.

Haber, R. N., and Hershenson, M. *The Psychology of Visual Perception.* New York: Holt, Rinehart, and Winston, 1980.

Haigler, H. J., and Aghajanian, G. K. Lysergic acid diethylamide and serotonin: a comparison of effects on serotenergic neurons and neurons receiving a serotonergic input. *Journal of Pharmacology and Experimental Therapeutics* 188: 688-699, 1974.

Hall, C. S. What people dream about. *Scientific American* 184: 60-63, 1951.

Hall, C. S., and Lindzey, G. *Theories of Personality* (3rd ed.). New York: Wiley, 1978.

Hall, C. S., and Van de Castle, R. L. *The Content Analysis of Dreams.* New York: Appleton-Century-Crofts, 1966.

Hall, J. S., and Crasilneck, H. B. Development of a hypnotic technique for treating chronic cigarette smoking. *International Journal of Clinical and Experimental Hypnosis* 18: 283-289, 1970.

Hamilton, W. *Lectures on Metaphysics.* New York: Sheldon, 1880.

Hart, J. T. Autocontrol of EEG alpha. Paper presented at the annual meeting of the Society for Psychophysiological Research, San Diego, October 1967.

Hartmann, E. L. *The Functions of Sleep.* New Haven: Yale University Press, 1973.

Hartmann, E., Baekeland, F., Zwilling, G., and Hoy, P. Sleep need: how much sleep and what kind? *American Journal of Psychiatry* 127: 1001-1008, 1971.

Harwood, C. W. Operant heart rate conditioning. *Psychological Record* 12: 279-284, 1962.

Hauri, P. Biofeedback technique in the treatment of serious, chronic insomniacs.

Paper presented at the annual meeting of the Biofeedback Society of America, Albuquerque, March 1978.

Hebb, D. O. *The Organization of Behavior.* New York: Wiley, 1949.

Helper, R. S., and Frank, I. M. Marijuana smoking and intraocular pressure. *JAMA* 217: 1392, 1971.

Heron, W., Bexton, W. H., and Hebb, D. O. Cognitive effects of decreased variation to sensory environment (abstract). *American Psychologist* 8: 366, 1953.

Heron, W., Doane, B. K., and Scott, T. H. Visual disturbances after prolonged perceptual isolation. *Canadian Journal of Psychology* 10: 13–18, 1956.

Hess, W. R. Das Schlafsyndrom als Folgedienzephaler Reizung *Helvetica Physiologica et Pharmacologica Acta* 2: 305–344, 1944.

Hilgard, E. R. *The Experience of Hypnosis.* New York: Harcourt, Brace, and World, 1965.

Hilgard, E. R. A neodissociation interpretation of pain reduction in hypnosis. *Psychological Review* 80: 396–411, 1973.

Hilgard, E. R. Neodissociation theory of multiple cognitive controls. In *Consciousness and Self-Regulation: Advances in Research.* G. E. Schwartz and D. Shapiro (eds.). New York: Plenum Press, 1976.

Hilgard, E. R. Controversies over consciousness and the rise of cognitive psychology. *Australian Psychologist,* 12: 7–27, 1977a.

Hilgard, E. R. *Divided Consciousness: Multiple Controls in Human Thought and Action.* New York: John Wiley and Sons, 1977b.

Hilgard, E. R. Divided consciousness in hypnosis: the implications of the hidden observer. In *Hypnosis: Developments in Research and New Perspectives.* E. Fromm and R. E. Shor (eds.). New York: Aldine, 1979.

Hilgard, E. R., and Hilgard, J. R. *Hypnosis in the Relief of Pain.* Los Altos, CA: Kaufmann, 1975.

Hofmann, A. LSD discoverer disputes 'chance' factor in finding. *Psychiatric News* 6: 23–26, 1971.

Honorton, C. Replicability, experimenter influence, and parapsychology: an empirical context for the study of mind. Paper presented at the Annual Meeting of the American Association for the Advancement of Science, Washington, D. C., February 1978.

Horowitz, M. J. Flashbacks: recurrent intrusive images after the use of LSD. *American Journal of Psychiatry* 126: 147–151, 1969.

Hothersall, D., and Brener, J. Operant conditioning of changes in heart rates in curarized rats. *Journal of Comparative and Physiological Psychology* 68: 338–342, 1969.

Hubel, D. H., and Wiesel, T. N. Brain mechanisms of vision. In *The Brain (Scien tific American Reprints).* San Francisco: W. H. Freeman, 1979.

Hughes, J., Smith, T. W., Kosterlitz, H. W., Fothergill, L. A., Morgan, B. A., and Morris, H. R. Identification of two related pentapeptides from the brain with potent opiate agonist activity. *Nature* 258: 577–579, 1975.

Hull, J., and Zubek, J. P. Personality characteristics of successful and unsuccessful sensory isolation subjects. *Perceptual and Motor Skills* 14: 231-240, 1962.

Hurston, Z. N. *Mules and Men*. Bloomington: Indiana University Press, 1978.

Hutchings, D. F., and Reinking, R. H. Tension headaches: what form of therapy is most effective? *Biofeedback and Self-Regulation* 1: 183-190, 1976.

Irwin, H. J. ESP and the human information processing system. *Journal of the American Society for Psychical Research* 72: 111-126, 1978a.

Irwin, H. J. Psi, attention, and processing capacity. *Journal of the American Society for Psychical Research* 72: 301-313, 1978b.

Isabell, H., and White, W. M. Clinical characteristics of addictions. *American Journal of Medicine* 14: 558-565, 1953.

Itard, J. M. G. *The Wild Boy of Aveyron*. Trans. by George Humphrey and Muriel Humphrey. New York: Appleton-Century-Crofts, 1932.

Jaffe, J. H. Drug addiction and drug abuse. In *The Pharmacological Basis of Therapeutics* (6th ed.). A. G. Goodman, L. S. Goodman, and A. Gilman (eds.). New York: Macmillan, 1980.

James, W. *Principles of Psychology*, vol. 1. New York: Holt, 1890.

James, W. Does consciousness exist? *Journal of Philosophy, Psychology, and Scientific Methods* 1: 477-491, 1904.

Janowsky, D. S., Meacham, M. P., Blaine, J. D., Schorr, M., and Bozzetti, L. P. Marijuana effects on simulated flying ability. *American Journal of Psychiatry* 133: 384-388, 1976.

Jarvik, M. E. The psychopharmacological revolution. *Psychology Today* 1: 51-58, 1967.

Jaynes, J. *The Origin of Consciousness in the Breakdown of the Bicameral Mind*. Boston: Houghton Mifflin, 1976.

Johnson, L. C., and MacLeod, W. L. Sleep and awake behavior during gradual sleep reduction. *Perceptual and Motor Skills* 36: 87-97, 1973.

Johnson, L. C., Slye, E., and Dement, W. C. EEG and autonomic activity during and after prolonged sleep deprivation. *Psychonomic Medicine* 27: 415-423, 1965.

Johnson, R. F. Q., Maher, B. A., and Barber, T. X. Artifact in the 'essence of hypnosis': an evaluation of trance logic. *Journal of Abnormal Psychology* 79: 212-220, 1972.

Johnson, W. G., and Turin, A. Biofeedback treatment of migraine headache: a systematic case study. *Behavior Therapy* 6: 394-397, 1975.

Jones, E. *The Life and Work of Sigmund Freud* (3 vols.). New York: Basic Books, 1953-1957.

Julesz, B. *Foundations of Cyclopean Perception*. Chicago: University of Chicago Press, 1971.

Kahn, E., Dement, W. C., Fisher, C., and Barmack, J. L. The incidence of color in immediately recalled dreams. *Science* 137: 1054, 1962.

Kahn, E., Fisher, C., and Edwards, A. Night terrors and anxiety dreams. In *The*

Mind in Sleep: Psychology and Psychophysiology. A. M. Arkin, J. S. Antrobus, and S. J. Ellman (eds.). Hillsdale, NJ: Lawrence Erlbaum Associates, 1978.

Kahneman, D. *Attention and Effort.* Englewood Cliffs, NJ: Prentice-Hall, 1973.

Kamiya, J. Conscious control of brain waves. *Psychology Today* 1: 57-60, 1968.

Kamiya, J. Operant control of the EEG alpha rhythm and some of its reported effects on consciousness. In *Altered States of Consciousness.* C. T. Tart (ed.). New York: Wiley, 1969.

Kasamatsu, A., and Hirai, T. Science of Zazen. *Psychologia,* 6: 86-91, 1963.

Kasamatsu, A., and Hirai, T. An electroencephalographic study on the Zen meditation. *Folia Psychiatrica et Neurologia Japonica* 20: 315-336, 1966.

Kasamatsu, A., and Hirai, T. An electroencephalographic study of the Zen meditation (Zazen). *Psychologia* 12: 205-225, 1969.

Katkin, E. S., and Murray, E. N. Instrumental conditioning of autonomically mediated behavior: theoretical and methodological issues. *Psychological Bulletin* 70: 52-68, 1969.

Katkin, E. S., Murray, E. N., and Lachman, R. Concerning instrumental autonomic conditioning: a rejoinder. *Psychological Bulletin* 71: 462-466, 1969.

Katz, M. M., Waskow, E. E., and Olsson, J. Characteristics of the psychological state produced by LSD. *Journal of Abnormal Psychology* 73: 1-14, 1968.

Kelly, H. A. *The Devil, Demonology and Witchcraft.* New York: Doubleday, 1974.

Kewman, D., and Roberts, A. H. Skin temperature biofeedback and migraine headaches. Paper presented at the annual conference of the Biofeedback Society of America, San Diego, CA, 1979.

Kimmel, H. D. Instrumental conditioning of autonomically mediated behavior. *Psychological Bulletin* 67: 337-345, 1967.

Kimmel, H. D. Instrumental conditioning of autonomically mediated responses in human beings. *American Psychologist* 29: 325-335, 1974.

Kimmel, H. D., and Hill, F. A. Operant conditioning of the GSR. *Psychological Reports* 7: 555-562, 1960.

Klonoff, H. Marijuana and driving in real-life situations. *Science* 186: 317-324, 1974.

Korner, A. F. REM organization in neonates: theoretical implications for development and the biological functions of REM. *Archives of General Psychiatry* 19: 330-340, 1968.

Krauss, H. H., Katzell, R., and Krauss, B. J. Effect of hypnotic time distortion upon free-recall learning. *Journal of Abnormal Psychology* 83: 140-144, 1974.

Krippner, S., Hickman, J., Auerhahn, N., and Harris, R. Clairvoyant perception of target material in three states of consciousness. *Perceptual and Motor Skills* 35: 439-446, 1972.

Krippner, S., and Rubin, D. (eds.). *The Kirlian Aura.* New York: Anchor Books, 1974.

Kristt, D. A., and Engel, B. T. Learned control of blood pressure in patients with high blood pressure. *Circulation* 51: 370-378, 1975.

Kroger, W. S. *Clinical and Experimental Hypnosis.* Philadelphia: J. B. Lippincott, 1977.

Kubzansky, P. E. The effects of reduced environmental stimulation on human behavior: a review. In *The Manipulation of Human Behavior.* A. D. Biderman and H. Zimmer (eds.). New York: John Wiley and Sons, 1961, pp. 51-95.

Kunnes, R. Double dealing in dope. *Human Behavior* 2: 22-27, 1973.

Lang, P. J., and Lazovik, A. D. Experimental desensitization of a phobia. *Journal of Abnormal and Social Psychology* 66: 519-525, 1963.

Lanyon, R. I., Barrington, C. C., and Newman, A. C. Modification of stuttering through EMG biofeedback: a preliminary study. *Behavior Therapy* 7: 96-103, 1976.

Levine, J. LSD—a chemical overview. In *Drugs and the Brain.* P. Black (ed.). Baltimore: Johns Hopkins Press, 1969.

Lilly, J. C. Mental effects of reduction of ordinary levels of physical stimuli in intact, healthy persons. *Psychiatric Research Reports* 5: 1-28, 1956.

Lilly, J. *Center of the Cyclone: An Autobiography of Inner Space.* New York: Julian, 1972.

Lindsey, P. H., and Norman, D. A. *Human Information Processing: An Introduction to Psychology* (2nd ed.). New York: Academic Press, 1977.

Lindsley, D. B. Psychological phenomena and the electro-encephalogram. *Electroencephalography and Clinical Neurophysiology* 4: 443-456, 1952.

Lindsley, D. B. Attention, consciousness, sleep, and wakefulness. In *Handbook of Physiology* vol. 3. Washington, D. C.: American Physiology Society, 1960.

Lindsley, D. B. Common factors in sensory deprivation, sensory distortion, and sensory overload. In *Sensory Deprivation: A Symposium.* P. Solomon, P. Kubzansky, P. Leiderman, J. Mendelson, R. Trumbull, and D. Wexler (eds.). Cambridge: Harvard University Press, 1961.

Lindsley, D. B., Bowden, J., and Magoun, H. Effect upon the EEG of acute injury to the brain stem activating system. *Electroencephalography and Clinical Neurophysiology* 1: 475-486, 1949.

Lisina, M. I. The role of orientation in the transformation of involuntary reactions into voluntary ones. In *Orienting Reflex and Exploratory Behavior.* L. G. Veronin, A. H. Leontiev, A. R. Luria, C. N. Sokolov, and O. S. Vinogradova (eds.). Washington, D. C.: American Institute of Biological Sciences, 1965.

Locke, J. *An Essay Concerning Human Understanding.* Oxford: Oxford University Press, 1975 (first published in 1690).

Loftus, E. F. *Eyewitness Testimony.* Cambridge: Harvard University Press, 1979.

Loftus, E. F. *Memory.* Reading, MA: Addison-Wesley, 1980.

London, P., Hart, J. T., and Leibovitz, M. P. EEG alpha rhythms and susceptibility to hypnosis. *Nature* 219: 71-72, 1968.

Loomis, A. L., Harvey, E. N., and Hobart, G. A. Potential rhythms of the cerebral cortex during sleep. *Science* 81: 597-598, 1935.

Loomis, A. L., Harvey, E. N., and Hobart, G. A. Cerebral states during sleep, as studied by human brain potentials. *Journal of Experimental Psychology* 21: 127-144, 1937.

Lubar, J. F., and Shouse, M. N. EEG and behavioral changes in a hyperkinetic child concurrent with training of the sensorimotor rhythm (SMR): a preliminary report. *Biofeedback and Self-Regulation* 1: 293-306, 1976.

Lubin, A., Moses, J., Johnson, L. C., and Naitoh, P. The recuperative effects of REM sleep and stage 4 sleep on human performance after complete sleep loss: experiment 1. *Psychophysiology* 2: 125-132, 1974.

Luce, G. G. *Research on Sleep and Dreams.* Bethesda, MD: National Institute of Mental Health, 1965.

Luria, A. R. *Higher Cortical Functions in Man.* New York: Basic Books, 1966.

Lynch, J. J., and Paskewitz, D. A. On the mechanism of the feedback control of human brain wave activity. *Journal of Nervous and Mental Disease* 153: 205-217, 1971.

MacNeill, M., and Zubek, J. P. Effects of prolonged visual deprivation (dark-rearing) on the weight of the sensory cortex of the rat. *Canadian Journal of Psychology* 21: 177-183, 1967.

Malcolm, N. Behaviorism as a philosophy of psychology. In T. W. Wann (ed.). *Behaviorism and Phenomenology: Contrasting Bases for Modern Psychology.* Chicago: University of Chicago Press, 1964.

Mandler, G., Preven, D. W., and Kuhlman, C. K. Effects of operant reinforcement on the GSR. *Journal of the Experimental Analysis of Behavior* 62: 552-559, 1962.

Marcus, E. M. Clinical considerations of the cerebral hemispheres and a general survey of neuropathology. In *An Introduction to the Neurosciences.* B. A. Curtis, S. Jacobson, E. M. Marcus (eds.). Philadelphia: W. B. Saunders, 1972.

Mars, L., and Devereux, G. Haitian voodoo and the ritualization of the nightmare. *Psychoanalytic Review* 38: 334-342, 1951.

Martindale, W. *Extrapharmacopoeia* (25th ed.). London: The Pharmaceutical Press, 1967.

Mathis, J. L. Sexual aspects of heroin addiction. *Medical Aspects of Human Sexuality* 4: 98-109, 1970.

McCarthy, L. E., and Borison, H. L. Antiemetic activity of nabilone, a cannabinol derivative, reversed by naloxone in awake cats. *Pharmacologist* 19: 230, 1977.

Melzack, R., and Perry, C. Self-regulation of pain: the use of alpha-feedback and hypnotic training for the control of chronic pain. *Experimental Neurology* 46: 452–469, 1975.

Meyer, D. *The Positive Thinkers.* Garden City, NY: Doubleday, 1965.

Midelfort, H. C. E. *Witch Hunting in Southwestern Germany, 1562–1684.* Stanford, CA: Stanford University Press, 1972.

Miller, N. E. Learning of visceral and glandular responses. *Science* 163: 434–445, 1969.

Miller, N. E. Postscript. In *Current Status of Physiological Psychology: Readings.* D. Singh, and C. T. Morgan (eds.). Monterey: Brooks-Cole, 1972.

Miller, N. E., and Banuzzizi, A. Instrumental learning by curarized rats of a specific visceral response, intestinal or cardiac. *Journal of Comparative and Physiological Psychology* 65: 1–7, 1968.

Miller, N. E., and DiCara, L. V. Instrumental learning of heart rate changes in curarized rats: shaping and specificity to a descriminative stimulus. *Journal of Comparative and Physiological Psychology* 63: 12, 1967.

Miller, N. E., and Dworkin, B. R. Visceral learning: recent difficulties with curarized rats and significant problems for human research. In *Cardiovascular Psychophysiology.* P. A. Obrist, A. H. Black, J. Brener, and L. V. DiCara (eds.). Chicago: Aldine, 1974.

Miller, N. E., and Dworkin, B. R. Critical issues in therapeutic applications of biofeedback. In *Biofeedback Theory and Research.* G. E. Schwartz, and J. Beatty (eds.). New York: Academic Press, 1977.

Miller, S., and Konorski, J. On a particular type of conditioned reflex. *Proceedings of the Biological Society* (Polish Section, Paris) 99: 1155–1157, 1928.

Mills, G. K., and Solyom, L. Biofeedback of EEG alpha in the treatment of obsessive ruminations: an exploration. *Journal of Behavior Therapy and Experimental Psychiatry* 5: 37–41, 1974.

Milner, B. Visually guided maze learning in man: effects of bilateral, frontal, and unilateral cerebral lesions. *Neuropsychologia* 3: 317–338, 1965.

Milner, B., Branch, C., and Rasmussen, T. Evidence for bilateral speech representation in some non–right-handers. *Transactions of the American Neurological Association,* 91: 306–308, 1966.

Montandon, H. E. Psychophysiological aspects of the Kirlian phenomenon: a confirmatory study. *Journal of the American Society for Psychical Research* 71: 45–49, 1977.

Moruzzi, G., and Magoun, H. W. Brainstem reticular formation and activation of the EEG. *Electroencephalography and Clinical Neurophysiology* 1: 455–473, 1949.

Moss, S., and Butler, D. C. The scientific credibility of ESP. *Perceptual and Motor Skills* 46: 1063–1079, 1978.

Moss, T., and Johnson, K. Bioplasma or corona discharge? In *The Kirlian Aura.* S. Krippner and D. Rubin (eds.). New York: Anchor Books, 1974.

Mowrer, O. H. Preparatory set (expectancy)– a determinant in motivation and learning. *Psychological Review* 85: 61–91, 1938.

Murphy, G., and Ballou, R. O. *William James on Psychical Research.* New York: Viking Press, 1969.

Murphy, P. J., Darwin, J., and Murphy, D. A. EEG feedback training for cerebral dysfunction: a research program with learning disabled adolescents. *Biofeedback and Self-Regulation* 2: 288, 1977.

Nanamoli, T. *Mindfulness of Breathing.* Kandy, Ceylon: Buddhist Publication Society, 1964.

Nanamoli, T. *Visuddhimagga: The Path of Purification.* Berkeley: Shambala, 1976.

National Institute of Drug Abuse. *Marijuana and Health. Third Annual Report to Congress from the Secretary of Health, Education and Welfare.* Washington, D. C.: U.S. Government Printing Office, 1976.

National Institute of Drug Abuse. *Marijuana Research Findings.* Research Monograph no. 14, 1976.

Natsoulas, T. Consciousness. *American Psychologist* 33: 906–914, 1978a.

Natsoulas, T. Toward a model for consciousness in the light of B. F. Skinner's contribution. *Behaviorism* 6: 139–176, 1978b.

Natsoulas, T. The unity of consciousness. *Behaviorism* 7: 45–63, 1979.

Nauta, W. J. H. Hypothalamic regulation of sleep in rats: experimental study. *Journal of Neurophysiology* 9: 285–316, 1946.

Nowlis, V. Research with the mood adjective checklist. In *Affect, Cognition, and Personality.* S. S. Tomkins and C. E. Izard (eds.). New York: Springer, 1965.

Nowlis, D., and Kamiya, J. The control of electroencephalographic alpha rhythms through auditory feedback and the associated mental activity. *Psychophysiology* 6: 476–484, 1970.

O'Connell, D. N., Shor, R. E., and Orne, M. T. Hypnotic age regression: an empirical and methodological analysis. *Journal of Abnormal Psychology Monograph Supplement* 76: 1–32, 1970.

Oesterreich, T. K. *Possession: Demoniacal and Other, Among Primitive Races in Antiquity, the Middle Ages, and Modern Times.* New Hyde Park, NY: University Books, 1966.

Orne, M. T. The nature of hypnosis: artifact and essence. *Journal of Abnormal and Social Psychology* 58: 277–299, 1959.

Orne, M. T. On the social psychology of the psychological experiment: with particular reference to demand characteristics and their implications. *American Psychologist* 17: 776–783, 1962.

Orne, M. T. On the simulating subject as a quasi-control group in hypnosis research: why, what, and how. In *Hypnosis: Developments in Research and New Perspectives.* E. Fromm and R. E. Shor (eds.). New York: Aldine, 1979.

Ornstein, R. E. *The Psychology of Consciousness.* San Francisco: W. F. Freeman, 1972

Ornstein, R. *The Psychology of Consciousness.* New York: Harcourt, Brace, Jovanovich, 1977.

Oswald, I. Drugs and sleep. *Pharmacological Review* 20: 272-303, 1968.

Oxford English Dictionary. Oxford: Oxford University Press, 1933.

Palmer, J. Scoring in ESP tests as a function of belief in ESP. Part I: The sheepgoat effect. *Journal of the American Society for Psychical Research* 65: 373-408, 1971.

Paskewitz, D. A. Biofeedback instrumentation: soldering closed the loop. *American Psychologist* 30: 371-378, 1975.

Pert, C. B., and Snyder, S. H. Opiate receptor: demonstration in nervous tissue. *Science* 179: 1011-1014, 1973.

Petersen, R. C. (ed.). *Marijuana Research Findings.* National Institute of Drug Abuse Research Monograph no. 14, Rockville, MD: National Institute of Drug Abuse, 1977.

Petersen, R. C. *Cocaine.* Statement of R. C. Petersen (NIDA, Alcohol, Drug Abuse, and Mental Health Administration Public Health Service, DHEW) Before the Select Committee on Narcotics Abuse and Control, House of Representatives, July 24, 1979.

Petersen, R. C. *Marijuana and Health.* DHEW Publication no. (ADM) 80-945. Eighth Annual Report to the U. S. Congress from the Secretary of DHEW. Washington, D. C.: U. S. Government Printing Office, 1980.

Plotkin, W. B., and Cohen, R. Occipital alpha and attributes of the 'alpha experience.' *Psychophysiology* 13: 16-21, 1976.

Post, R. M. Cocaine psychosis: a continuum model. *American Journal of Psychiatry* 132: 225-231, 1975.

Powell, D. H. Helping habitual smokers using flooding and hypnotic desensitization techniques. *International Journal of Clinical and Experimental Hypnosis* 28: 192-196, 1980.

Pratt, J. G. *ESP research today: A Study of Developments in Parapsychology Since 1960.* Metuchen, NJ: Scarecrow Press, 1973a.

Pratt, J. G. A decade of research with a selected ESP subject: an overview and reappraisal of the work with Pavel Stepanek. *Proceedings of the American Society for Psychical Research* 30: 1-78, 1973b.

Pratt, J. G., and Roll, W. G. The Seaford disturbances. *Journal of Parapsychology* 22: 79-124, 1958.

Pratt, J. G., and Woodruff, J. L. Size of stimulus symbols in extrasensory perception. *Journal of Parapsychology* 3: 121-158, 1939.

Puccetti, R. The case for mental duality: evidence from split-brain data and other considerations. *Behavioral and Brain Sciences* 4: 93-124, 1981.

Raikov, V. L. Age regression to infancy by adult subjects in deep hypnosis. *American Journal of Clinical Hypnosis* 22: 156-163, 1980.

Rao, K. Ramakrishna. *Experimental Parapsychology.* Springfield, IL: Charles C Thomas, 1966.

Rao, K. Ramakrishna. On the nature of psi: an examination of some attempts to explain ESP and PK. *Journal of Parapsychology* 41: 294-351, 1977.

Rao, K. Ramakrishna. On 'the scientific credibility of ESP.' *Perceptual and Motor Skills* 49: 415-429, 1979.

Ray, O. *Drugs, Society, and Human Behavior.* St. Louis: C. V. Mosby, 1978.

Reading, C., and Mohr, P. D. Biofeedback control of migraine: a pilot study. *British Journal of Social and Clinical Psychology* 15: 429-433, 1976.

Rechtschaffen, A., and Dement, W. C. Narcolepsy and hypersomnia. In *Sleep: Physiology and Pathology.* A. Kales (ed.). Philadelphia: J. B. Lippincott, 1969.

Rechtschaffen, A., Verdone, P., and Wheaton, J. Reports of mental activity during sleep. *Canadian Psychiatric Association Journal* 8: 409-414, 1963.

Rechtschaffen, A., Wolpert, E. A., Dement, W. C., Mitchell, S. A., and Fisher, C. Nocturnal sleep of narcoleptics. *Electroencephalography and Clinical Neurophysiology* 15: 599-609, 1963.

Resnick, R. B., Kestenbaum, R. S., and Schwartz, L. K. Acute systematic effects of cocaine in man: a controlled study by intranasal and intravenous routes of administration. *Science* 195: 696-698, 1977.

Restak, R. The brain makes its own narcotics. *Saturday Review* March 5, 1977, pp. 8-11.

Rhine, J. B. *Extrasensory Perception.* Boston: Bruce Humphries, 1964. (first published in 1934).

Rhine, J. B. Parapsychology and dualism (editorial). *Journal of Parapsychology* 9: 225-228, 1945.

Rhine, J. B. *New World of the Mind.* New York: William Sloan, 1953.

Rhine, J. B., and Brier, R. (eds.). *Parapsychology Today.* New York: Citadel Press, 1968.

Rhine, J. B., and Pratt, J. G. *Parapsychology: Frontier Science of the Mind.* Springfield, IL: Charles C Thomas, 1957.

Rhine, L. E. *Hidden Channels of the Mind.* New York: Sloan Associates, 1961.

Rhine, L. E. *Mind Over Matter.* New York: Macmillan, 1970.

Ricalla, L. M. Healing by laying on of hands: myth or fact? *Ethics in Science and Medicine* 2: 167-171, 1975.

Rinkel, M. Psychedelic drugs. *American Journal of Psychiatry* 122: 1415-1416, 1966.

Robertson, M. H. Theoretical implications of sensory deprivation. *Psychological Records* 11: 33-42, 1961.

Robertson, M. H., and Wolter, D. J. The effect of sensory deprivation upon scores on the Wechsler Adult Intelligence Scale. *Journal of Psychology* 56: 213-218, 1963.

Roffwarg, H. P., Muzio, J. N., and Dement, W. C. Ontogenetic development of the human sleep-dream cycle. *Science* 152: 604-619, 1966.

Rosenthal, R. *Experimenter Effects in Behavioral Research.* New York: Appleton-Century-Crofts, 1966.

Rosenzweig, N. Sensory deprivation and schizophrenia: clinical and theoretical similarities. *American Journal of Psychiatry* 116: 326-329, 1959.

Rubin, S. *Current Research in Hypnopaedia.* New York: American Elsevier, 1968.

Sampson, H. Psychological effects of deprivation of dreaming sleep. *Journal of Nervous and Mental Disease* 143: 305-317, 1966.

Sargant, W. *The Mind Possessed.* New York: Penguin, 1975.

Sargent, J. D., Green, E. E., and Walters, E. D. Preliminary report on the use of autogenic feedback techniques in the treatment of migraine and tension headaches. *Psychosomatic Medicine* 35: 129-135, 1973.

Sattler, J. M. Racial 'experimenter effects' in experimentation, testing, interviewing, and psychotherapy. *Psychological Bulletin* 73: 137-160, 1970.

Schedivy, D. I., and Kleinman, K. M. Lack of correlation between frontalis EMG and either neck EMG or verbal ratings of tension. *Psychophysiology* 14: 182-186, 1977.

Schlaadt, R. G., and Shannon, P. T. *Drugs of Choice: Current Perspectives in Drug Use.* Englewood Cliffs, NJ: Prentice-Hall, 1982.

Schlosberg, H. The relationship between success and the laws of conditioning. *Psychological Review* 44: 379-394, 1937.

Schmeidler, G. R., and McConnell, R. A. *ESP and Personality Patterns.* New Haven: Yale University Press, 1958.

Schmidt, H. Toward a mathematical theory of psi. *Journal of the American Society for Psychical Research* 69: 301-319, 1975.

Schultz, J. H., and Luthe, W. *Autogenic Therapy.* Vol. 1. New York: Grune and Stratton, 1969.

Schwartz, D. G., Weinstein, L. N., and Arkin, A. M. Qualitative aspects of sleep mentation. In *The Mind in Sleep: Psychology and Psychophysiology.* A. M. Arkin, J. S. Antrobus, and S. J. Ellman (eds.). Hillsdale, NJ: Lawrence Erlbaum Associates, 1978.

Schwartz, G. E., and Beatty, J. *Biofeedback Theory and Research.* New York: Academic Press, 1977.

Scott, T. H., Bexton, W. H. Heron, W., and Doane, B. K. Cognitive effects of perceptual isolation. *Canadian Journal of Psychology* 13: 200-209, 1959.

Scriven, M. The frontiers of psychology: psychoanalysis and parapsychology. In *Philosophical Dimensions of Parapsychology.* J. M. O. Wheatley and H. L. Edge (eds.). Springfield, IL: Charles C Thomas, 1976.

Shah, I. *The Way of the Sufi.* New York: Dutton, 1970.

Sharpless, S. K. Hypnotics and sedatives. In *The Pharmacological Basis of Therapeutics.* L. Goodman and A. Gilman (eds.). New York: Macmillan, 1970.

Shearn, D. W. *Operant Conditioning of Heart Rate.* Ph.D. diss., Indiana University, 1960.

Sheer, D. E. (ed.). *Electrical Stimulation of the Brain.* Austin: University of Texas Press, 1961.

Shor, R. E. The fundamental problem in hypnosis research as viewed from historic perspectives. In *Hypnosis: Developments in Research and New Perspectives*. E. Fromm, and R. E. Shor (eds.). New York: Aldine, 1979.

Shor, R. E., and Orne, E. C. *The Harvard Group Scale of Hypnotic Susceptibility: Form A*. Palo Alto: Consulting Psychologists Press, 1962.

Shouse, M. N., and Lubar, J. F. Management of the hyperkinetic syndrome with methylphenidate and SMR biofeedback training. *Biofeedback and Self-Regulation* 2: 290, 1977.

Shouse, M. N., and Lubar, J. F. Operant conditioning of EEG rhythms and Ritalin in the treatment of hyperkinesis. *Biofeedback and Self-Regulation* 4: 299–312, 1979.

Shurley, J. T. Profound experimental sensory isolation. *American Journal of Psychiatry* 117: 539–545, 1960.

Shurley, J. T. Problems and methods in experimental sensory input alteration and variance. Unpublished paper, 1961.

Simantov, R., Goodman, R., Aposhian, D., and Snyder, S. H. Phylogenetic distribution of a morphine-like ligand 'enkephalin.' *Brain Research* 111: 204–211, 1976.

Skinner, B. F. *Science and Human Behavior*. New York: Macmillan, 1953.

Skinner, B. F. Behaviorism at fifty. In *Behaviorism and Phenomenology: Contrasting Bases for Modern Psychology*. T. W. Wann (ed.). Chicago: University of Chicago Press, 1964.

Skinner, B. F. *About Behaviorism*. New York: Alfred A. Knopf, 1974.

Slaughter, J., Hahn, W., and Rinaldi, R. Instrumental conditioning of heart rate in the curarized rat with varied amounts of pretraining. *Journal of Comparative and Physiological Psychology* 72: 356–359, 1970.

Smith, D. E., and Rose, A. J. LSD: its use, abuse, and suggested treatment. *Journal of Psychedelic Drugs* 1: 117–123, 1967–1968.

Smith, H. Do drugs have religious import? In *LSD: The Consciousness-Expanding Drug*. D. Solomon (ed.). New York: G. P. Putnam's Sons, 1964.

Snyder, F. The phenomenology of dreaming. In *The Psychodynamic Implications of the Physiological Studies on Dreams*. H. Madow and L. H. Snow (eds.). Springfield, IL: Charles C Thomas, 1970.

Snyder, S. H. Cannabis. *Psychology Today* 4: 37–40, 1971.

Snyder, S. H. The brain's own opiates. *Chemical and Engineering News* 55: 26–35, 1977.

Sokolov, E. N. *Perception and the Conditioned Reflex*. New York: Pergamon Press, 1963.

Spanos, N. P. Witchcraft in histories of psychiatry: a critical analysis and an alternative conceptualization. *Psychological Bulletin* 85: 417–439, 1978.

Spanos, N. P., and Gottlieb, J. Ergotism and the Salem village witch trials. *Science* 194: 1390–1394, 1976.

Spanos, N. P., Ham, M. W., and Barber, T. X. Suggested ('hypnotic') visual hallucinations: experimental and phenomenological data. *Journal of Abnormal Psychology* 81: 96–106, 1973.

Sperry, R. W. Cerebral organization and behavior. *Science* 133: 1749–1757, 1961.

Sperry, R. W. The great cerebral commissure. *Scientific American* 210: 42–52, 1964.

Sperry, R. W. Lateral specialization in the surgically separated hemispheres. In *The Neurosciences: Third Study Program.* F. O. Schmitt and F. G. Wordon (eds.). Cambridge: MIT Press, 1974.

Spiegel, H. An eye-roll sign for hypnotizability. Paper presented at the annual meeting of the Society for Clinical and Experimental Hypnosis, Philadelphia, October, 1970a.

Spiegel, H. A single-treatment method to stop smoking using ancillary self-hypnosis. *International Journal of Clinical and Experimental Hypnosis* 18: 235–250, 1979b.

Stambaugh, E. E., and House, A. E. Multimodality treatment of migraine headache: a case study utilizing biofeedback, relaxation, autogenic and hypnotic treatments. *American Journal of Clinical Hypnosis* 19: 235–240, 1977.

Stanford, R. G. An experimentally testable model for spontaneous psi events. I. Estrasensory events. *Journal of the American Society for Psychical Research* 68: 34–57, 1974.

Stanford, R. G. Are parapsychologists paradigmless in psiland? In *The Philosophy of Parapsychology.* B. Shapin and L. Coly (eds.). New York: Parapsychology Foundation, 1977a.

Stanford, R. G. Conceptual frameworks of contemporary psi research. In *Handbook of Parapsychology.* B. Wolman (ed.). New York: Van Nostrand Reinhold, 1977b.

Stanton, H. E. Weight loss through hypnosis. *American Journal of Clinical Hypnosis,* 18: 34–38, 1975.

Sterling-Smith, R. S. A special study of drivers most responsible in fatal accidents. *Summary for Management Report,* Contract DOT HS 310-3-595. Washington, D. C.: Department of Transportation, 1976.

Sterman, M. B. Neurophysiological and clinical studies of sensorimotor EEG biofeedback training: some effects on epilepsy. *Seminars in Psychiatry* 5: 507–525, 1973.

Sterman, M. B., and Friar, L. Suppression of seizures in an epileptic following sensorimotor EEG feedback training. *Electroencephalography and Clinical Neurophysiology* 33: 89–95, 1972.

Sterman, M. B., and MacDonald, L. R. Effects of central cortical EEG feedback training on seizure incidence in poorly controlled epileptics. *Epilepsia* 19: 207–222, 1978.

Stoyva, J., Budzynski, T., Sittenfeld, P., and Yaroush, R. A two-step EMG-theta feedback training in sleep onset insomnia: preliminary results. Paper presented at the annual meeting of the Biofeedback Research Society, Colorado Springs, February 1974.

Stromeyer, C. F., and Psotka, J. The detailed texture of eidetic images. *Nature* 225: 346-349, 1970.

Suedfeld, P. *Restricted Environmental Stimulation: Research and Clinical Applications.* New York: John Wiley and Sons, 1980.

Sugi, Y., and Akutsu, K. *Science of Zazen—Energy Metabolism.* Tokyo: University Press of Tokyo, 1964.

Targ, R., and Puthoff, H. ESP experiments with Uri Geller. In *Research in Parapsychology, 1973.* W. G. Roll, R. L. Morris, and J. D. Morris (eds.). Metuchen, NJ: Scarecrow Press, 1974.

Tart, C. T. Card guessing tests: learning paradigm or extinction paradigm? *Journal of the American Society for Psychical Research* 60: 46-55, 1966.

Tart, C. T. (ed.). *Altered States of Consciousness.* Garden City, NY: Doubleday, 1972.

Tart, C. T. *States of Consciousness.* New York: Dutton, 1975.

Tart, C. T. Putting the pieces together: a conceptual framework for understanding discrete states of consciousness. In *Alternate States of Consciousness: Multiple Perspectives on the Study of Consciousness.* N. E. Zinberg (ed.). New York: Free Press, 1977a.

Tart, C. T. Toward conscious control of psi through immediate feedback training: some considerations of internal processes. *Journal of the American Society for Psychical Research* 71: 375-407, 1977b.

Tart, C. T., Palmer, J., and Redington, D. J. Effects of Immediate feedback on ESP performance: a second study. *Journal of the American Society for Psychical Research* 73: 151-165, 1979a.

Tart, C. T., Palmer, J., and Redington, D. J. Effects of immediate feedback on ESP performance over short time periods. *Journal of the American Society for Psychical Research* 73: 291-301, 1979b.

Taylor, N. *Flight from Reality.* New York: Duell, Sloan and Pearce, 1949.

Tilley, A. J., and Empson, J. A. C. REM sleep and memory consolidation. *Biological Psychology* 6: 293-300, 1978.

Tinklenberg, J. R., and Woodrow, K. M. Drug use among youthful assaultive and sexual offenders. In *Aggression Research Publication.* S. H. Frazier (ed.). Association for Research in Nervous and Mental Disease, 1974.

Titchener, E. B. *Experimental Psychology of the Thought Process.* New York: Macmillan, 1909.

Travis, T. A., Kondo, C. Y., and Knott, J. R. Subjective aspects of alpha enhancement. *British Journal of Psychiatry* 127: 122-126, 1975.

Treisman, A., and Geffen, G. Selective attention: perception or response? *Quarterly Journal of Experimental Psychology* 19: 1-18, 1967.

Trevor-Roper, H. R. *The European Witch-Craze of the Sixteenth and Seventeenth Centuries and Other Essays.* New York: Harper & Row, 1969.

Trowill, J. A. Instrumental conditioning of heart rate in the curarized rat. *Journal of Comparative and Physiological Psychology* 63: 7-11, 1967.

True, R. M. Experimental control in hypnotic age regression states. *Science* 110: 583-584, 1949.

Turner, R. K., and Taylor, P. D. Conditioning treatment of nocturnal enuresis in adults: preliminary findings. *Behavioral Research and Therapy* 12: 41-52, 1974.

Ungerstedt, U. On the anatomy, pharmacology, and function of the nigrostriatal dopamine system. *Acta Physiological Scandinavica* 82: 95-122, 1971.

Vernon, J. A., and McGill, T. E. Time estimation during sensory deprivation. *Journal of General Psychology* 69: 11-18, 1963.

Vojtechovský, M., Safratová, V., Votava, Z., and Feit, V. The effects of sleep deprivation on learning and memory in healthy volunteers. *Activitas Nervosa Superior* 13: 143-144, 1971.

Wada, J. A new method for the determination of the side of cerebral speech dominance: a preliminary report on the intracarotid injection of sodium amytal in man. *Medical Biology*, 14: 221-222, 1949.

Walker, E. H. Foundations of paraphysical and parapsychological phenomena. In *Quantum Physics and Parapsychology*. L. Oteri (ed). New York: Parapsychology Foundation, 1975.

Walker, N. S., Garrett, J. B., and Wallace, B. Restoration of eidetic imagery via hypnotic age regression: a preliminary report. *Journal of Abnormal Psychology* 85: 335-337, 1976.

Wallace, B. Restoration of eidetic imagery via hypnotic age regression: more evidence. *Journal of Abnormal Psychology* 87: 673-675, 1978.

Wallace, B. Hypnotic susceptibility and the perception of afterimages and dot stimuli. *American Journal of Psychology* 92: 681-691, 1979.

Wallace, B., and Garrett, J. B. Hypnotic susceptibility and autokinetic movement frequency. *Perceptual and Motor Skills* 36: 1054, 1973.

Wallace, B., Garrett, J. B., and Anstadt, S. P. Hypnotic susceptibility, suggestion, and reports of autokinetic movement. *American Journal of Psychology* 87: 117-123, 1974.

Wallace, B., Knight, T. A., and Garrett, J. B. Hypnotic susceptibility and frequency reports to illusory stimuli. *Journal of Abnormal Psychology* 85: 558-563, 1976.

Wallace, R. K., and Benson, H. The physiology of meditation. *Scientific American* 226: 85-90, 1972.

Wallace, R. K., Benson, H., and Wilson, A. F. A wakeful hypometabolic physiological state. *American Journal of Physiology* 221: 795-799, 1971.

Wallechinsky, D., and Wallace, I. *The People's Almanac*. Garden City, NY: Doubleday, 1975.

Walsh, D. H. Interactive effects of alpha feedback and instructional set on subjective state. *Psychophysiology* 11: 428-435, 1974.

Walsh, R. N. Initial meditative experiences. Part II. *Journal of Transpersonal Psychology* 10: 1-28, 1978.

Walter, W. G. The location of cerebral tumors by electroencephalography. *Lancet* 2: 305–308, 1936.

Walter, W. G., and Dovey, V. J. Electro-encephalography in cases of subcortical tumour. *Journal of Neurology, Neurosurgery, and Psychiatry* 7: 57–65, 1944.

Walters, R. H., and Quinn, M. J. *A Comparison of the Effects of Social Deprivation and Sensory Deprivation on Autokinetic Judgements.* Unpublished manuscript, 1961.

Washburn, M. C. Observations relevant to a unified theory of meditation. *Journal of Transpersonal Psychology* 10: 45–65, 1978.

Watson, J. B. Psychology as the behaviorist views it. *Psychological Review* 20: 158–177, 1913.

Webb, W. B. Sleep research past and present. In *Sleep: An Active Process.* W. B. Webb (ed.). Glenview, IL: Scott, Foresman, 1973.

Webb, W. B. Sleep as an adaptive response. *Perceptual and Motor Skills* 37: 511–514, 1974.

Webb, W. B., and Agnew, H. W., Jr. Stage 4 sleep: influence of time course variables. *Science* 174: 1354–1356, 1971.

Webb, W. B., and Agnew, H. W., Jr. The effects of a chronic limitation of sleep length. *Psychophysiology* 11: 265–274, 1974.

Weber, E. S. P., and Fehmi, L. G. The therapeutic use of EEG biofeedback. Paper presented at the annual meeting of the Biofeedback Research Society, Colorado Springs, February 1974.

Weil, A. T. *The Natural Mind: A New Way of Looking at Drugs and the Higher Consciousness.* Boston: Houghton Mifflin, 1972.

Weil, A. T., Zinberg, N. E., and Nelson, J. N. Clinical and physiological effects of marihuana in man. *Science* 162: 1234–1242, 1968.

Weitzenhoffer, A. M., and Hilgard, E. R. *Stanford Hypnotic Susceptibility Scale, Forms A and B.* Palo Alto: Consulting Psychologists Press, 1959.

Weitzenhoffer, A. M., and Hilgard, E. R. *Stanford Hypnotic Susceptibility Scale: Form C.* Palo Alto: Consulting Psychologists Press, 1962.

Welwood, J. Meditation and the unconscious. *Journal of Transpersonal Psychology* 9: 1–26, 1977.

Wesson, D. R., and Smith, D. E. Barbiturate use as an intoxicant: a San Francisco perspective. Testimony given to the Subcommittee to Investigate Juvenile Delinquency, San Francisco, December 15, 1971.

Wetii, C. V., and Wright, R. K. Death caused by recreational cocaine use. *JAMA* 241: 2519–2522, 1979.

Wexler, D., Mendelson, J., Leiderman, P. H., and Solomon, P. Sensory deprivation: a technique for studying the psychiatric aspects of stress. *Archives of Neurology and Psychiatry* 79: 225–233, 1958.

Wheeler, L., Reis, H. T., Wolff, E., Grupsmith, E., and Mordkoff, A. M. Eye-roll and hypnotic susceptibility. *International Journal of Clinical and Experimental Hypnosis* 22: 327–334, 1974.

Whitlock, F. A. The psychiatry and psychopathology of paranormal phenomena. *Australian and New Zealand Journal of Psychiatry* 12: 11-19, 1978.

Whitwell, J. R. *Historical Notes on Psychiatry*. London: H. K. Lewis, 1936.

Wickramasekera, I. E. Electromyographic feedback training and tension headache: preliminary observations. *American Journal of Clinical Hypnosis* 15: 83-85, 1972.

Wickramasekera, I. E. Temperature feedback for the control of migraine. *Journal of Behavior Therapy and Experimental Psychiatry* 4: 343-345, 1973.

Williams, H. L., and Lubin, A. *Impaired Performance in a Case of Prolonged Sleep Loss*. Mimeographed paper. Washington, D. C.: Walter Reed Army Institute of Research, 1959.

Winkel, G. H., and Sarason, I. G. Subject, experimenter and situational variables in research on anxiety. *Journal of Abnormal and Social Psychology* 68: 601-608, 1964.

Wolpe, J. For phoria: a hair of the hound. *Psychology Today* 3: 34-37, 1969.

Woodruff, J. L., and Rhine, J. B. An experiment in precognition using dice. *Journal of Parapsychology* 6: 243-262, 1942.

Worthington, T. S. The use in court of hypnotically enhanced testimony. *International Journal of Clinical and Experimental Hypnosis* 27: 402-416, 1979.

Zepelin, H., and Rechtschaffen, A. Mammalian sleep, longevity, and energy metabolism. *Brain, Behavior, and Evolution* 10: 425-470, 1974.

Zinberg, N. E. *Alternate States of Consciousness: Multiple Perspectives on the Study of Consciousness*. New York: Free Press, 1977.

Ziskind, E. An explanation of mental symptoms found in acute deprivation: researches, 1958-1963. *American Journal of Psychiatry* 121: 939-946, 1965.

Zubek, J. P. *Sensory Deprivation: Fifteen Years of Research*. New York: Appleton-Century-Crofts, 1969.

Zubek, J. P., and MacNeill, M. Effects of immobilization: behavioral and EEG changes. *Canadian Journal of Psychology* 20: 316-336, 1966.

Zubek, J. P., Pushkar, W., Sansom, W., and Gowing, J. Perceptual changes after prolonged sensory isolation (darkness and silence). *Canadian Journal of Psychology* 15: 83-100, 1961.

Zubek, J. P., Sansom, W., and Prysianiuk, A. Intellectual changes during prolonged perceptual isolation (darkness and silence). *Canadian Journal of Psychology* 14: 233-243, 1960.

Zubek, J. P., and Wilgosh, L. Prolonged immobilization of the body: changes in performance and in the electroencephalogram. *Science* 140: 306-308, 1963.

Author Index

Subject Index